WILLIAMS-SONOMA

Savoring

Fish & Shellfish

Best Recipes from the Award-Winning International Cookbooks

GENERAL EDITOR

Chuck Williams

AUTHORS

Georgeanne Brennan • Kerri Conan • Lori de Mori • Abigail Johnson Dodge

Janet Fletcher • Joyce Goldstein • Diane Holuigue

Joyce Jue • Cynthia Nims • Ray Overton • Jacki Passmore

Julie Sahni • Michele Scicolone • Marilyn Tausend

Oxmoor House®

6 INTRODUCTION

NORTH AMERICA

16 Clambake Dinner

18 Seafood Cocktail in Spicy Red Sauce

19 Scallops with White Wine and Herbs

21 Salmon Pirog

22 Panfried Trout with Mushrooms and Bacon

23 Crab Cakes with Herbed Tartar Sauce

24 Red Snapper with Chile Sauce and Cheese

27 Grilled Ahi Tuna Niçoise

28 Grilled Halibut Teriyaki

29 Scallop Ceviche with Avocado Balls

30 Lemon Catfish with Slaw in Parchment

33 Squid in Sauce of Three Chiles

34 Fish and Chips

35 Trout in Herb Sauce

37 Dungeness Crab Boil with Shallot Butter

38 Petrale Sole Doré with Lemon-Caper Butter

39 Shrimp with Orange and Tequila

40 Fish Tacos

42 Fritto Misto of Squid, Artichokes, and Lemon

43 Steamed Thai Red Curry Mussels

45 Grilled Salmon with Shaved Fennel Salad

ASIA

52 Scallops and Snow Peas with Crabmeat Sauce

55 Spice-Rubbed Grilled Shrimp

56 Balinese Fish with Lemongrass and Lime

57 Scallops in Thick Red Curry Sauce

59 Flaked Pomelo and Shrimp Salad

61 West Lake Fish

63 Seafood Clay Pot

64 Hanoi-Style Fried Fish

65 Steamed Fish with Ginger and Green Onions

66 Shrimp wih Cashew Nuts

68 Spicy Fish Cakes

71 Tandoori Grilled Fish

72 Stir-Fried Crab with Black Beans

75 Shrimp with Chile and Garlic in Wine Sauce

76 Braised Fish with Eggplant and Potato

77 Mussels with Garlic and Basil

79 Sichuan Chile and Garlic Fish

80 Masala Shrimp Stir-Fry

82 Spicy Fish

83 Fried Shrimp in the Shell with Tamarind

85 Malabar Braised Fish in Sour Gravy

87 "Broken Tile" Fish with Sweet-and-Sour Sauce

88 Chile Crab

90 Shrimp in Spiced Cream Sauce

91 Catish Simmered in a Clay Pot

92 Stir-Fried Okra and Shrimp with Sambal

95 Fried Cuttlefish "Pinecones" with Pepper-Salt

96 Steamed Whole Fish with Pickled Plums

98 Steamed Pork and Shrimp Dumplings

FRANCE

107 Vegetables and Salt Cod with Mayonnaise

108 Warm Oysters with Tomato Vinaigrette

110 Sardines with Olive Oil and Tomatoes

111 Lingcod with a Black Olive Crust

113 Lobster in the Style of Cherbourg

114 Salmon in Cream and Muscadet Sauce

116 Spicy Salt Cod Fritters

117 Squid Braised with Peas

CONTENTS

119 Mussels in White Wine
120 Red Mullet in Parchment
121 Baked Stuffed Sardines
122 Steamed Cod with Vegetables
124 Crab with its Butter and Seaweed
126 Grilled Anchovies with Banyuls Vinegar
127 Sole Cooked in Butter
129 Shrimp with Fennel
130 Cuttlefish Stuffed with Tapenade
133 Scallops Gratin
134 Sea Robin Monte Carlo
135 Grilled Tuna with Herbs
137 Onion and Anchovy Tart
138 Sea Bass on a Bed of Vegetables
139 Swordfish, Toulon Style
140 Deep-Fried Baby Fish
142 Sea Bass with Vegetables
143 Niçoise Sandwiches
145 Monkfish with Olives and Artichokes
146 Mediterranean Fish Soup

ITALY

154 Grilled Sea Bream with Wild Fennel
157 Shrimp Salad with Tomatoes
and Capers
157 Monkfish with Lemon and Capers

158 Stuffed Mussels
159 Hot Anchovy and Garlic Dip
161 Fillet of Sole with Mushrooms
162 Stuffed Clams
164 Mussels with Black Pepper
165 Smoked Swordfish Toasts
167 Roasted Fish with Pine Nuts and Raisins
168 Squid with Spinach
168 Red Mullet in White Wine, Garlic,
and Parsley
170 Red Mullet in Tomato Sauce
171 Tuna with Garlic, Basil, and Tomato
172 Sea Bass with Potatoes and Olives
174 Oven-Roasted Trout with Potatoes
175 Clams with White Wine, Garlic,
and Tomatoes
176 Whipped Salt Cod
179 Sea Bass in Parchment with
Caper Sauce
179 Roast Eel Kabobs
180 Fried Soft-Shell Crabs
181 Salt Cod with Leeks
182 Seafood Stew

SPAIN AND PORTUGAL

191 Monkfish with Greens
191 Scallops Baked in White Wine

193 Sizzling Shrimp with Garlic
195 Monkfish with Pine Nut Sauce
195 Trout in the Style of Bragança
196 Salt Cod, Bay of Biscay Style
197 Shrimp with Curry
198 Clams in White Wine
201 Shrimp with Hot Sauce
202 Tuna with Peppers and Potatoes
202 Swordfish with Tomatoes
and Anchovies
205 Peppers Stuffed with Salt Cod
206 Stuffed Squid
206 Salt Cod and Potato Gratin
208 Mullet with Orange-Wine Sauce
211 Fish in a Tart Vinaigrette
212 Salt Cod with Chickpeas
213 Squid with Peas
214 Hake with Cider
217 Clams with Sausage and Tomatoes
218 Tuna with Garlic and Chile
218 Crab in a Cart

221 GLOSSARY
227 INDEX
231 ACKNOWLEDGMENTS

Top: South of Cancún, Mexico, the town of Tulúm offers intriguing views of the palm-fringed beaches fronting the inviting waters of the Caribbean. **Above:** From these rocky Provençal waters come the prized *rouget barbet*, or red mullet, and the *rouget grondin*, or sea robin. **Right:** These bright red fish were caught in a coral reef off Boracay Island in the central Philippines. Only moments out of the water, they are already on their way to market.

*S*eafood is the last great wild edible on the planet. Despite the growing popularity of managed aquaculture and fish farms, much of the seafood that ends up on our tables has been drawn from the world's rivers, lakes, bays, and oceans using skills handed down through generations of men and women who make their living on the water. Fishing can require resources as modern as a satellite positioning system or as old-fashioned as a rod, a hook, and a chunk of bait. And across the world, seafood is both a staple and a treasure.

Garlic-sizzled shrimp brought to a terrace table along the Amalfi coast in Italy; tuna poke sparked with sesame and ginger and served overlooking the Pacific in Honolulu; caper-dotted sole meunière at a French bistro; clams with spicy chorizo for a late-night dinner in Barcelona; shrimp dumplings in translucent wrappers at a Hong Kong dim sum parlor; succulent catfish glazed with caramel sauce streetside in Hanoi: all these delicacies offer the taste of salt and fresh waters and the lands that surround them.

Shaped by the natural abundance of America's lengthy coastlines, inland lakes, and grand rivers, seafood is a vibrant part of American gastronomy. From New England's seasonal clambakes and lobster boils and Wisconsin's Friday-night fish fries to the sushi and sashimi of Hawaii and the prized plank-roasted salmon of Alaska and the Pacific Northwest, every region has its specialty, beloved by locals and sought out by visitors.

Mexico, too, has thousands of miles of coastline and a wealth of mountain lakes. Beachside stands sell seafood cocktails and ceviches made from mussels, clams, fish, and shrimp tossed with lime juice, whose acidity "cooks" the seafood, leaving it tangy and fresh-tasting, especially when garnished with peppers, cilantro, or unctuous green avocado. Fish tacos are another handheld treat, especially popular along the rustic beaches of Baja. Tequila-drenched shrimp with orange, squid in a sauce of three chiles, snapper with smoked chipotle chiles: these Mexican dishes demonstrate how a few vivid flavors can highlight fresh seafood.

Whole fish are a symbol of abundance throughout China, and few celebratory banquets would be complete without one. But seafood has a place on the everyday table too, in the shape of the steamed pork and shrimp dumplings beloved by dim sum fanciers; in a clay pot stew brimming with squid, fish, and prawns; or in a simple stir-fry of shrimp and cashew nuts.

Water has always been crucial to the prosperity of Southeast Asia. Centuries of trading, colonization and migration, all made possible by long coasts, meandering rivers, and spreading deltas, shaped the region's history and defined its tables. As a result, fish and shellfish appear on the table at almost every meal, always flavored with a lively array of aromatic herbs and spices.

Bounded by the sea on two sides, India is also rich in bays and rivers, which produce a wide array of fish and shellfish, including succulent, dramatically striped tiger prawns. From the coastal cities of Goa to the riverside villages of Bengal, Indian seafood is rubbed with tandoori-style spices and grilled, braised with myriad vegetables, or sautéed in lush Moghul sauces.

In the heart of Paris, men still fish in the Seine, hoping to pull in enough to make a *friture*, or fried-fish supper. While French cuisine is filled with recipes for delicate freshwater fish, it also abounds with lustier options for the more robust specimens hauled from the Mediterranean and the Atlantic: sardines, anchovies, red mullet, swordfish, tuna, sea bass, sole, and monkfish, along with mussels, crabs, scallops, oysters, and lobster. Wine, herbs, butter, and cream often find their way into the north's dishes, while olive oil, tomatoes, garlic, and olives denote a Provençal dish.

Similar fish turn up along Italy's coasts, flanked by the Mediterranean and the Adriatic. Sicily and Sardinia contribute their own renowned fish dishes, including stuffed swordfish laced with lemon juice, capers, and oregano, as does Tuscany, serving up whole fish perfumed with rosemary, sprinkled with balsamic vinegar, and dotted with raisins and pine nuts.

Although salt cod is used in both France and Italy, nowhere in southern Europe is it more revered than on the Iberian peninsula. And with good reason: sailing farther west, Spanish, Basque, and Portuguese fishermen discovered ever more abundant stocks of cod. Salted and dried wood-hard, the fish's superb keeping qualities made it an indispensable staple. These days, it has been supplemented by squid, swordfish, eels and monkfish, along with clams and mussels, often combined with spicy linguiça, chorizo, or slivers of jamon Serrano.

Whether you're fishing on a placid lake or choosing mussels at your neighborhood market, the following pages will bring you an abundance of fresh and delicious ways to make the most of your day's catch.

Left: Fishing boats rest along France's Brittany coast during low tide. **Above, left:** What constitutes a bouillabaisse, the famed fish soup of Marseilles, is the subject of vigorous debate among gastronomes. Once the humble fisherman's *plat pauvre,* the dish has evolved into an expensive culinary art form, scented with saffron and using only the freshest locally caught fish. **Above, right:** An Italian fisherman proudly shows off his early-morning catch.

NORTH AMERICA

*L*ocal *seafood is a favorite first course for Americans who live near a coast or well-stocked lake or river. For much of American history, fish and seafood were workingmen's food. Lobsters were so common in seventeenth-century New England that fishermen used them as bait for cod and people complained of having to eat them too often. Oyster bars thrived in many cities, and no patron would think of ordering less than a dozen (more likely two), if downing them freshly shucked and raw. Rich, creamy oyster stews and pan roasts were also offered as alternatives. Such places still thrive in San Francisco, Seattle, New York, and New Orleans.*

Gulf oysters served in myriad ways—raw on the half shell, fried in po'boys and oyster loaves, or simmered in gumbo—are still a hallmark of Southern coastal cooking. In the fine dining establishments of New Orleans, customers traditionally started their meal with oysters Rockefeller (baked with herbed spinach with Pernod), oysters Bienville (with shrimp sauce), or a few of each.

American diners have recently discovered sushi bars and the pleasures of raw seafood Japanese style: slices of tuna or yellowtail sashimi served with dipping sauce or draped over pearly rice. Like sashimi, Hawaiian poke (marinated raw tuna) appeals to those with a taste for culinary adventure.

Along the Atlantic Coast, beachside seafood rituals are summer highlights. Around Chesapeake Bay, a blue-crab feast can materialize at a park, in a backyard, or at the shore. Newspaper is draped over picnic tables and crab pots are filled with beer, vinegar, and Old Bay seasoning. When the hot crabs are served, diners roll up their sleeves, and the messy picking begins.

The New England equivalent is a lobster boil or clambake, the latter based on methods that Native Americans shared with early settlers. Authentic clambakes transpire at the shore, in a pit lined with hot stones and seaweed. Clams, potatoes, corn on the cob, and sometimes lobsters are piled into the pit, covered with seaweed, and left to steam to perfection. For many New Englanders, childhood memories include family trips to the Massachusetts shore for a clambake or to Maine for lobster drenched in drawn butter.

Down South, most catfish is now locally farmed, but the succulent fish still finds its way into many southerners' cast-iron frying pans. Traditionally, cooks dip the fillets in cayenne-spiked cornmeal and then fry them crisp in hot, deep lard. Coleslaw and hush puppies—deep-fried balls of well-seasoned cornmeal batter—complete a catfish feast. Contemporary chefs are exploring the possibilities of this popular and inexpensive fish, serving it steamed French style in parchment packets or caramelized with Vietnamese spices in Asian clay pots.

In the Pacific Northwest, the abundance of rivers, coastline, and high-quality grape-growing areas has provided for some superb food and wine marriages: grilled Pacific salmon with Oregon Pinot Noir, Thai-style mussels with Washington Riesling, steamed local manila clams with Oregon Pinot Gris. California, too, offers an abundance of local seafood, from San Francisco's famous Dungeness crabs served with a chilled Napa Chardonnay and hot sourdough bread to a crunchy *fritto misto* of Monterey Bay squid and Watsonville artichokes or golden petrale sole showered with Meyer lemon juice.

More than half the states in Mexico abut the waters of the Pacific Ocean, the Gulf of Mexico, the Sea of Cortés, or the Caribbean. Along these coastlines, ceviche or seafood cocktails featuring local seafood "cooked" in lemon or lime juice are among the most common *entradas*, or appetizers, served to start a meal. In Baja California, ceviche may be scooped onto a tortilla and served as a handheld snack. Up and down the long coastline of Veracruz, small palm-thatched *palapas*, or beach shacks, sell tacos filled with lightly battered, fried and shredded fish, piled with tangy tomato salsa and crunchy raw cabbage.

On an Acapulco beach, dinner can be as simple as just-caught fish cooked on sticks over a fire of dried coconut shells. In the highlands of Puebla, where dark volcanic soil covers the hillsides and both fast-moving rivers and lazy streams water the valleys, garlic-anointed fish may be wrapped and steamed in corn husks like a tamale. But most main-course dinners are not plain grilled or fried fish. They are served in or with a sauce, and when you order, it is often by the name of the sauce—a *pipián verde* (green pumpkinseed sauce), a *mole negro*, or a *salsa de hierbas*, an herby amalgamation of cilantro, parsley, Mexican oregano, garlic, olive oil, and wine. These dishes are presented alone or, at the most, with a mound of rice—typical of the simplicity with which fresh seafood can be treated throughout North America.

Freshwater fish, such as catfish, black bass, and trout, were once abundant in the streams and lakes of the high tablelands. Pollution and overfishing have destroyed many of the wild stocks, and so much of the fish available in these areas is now farmed.

Left: A collection of colorful buoys, used to mark the location of lobster traps beneath the water's surface, hangs on a wall in Rock Harbor, Maine. **Above, left:** Settled in the 1600s, Cape Cod, a long, narrow, curved peninsula off southern Massachusetts, is a popular summertime vacation destination. **Above, right:** Steamer clams, which flourish in the cold northern waters of America, are a delicious treat in a clambake, quickly steamed, or breaded and deep-fried.

Clambake Dinner

New England • America

The first New England clambakes date back to the early 1600s, when Native Americans demonstrated hot-pit cooking to the Massachusetts Bay colonists. The spirit of this seaside dinner, plain or fancy, still draws New Englanders to the summer table.

4 live lobsters, 1 lb (500 g) each

8 small red potatoes, each about 2 inches (5 cm) in diameter, unpeeled

4 ears corn, husks and silk removed

2 small white onions, each about 2½ inches (6 cm) in diameter, halved

48 small hard-shelled clams such as littleneck or mahogany, scrubbed

1⅓ cups (11 oz/345 g) salted or unsalted butter

2 lemons, quartered

¼ cup (⅓ oz/10 g) chopped fresh flat-leaf (Italian) parsley

Serves 4

1 Set a large steaming rack in the bottom of a large lobster kettle or other large, wide pot. Fill the pot about one-third full with water. Cover and bring to a boil over high heat. Plunge the lobsters, headfirst, into the boiling water. Cover and boil until the lobsters are partially cooked and their shells are beginning to turn bright red, about 3 minutes. Using long tongs, transfer the lobsters to a large plate.

2 Return the water to a boil and add the potatoes, corn, and onions. Return the lobsters to the pot along with any accumulated juices. Cover the pot tightly with a double layer of aluminum foil and the lid. Cook for 10 minutes. Uncover and scatter the clams around the lobsters, discarding any clams that fail to close to the touch. Re-cover with the foil layers and the lid and continue cooking until the lobsters are bright red, the potatoes are tender when pierced, and the clams have opened, 6–8 minutes longer. In a small saucepan, melt the butter and keep warm.

3 Using the tongs, remove the lobsters, clams, corn, potatoes, and onions to a large platter or cutting board. Discard any clams that failed to open. Ring the edge of the platter with lemon wedges and sprinkle the entire platter with the parsley. Divide the melted butter among small ramekins. Serve at once.

CLAMS AND LOBSTER

The rough waters of the Atlantic harbor two of New England's most cherished natural resources, clams and lobsters. Two main types of clams are harvested along the coast. Small hard-shelled clams, such as the cherrystone, littleneck, and Maine mahogany, are excellent raw, steamed, or added to soups and sauces. Larger hard-shelled species, known as quahogs or chowder clams, are meatier but also tougher and are usually processed for use in chowders, stuffings, and savory pies. Soft-shelled clams have oval shells and a telltale black "foot," or neck, protruding from one end. These sweet clams are great for steaming and are also delicious battered and fried.

Until the early 1800s, lobsters were so ordinary that they were fed to children, prisoners, and servants, or used as fertilizer. Although tastes have changed, the local lobstering industry has altered little. In the predawn hours, hardy New England lobstermen head out to sea in search of a good day's haul, many choosing to follow the livelihood of their fathers and grandfathers.

Seafood Cocktail in Spicy Red Sauce

Ceviche Rojo de Camarón y Sierra • Veracruz • Mexico

This is a particularly refreshing example of ceviche, the centuries-old dish in which seafood is cooked by contact with acidic citrus juice instead of heat. Ricardo Muñoz Zurita, who grew up in Tabasco and Veracruz, likes to use sierra, the colorful Spanish mackerel from the Gulf of Mexico, but substituting black sea bass, rockfish, or red snapper works equally well. This cooling treat is perfect when served with a cold beer or tangy limeade.

1 Place the fish in a shallow glass dish. Add the lime juice, cover, and marinate for up to 2 hours at room temperature, or until opaque. (The fish will not "cook" as quickly if refrigerated.)

2 Stir in the shrimp, onion, garlic, salt, and pepper. Cover again and refrigerate for 30 minutes or so.

3 Drain the fish mixture to remove the excess lime juice. Add the chopped cilantro, ketchup, and *adobo* sauce. Mix well.

4 Spoon into glass dishes, garnish with the avocado slices, and serve.

½ lb (250 g) lean white-fleshed fish fillet (see note), cubed

½ cup (4 fl oz/125 ml) fresh lime juice

½ lb (250 g) bay shrimp (prawns)

½ cup (2½ oz/75 g) minced white onion

2 teaspoons minced garlic

2 teaspoons sea salt

½ teaspoon freshly ground pepper

¼ cup (⅓ oz/10 g) finely chopped fresh cilantro (fresh coriander)

1 cup (8 fl oz/250 ml) tomato ketchup

1 tablespoon sauce from *chiles chipotles en adobo*

1 avocado, preferably Haas, pitted, peeled, and sliced

Serves 6

Scallops with White Wine and Herbs

New England · America

Bay scallops are found in the calm waters that border Long Island, New York, and Massachusetts, but most New Englanders agree that the best scallops are harvested just off Nantucket Island. Commercial scallopers are joined by locals (and some savvy visitors) who gather their equipment and set off at low tide in search of the treasured shellfish.

¾ lb (375 g) bay scallops or sea scallops

1 tablespoon all-purpose (plain) flour

2 tablespoons plus ¼ cup (4 oz/125 g) unsalted butter

½ cup (4 fl oz/125 ml) dry white wine

1 shallot, minced

1 tablespoon minced fresh tarragon

Kosher salt and freshly ground pepper to taste

3 tablespoons pine nuts, lightly toasted

Serves 4

1 Remove any remaining white muscle from the side of each scallop. If using sea scallops, cut each in half horizontally to form 2 rounds. Rinse the scallops and pat dry, then sprinkle with the flour, coating evenly. In a large frying pan over medium-high heat, melt the 2 tablespoons butter until foamy. Add the scallops and cook, stirring frequently, until slightly browned on the edges, about 3 minutes. Transfer to a plate and cover with aluminum foil.

2 Add the wine and shallot to the same pan, bring to a boil over medium-high heat, and deglaze the pan, scraping up any browned bits on the bottom. Boil, stirring occasionally, until reduced to 2 tablespoons, about 4 minutes. Remove from the heat and gradually whisk in the remaining ¼ cup (4 oz/125 g) butter, a few pieces at a time, until emulsified, about 3 minutes. Return the scallops and any accumulated juices to the pan and stir in the tarragon. Gently warm over very low heat until the scallops are heated through. Do not overheat, or the sauce will separate and the scallops will toughen. Season with salt and pepper. Spoon the scallops and sauce onto individual plates. Sprinkle with the pine nuts and serve at once.

Salmon Pirog

Alaska · America

This traditional Alaskan dish garnished with dilled sour cream reflects the heritage that the Last Frontier shares with Russia, its nearest neighbor to the west.

DOUGH

3 cups (15 oz/470 g) all-purpose (plain) flour

1 teaspoon salt

¾ cup (6 oz/185 g) chilled unsalted butter, cut into ½-inch (12-mm) pieces

1 tablespoon fresh lemon juice

4–6 tablespoons (2–3 fl oz/60–90 ml) ice water

2 tablespoons canola oil

½ small head green cabbage, about ½ lb (250 g), trimmed and finely shredded

2 tablespoons minced fresh flat-leaf (Italian) parsley

4 teaspoons minced fresh dill

Salt and freshly ground pepper to taste

¾ lb (375 g) fresh mushrooms, brushed clean and very finely chopped

¾ cup (4 oz/125 g) finely chopped yellow onion

1 piece salmon fillet, 1½ lb (750 g), skin removed

1 egg

1 cup (5 oz/155 g) cooked long-grain white rice

½ cup (4 oz/125 g) sour cream

Serves 4

1 To make the dough, in a bowl, stir together the flour and the 1 teaspoon salt. Add the butter and toss to coat. Using a pastry blender or 2 knives, cut the butter into the flour mixture until it has a coarse, sandy texture. Stir in the lemon juice and then the ice water, 1 tablespoon at a time, using only as much as needed for the dough to hold its shape when pinched between your fingers. Turn the dough out onto a work surface and divide in half. Form each half into a ball, enclose separately in plastic wrap, and refrigerate for at least 30 minutes or for up to 1 day.

2 In a frying pan over medium heat, warm 1 tablespoon of the canola oil. Add the shredded cabbage and 2 tablespoons water and cook, stirring often, until very tender, 8–10 minutes. Stir in 1 tablespoon of the parsley with 1 teaspoon of the dill and season with salt and pepper. Transfer to a bowl and wipe out the frying pan.

3 In the frying pan over medium-high heat, warm the remaining 1 tablespoon canola oil. Add the mushrooms and onion and sauté until the mushrooms are tender and the liquid they give off has evaporated, 5–7 minutes. Season with salt and pepper. Add the remaining 1 tablespoon parsley and 1 teaspoon of the dill. Remove from the heat.

4 Use needle-nose pliers or tweezers to remove any fine pin bones from the salmon. Cut against the grain into slices about ½ inch (12 mm) thick. In a small bowl, lightly beat together the egg, a pinch of salt, and 2 tablespoons water to make an egg wash.

5 Preheat the oven to 375°F (190°C). On a lightly floured work surface, roll out 1 dough ball into a rectangle about 10 inches (25 cm) wide and 14 inches (35 cm) long. Trim the edges. Cut the dough in half lengthwise and then crosswise, making 4 smaller rectangles. Lightly brush the egg wash evenly over the rectangles. Spread one-fourth of the rice over each rectangle, leaving a 1-inch (2.5-cm) border uncovered around the edges. Spoon an even layer of one-fourth of the cabbage over each rice base. Lay the salmon slices on top of the cabbage, cutting and rearranging the pieces as needed so the salmon evenly covers the cabbage and dividing the salmon evenly among the rectangles. Season lightly with salt and pepper. Spread the mushroom mixture over the salmon, dividing it among the rectangles.

6 Roll out the remaining dough ball into a rectangle about 12 inches (30 cm) wide and 16 inches (40 cm) long. Trim the edges. Cut the dough in half lengthwise first and then crosswise, making 4 smaller rectangles. Lay these pastry pieces over the filling, lining up the edges with the pastry base, very gently stretching the dough a bit if needed. Press firmly along the edges to seal, trim with a small knife to neaten, and then use the tines of a fork to crimp the edges. Brush the pastry top with egg wash and, using the tip of a sharp knife, cut a few vents in the top of each pastry. Transfer the pastries to an ungreased baking sheet.

7 Bake until well browned, about 20 minutes. Meanwhile, in a bowl, stir together the sour cream and the remaining 2 teaspoons dill. Cover and refrigerate until ready to serve. Remove the pastries from the oven and immediately divide among individual plates. Spoon some of the dilled sour cream alongside and serve at once.

Panfried Trout with Mushrooms and Bacon

The Mountain States • America

With ingredients like wine, fish stock, and cream, this dish is obviously a modern invention. But it does take its inspiration from the past and from three of the Mountain States' indigenous ingredients—trout, mushrooms, and pine nuts—transforming (but not disguising) them into something fresh and new. The trout and its creamy French-inspired mushroom sauce are sophisticated enough to serve to company. At the dinner table, pour a white wine much like the one you use in the dish.

1 In a frying pan over medium heat, fry the bacon slices, turning once or twice, until browned and almost crisp, about 8 minutes. Transfer to paper towels to drain; keep warm.

2 Pour off all but about 2 tablespoons of the bacon drippings. Return the pan to medium-low heat. Add the pine nuts to the bacon drippings and cook, stirring occasionally, until crisp and lightly browned, 3–4 minutes. Using a slotted spoon, transfer the nuts to a plate and reserve.

3 Return the pan to medium heat. Add the mushrooms to the bacon drippings and add the ¼ teaspoon salt and the ¼ teaspoon pepper. Cover and cook, stirring once or twice, until the mushrooms render their juices and are beginning to soften, about 5 minutes. Uncover, add the stock and the wine, and raise the heat to high. Bring to a brisk simmer and deglaze the pan, stirring to scrape up any browned bits on the pan bottom. Cook, stirring occasionally, until the liquid is reduced by half, 3–4 minutes. Stir in the cream, reduce the heat to medium, and simmer, uncovered, until the sauce thickens slightly and coats the mushrooms, about 3 minutes. Stir the pine nuts into the sauce. Keep warm.

4 Meanwhile, in a large frying pan over medium-high heat, warm the corn oil. Spread the cornmeal on a plate. One at a time, dip the trout in the cornmeal, coating them evenly on both sides. Again one at a time, shake off the excess cornmeal and carefully lower the trout into the hot oil. When both are in the pan, cook until browned on the first side, about 5 minutes. Using a large spatula, carefully turn the trout. Cook until browned on the second side and opaque throughout but still moist, 4–5 minutes longer.

5 Transfer the trout to warmed individual plates. Taste the sauce and adjust the seasoning. Spoon the sauce around (not over) the trout, dividing it evenly and using it all. Sprinkle the sauce with the chives. Top each trout with 2 bacon slices and serve.

---

4 slices thick-cut bacon

2 tablespoons pine nuts

¾ lb (375 g) full-flavored fresh mushrooms such as cremini, brushed clean and thickly sliced

¼ teaspoon salt, plus salt to taste

¼ teaspoon freshly ground pepper, plus pepper to taste

½ cup (4 fl oz/125 ml) chicken or fish stock

⅓ cup (3 fl oz/80 ml) medium-dry white wine such as Chardonnay

⅓ cup (3 fl oz/80 ml) heavy (double) cream

2 tablespoons corn oil

⅓ cup (2 oz/60 g) yellow cornmeal

2 rainbow trout, about ¾ lb (375 g) each, cleaned

1 tablespoon minced fresh chives

Serves 2

Crab Cakes with Herbed Tartar Sauce

The Mid-Atlantic · America

The Chesapeake Bay area harbors the blue crab, the East Coast's finest crab variety. The name befits this small, dark blue to blue-green crustacean, which turns a brilliant red when boiled. Maryland chefs regularly use the flavorful meat for crab cakes.

CRAB CAKES

⅓ cup (3 fl oz/80 ml) mayonnaise

1 egg

2 teaspoons Worcestershire sauce

1 or 2 dashes Tabasco sauce or other hot-pepper sauce

2 small green (spring) onions, including tender green tops, minced

⅓ cup (1½ oz/45 g) plus 1½ cups (6 oz/185 g) fine dried bread crumbs

3 tablespoons minced red bell pepper (capsicum)

2 tablespoons minced fresh flat-leaf (Italian) parsley

1 lb (500 g) fresh lump crabmeat, picked over for shell fragments and cartilage

¾ teaspoon kosher salt

¼ teaspoon freshly ground pepper

HERBED TARTAR SAUCE

¾ cup (6 fl oz/180 ml) mayonnaise

3 tablespoons drained sweet pickle relish

2 tablespoons minced fresh herbs such as flat-leaf (Italian) parsley, chives, basil, or mint, or a combination

1 tablespoon sour cream

1 tablespoon minced red onion

1 teaspoon fresh lemon juice

1 or 2 dashes Tabasco sauce or other hot-pepper sauce

Coarse salt and freshly ground pepper to taste

2 tablespoons unsalted butter

2 tablespoons canola oil

Lemon wedges

Serves 8 as a first course, or 4 as a main course

1 To make the crab cakes, in a bowl, stir together the mayonnaise, egg, Worcestershire sauce, and hot-pepper sauce until well blended. Add the green onions, ⅓ cup (1½ oz/45 g) bread crumbs, bell pepper, and parsley and mix until blended. Add the crabmeat, salt, and pepper and mix gently. Pour the remaining 1½ cups (6 oz/185 g) bread crumbs onto a plate. Divide the crabmeat mixture into 8 equal portions. Lightly dampen your hands and shape each portion into a patty about 3 inches (7.5 cm) in diameter. Coat the patties with the bread crumbs. Place on a clean plate, cover with plastic wrap, and refrigerate for at least 2 hours or for up to 8 hours before cooking.

2 Meanwhile, make the tartar sauce: In a bowl, stir together the mayonnaise, relish, herbs, sour cream, red onion, and lemon juice until well blended. Season to taste with hot-pepper sauce, salt, and pepper. Cover and refrigerate until ready to serve.

3 In a large frying pan over medium heat, combine the butter and the canola oil. Heat until the butter is melted and foaming and then add half of the crab cakes. Cook, turning once or twice, until browned, about 5 minutes on each side. Transfer to a clean plate and cover with aluminum foil. Repeat with the remaining crab cakes. Divide the cakes among individual plates. Place the lemon wedges alongside and pass the tartar sauce at the table.

Red Snapper with Chile Sauce and Cheese

Pescado Marco · Mexico City · Mexico

In the early afternoon, polished cars block the street outside the bar-restaurant Guadiana in Mexico City, the chauffeurs oblivious to those trying to drive past. Inside, people conduct business while drinking tequila or wine and enjoying the superb food of owner Marco Beteta. This dish is a popular item on his menu.

1 In a saucepan over medium heat, warm the oil. Add the onion slices and sauté until they are translucent, about 5 minutes. Add the garlic and sauté for 1 minute longer. Stir in the flour and cook, stirring, until golden, about 3 minutes. Gradually pour in the water while stirring constantly. Add the tomatoes, bay leaf, bouillon granules, and allspice. Bring to a simmer and cook until thickened, about 10 minutes. Remove from the heat and let cool slightly.

2 Working in batches, pour the sauce into a blender, add the chiles, and process until smooth. Pass the purée through a medium-mesh sieve, pressing down with the back of a spoon, and set aside.

3 In a frying pan large enough to hold the fish in a single layer, fry the bacon over medium heat until almost crisp, about 3 minutes. Using a slotted spoon, transfer to paper towels to drain. Pour off the bacon fat, wipe out the pan, and return to medium-high heat. Pour in the chile sauce, lime juice, and Worcestershire and Maggi sauces. Season with salt and pepper. Bring to a boil, reduce the heat to low, and simmer for 5 minutes to blend the flavors.

4 Rinse the fish fillets and pat dry. Sprinkle them with salt and pepper and carefully lay them in the sauce. Cook until the flesh is opaque throughout, 4–5 minutes. Turn the fillets halfway through cooking if the sauce does not cover the fish, or spoon the simmering sauce over the top.

5 When the fish is ready, place a cheese slice on top of each fillet, cover the pan, and cook just until the cheese melts. Transfer to a warmed platter or individual plates, sprinkle the chopped bacon over the top, and serve at once.

¼ cup (2 fl oz/60 ml) safflower or canola oil

½ white onion, sliced

4 cloves garlic

2½ tablespoons all-purpose (plain) flour

4 cups (32 fl oz/1 l) water

6 tomatoes, sliced

1 bay leaf

1 teaspoon chicken bouillon granules

½ teaspoon ground allspice

2 *chiles chipotles en adobo*

⅓ lb (5 oz/155 g) bacon, chopped

Juice of ½ lime

6 drops Worcestershire sauce

3 drops Maggi seasoning sauce or 2 drops *each* dark soy sauce and Worcestershire sauce

Sea salt and freshly ground pepper to taste

6 red snapper fillets or other firm white-fleshed fish fillets, about 6 oz (185 g) each

6 thin slices white Cheddar or Monterey jack cheese

Serves 6

THE FISH OF MEXICO

With thousands of miles of shoreline, Mexico is blessed with an abundance of seafood. More than half of the states are washed by the waters of the Pacific Ocean, the Gulf of Mexico, the Caribbean, or the Sea of Cortés, and each has its own culinary specialties. It is on the Gulf of Mexico, however, where the most varieties and the most elaborate preparations are found. At the market of Villahermosa, for example, you might spot *pejelagartos*, rows of smoked fish with a crocodile-like skin, run through, mouth to tail, with wooden sticks. Appearance aside, they make a tasty taco filling. In Campeche, *pan de cazón*, a double-decker tortilla sandwich with layers of sand shark meat, black beans, and a feisty habanero chile sauce, is a traditional dish. And at the tip of the Yucatán peninsula, you might be served *tikin-xic*, large fillets of fish rubbed with achiote paste and grilled over a smoldering fire built right on the sand. In all of the coastal communities, restaurants offer whatever was caught that day prepared almost any way imaginable.

One shouldn't leave, though, without sampling the spectacular *huachinango a la Veracruzana*, red snapper with an olive, caper, and tomato sauce, or that other classic dish, *robalo en hoja santa*, sea bass wrapped in the leaves of an herb with a sense-tickling aroma.

Grilled Ahi Tuna Niçoise

California · America

California cooks often adapt the familiar *salade niçoise* by making it with fresh Pacific tuna instead of the traditional canned tuna. Ahi, a meaty, red-fleshed tuna from the waters off Hawaii and Southern California, works beautifully in this French classic. Serve the salad with a chilled dry rosé and crusty French bread.

DRESSING

2 large cloves garlic, peeled but left whole

8 anchovy fillets

Large pinch of salt, plus salt to taste

3 tablespoons red wine vinegar

½ cup (4 fl oz/125 ml) plus 1 tablespoon extra-virgin olive oil

Freshly ground pepper to taste

4 ahi tuna steaks, about 6 oz (185 g) each

2 tablespoons extra-virgin olive oil

½ teaspoon fennel seed, crushed in a mortar

Salt and freshly ground pepper to taste

4 eggs

¾ lb (375 g) small boiling potatoes

½ lb (250 g) slender green beans, ends trimmed

½ red onion, very thinly sliced

½ fennel bulb, very thinly sliced crosswise

2 tablespoons capers, coarsely chopped

¼ cup (⅓ oz/10 g) coarsely chopped fresh basil

3 small tomatoes, cut in half or into wedges

24 Niçoise olives

Serves 6

1 To make the dressing, combine the garlic, anchovies, and pinch of salt in a mortar and pound to a paste. Transfer to a bowl. Whisk in the vinegar, then whisk in the oil. Season with pepper and more salt to taste. Set aside to allow the flavors to mellow.

2 Prepare a medium-hot fire in a charcoal grill, preheat a gas grill, or preheat a broiler (grill). Rub the tuna all over with the olive oil. Season with the fennel seed, salt, and pepper. Grill or broil on both sides until opaque throughout, 6–8 minutes. Set aside to cool.

3 Put the eggs in a small saucepan and add water to cover by 1 inch (2.5 cm). Bring to a boil over high heat, cover, and remove from the heat. Let stand for 8 minutes, then drain and place under running cold water until cool. Drain again, then peel and set aside.

4 Put the potatoes in a saucepan and add salted water to cover by 1 inch (2.5 cm). Bring to a boil over high heat, then adjust the heat to maintain a gentle simmer. Cook, uncovered, until the potatoes are just tender when pierced, about 15 minutes. Drain and, when cool enough to handle, peel the potatoes. Bring a saucepan three-fourths full of salted water to a boil. Add the green beans and boil until tender, about 5 minutes. Drain and place under running cold water until cool. Drain again and pat dry. Cut in half.

5 Put the tuna in a large bowl, breaking it up with your hands. Halve or slice the potatoes and add to the bowl along with the green beans, red onion, fennel, capers, and basil. Add the dressing and toss gently. Add the tomatoes and toss again gently. Adjust the seasoning. Transfer the salad to a shallow serving bowl. Cut the eggs lengthwise into quarters and arrange around the edge of the salad. Scatter the olives over all.

Grilled Halibut Teriyaki

Pacific Northwest • America

Halibut is one of the most distinctive fish of the Pacific Northwest, with much of the catch coming from the deep, frigid waters of the Gulf of Alaska. The large flatfish is related to flounder and sole but is unique in its potential size, which can reach well over a hundred pounds. Serve these teriyaki-glazed halibut steaks with steamed white rice with toasted sesame seeds stirred in just before serving.

¾ cup (6 fl oz/180 ml) soy sauce

¾ cup (6 fl oz/180 ml) mirin

2 tablespoons minced green (spring) onion, including tender green tops, plus sliced green onion for garnish

1 tablespoon peeled and minced or grated fresh ginger

4 halibut steaks, about ½ lb (250 g) each

2 teaspoons cornstarch (cornflour) dissolved in 1 tablespoon water

Serves 4

1 To make the teriyaki sauce, in a small saucepan over medium-high heat, combine the soy sauce, mirin, minced green onion, and ginger and bring just to a boil. Let cool completely. Transfer 1 cup (8 fl oz/250 ml) of the cooled sauce to a shallow dish. Add the halibut steaks, turning to coat. Marinate for about 30 minutes at room temperature, turning the steaks once or twice.

2 Prepare a fire in a charcoal grill. Reheat the remaining teriyaki sauce over medium heat, then add the cornstarch mixture and stir until the sauce has thickened, about 2 minutes. Set the teriyaki glaze aside.

3 Brush the grill rack lightly with oil. Lift the steaks from the marinade, allowing the excess liquid to drip off, and set on the grill. Grill, turning once, until there is a touch of translucency at the center of the steaks when tested with a knife (the steaks will continue to cook through once taken from the grill), 3–5 minutes on each side. Remove the steaks from the grill, brush both sides with the teriyaki glaze, and divide among warmed individual plates. Scatter the sliced green onion over the tops.

Scallop Ceviche with Avocado Balls

Ceviche de Callo de Hacha con Aguacate • Colima • Mexico

Almost every indentation of Mexico's Pacific shoreline that includes sandy beaches will also have its contingent of palm-thatched *palapas*, where the local seafood specialties such as ceviche are served. Each cook has her or his own version, and this unusual one, made with scallops, comes from a *palapa* on the isolated gray sand beach at Boca de Pascuales, in the tiny, hot, and humid state of Colima.

1 lb (500 g) bay scallops

½ cup (4 fl oz/125 ml) fresh lime juice, plus extra if needed

3 avocados, preferably Hass

1 ripe tomato, diced

1 tablespoon finely chopped fresh cilantro (fresh coriander)

1 serrano chile, minced

⅓ cup (3 fl oz/80 ml) extra-virgin olive oil

Sea salt to taste

Serves 6

1 Put the scallops in a glass bowl and toss with the ½ cup (4 fl oz/125 ml) lime juice. Cover and let marinate at room temperature for 10–15 minutes.

2 Halve the avocados and remove the pits. With a small melon baller, spoon out balls of the avocado flesh, or make ½-inch (12-mm) hatched cuts through the flesh and scoop out the small cubes. Drain the scallops and stir in the tomato, cilantro, chile, and oil. When well mixed, add the avocado and gently toss together. Sprinkle in the salt and, if needed, add more lime juice.

3 Serve in tall wineglasses, small clear glass bowls, or the fluted shells of the scallops.

Lemon Catfish with Slaw in Parchment

The South · America

Catfish is the South's most versatile freshwater catch, turning up on dinner tables fried, steamed, poached, baked, grilled, wrapped in parchment, or "dished up" in soups and stews. Today, most of the catfish sold in markets and appearing on menus are farm-raised. Mississippi is the uncontested Catfish Capital of the World, raising more of this lean, mild-tasting fish than any other place on earth. Pour a young, fruity Chardonnay or an ice-cold beer to accompany this dish, and you will have a meal to remember.

8 catfish fillets, 6–8 oz (185–250 g) each, skinned

Salt and freshly ground pepper to taste

VINAIGRETTE

¼ cup (2 fl oz/60 ml) dry white wine

¼ cup (2 fl oz/60 ml) fresh lemon juice

Finely grated zest of 1 lemon

2 teaspoons Dijon mustard

1 teaspoon Asian sesame oil

⅓ cup (3 fl oz/80 ml) canola oil

1 teaspoon salt

1 teaspoon freshly ground pepper

1 teaspoon sugar

2 tablespoons sesame seeds

COLESLAW

½ small head red cabbage, thinly sliced (about 2 cups/6 oz/185 g)

½ small head green cabbage, thinly sliced (about 2 cups/6 oz/185 g)

6 green (spring) onions, including tender green tops, chopped

1 tablespoon peeled and chopped fresh ginger

1 carrot, peeled and shredded

1 red bell pepper (capsicum), seeded and cut into 2-inch (5-cm) matchsticks

1 yellow bell pepper (capsicum), seeded and cut into 2-inch (5-cm) matchsticks

½ cup (⅔ oz/20 g) chopped fresh dill

16 thin lemon slices

Fresh dill sprigs

Serves 8

1 Pat the catfish fillets dry with paper towels. Season on both sides with salt and pepper.

2 To make the vinaigrette, in a bowl, whisk together the wine, lemon juice and zest, and mustard. In a small measuring pitcher, combine the sesame oil and the canola oil. Slowly add the oil to the bowl in a thin, steady stream, whisking constantly, until the vinaigrette is thick and emulsified. Whisk in the salt, pepper, and sugar. Stir in the sesame seeds.

3 To make the coleslaw, in a large bowl, toss together the red cabbage, green cabbage, green onions, ginger, carrot, red and yellow bell peppers, and half of the chopped dill. Add half of the vinaigrette and toss to coat the vegetables evenly.

4 Preheat the oven to 400°F (200°C).

5 Cut 8 pieces of parchment (baking) paper, each about 12 by 18 inches (30 by 45 cm). Lay the pieces on a work surface and lightly oil the top surface of the parchment.

6 Divide the coleslaw evenly among the pieces of parchment, placing each portion slightly off center. Place a catfish fillet over each mound of slaw. Lay 2 lemon slices over each catfish fillet. Drizzle the remaining vinaigrette evenly over each portion, then top with the remaining chopped dill, dividing evenly.

7 Fold the parchment in half over the fish by bringing the short sides together and folding them to seal. Fold in the sides so that none of the juices or steam can escape. (The packets can be refrigerated for up to 4 hours before continuing.)

8 Place the packets on a baking sheet and place in the oven. Bake until the paper begins to brown and puff, 22–25 minutes. Remove from the oven and let stand for 5 minutes.

9 Place the packets on warmed individual plates. Carefully slit an X in the top of each packet to let the steam escape.

10 Garnish each packet with a sprig of fresh dill, then serve at once.

Squid in Sauce of Three Chiles

Calamares en Salsa de Tres Chiles • Mexico City • Mexico

At Restaurante Isadora in Mexico City, Carmen Ortuña creates intriguing dishes that combine traditional ingredients in an innovative way; this one is no exception.

1 lb (500 g) squid

Salt and freshly ground pepper to taste

1 *each* fresh ancho chile, mulato chile, and guajillo chile

1½ teaspoons olive oil

1½ teaspoons minced garlic, plus 1 clove, minced

Juice of 1 lime

2 teaspoons Worcestershire sauce

½ cup (4 fl oz/125 ml) dry white wine

1 cup (8 fl oz/250 ml) bottled clam juice

2 tablespoons unsalted butter

Steamed white rice for serving

¼ cup (½ oz/15 g) finely chopped fresh flat-leaf (Italian) parsley

Serves 4

1 First, clean the squid: Working with 1 squid at a time, pull the head from the body. Cut off and reserve the tentacles; discard the head. Squeeze out and discard the small, hard "beak" at the base of the tentacles; leave the tentacles whole. Using your fingers, pull out any internal matter from the body, including the quill-like cartilage, and discard. Peel off the mottled skin that covers the body. Rinse the body well. Cut the body crosswise into rings ¼ inch (6 mm) wide. Leave the tentacles whole. Pat dry and sprinkle with salt and pepper. Set aside.

2 Cut each chile in half from top to bottom. Remove the seeds and veins. Slice the chiles crosswise into narrow strips ¾ inch (2 cm) long. In a saucepan over medium-low heat, warm the oil. Add the 1½ teaspoons minced garlic and sauté for about 1 minute. Add the chiles, lime juice, Worcestershire sauce, and wine and cook for 2 minutes. Add the clam juice. Bring to a boil, reduce the heat to low, and simmer for 10 minutes.

3 Melt the butter in a frying pan over medium heat. Add the minced garlic clove and sauté until translucent, about 30 seconds. Add the squid and sauté until opaque, just a couple of minutes. Stir in the chile sauce and heat through.

4 Scoop some rice onto warmed plates and spoon the squid and sauce over it. Garnish with the parsley and serve at once.

COMIDA NEGRA

An oft-stated principle of cooking is that the appearance of a dish is almost as important as its taste. If food is garnished with a bit of color, it will appeal to the eater. The unadorned black (*negro*) dishes of Mexico, however, refute that premise. The supreme dishes of most regions are singularly monochromatic.

One of the most prized of Yucatecan dishes is relleno *negro*, stuffed turkey seasoned with *chirmole*, a paste of burnt black chile. In states bordering the Gulf of Mexico, *calamares en su tinta* is a favorite. Tiny squid are cooked in a subtly flavored but disconcertingly black sauce made from liquid that has been extracted from the squid's ink sacs. Even the accompanying rice turns gray.

In Mexico City's sophisticated restaurants, *huitlacoche*, a black fungus that grows on ears of corn, is a great delicacy in soups and as a crepe filling. The exotic mushroomy flavor of the fungus, often compared with that of truffles, transforms even a simple taco or quesadilla. To convey the idea of what it looks like, the Aztec-derived name roughly translates as "sleeping excrement."

Remember, too, that the queen of all fiesta dishes is *mole poblano,* with its chile-rich black sauce, and, in Oaxaca, the *mole negro.*

Fish and Chips

New England • America

Sprinkle a little malt vinegar on this batter-fried fish, and you will have a dish worthy of serving in any London pub, although many New Englanders opt to enjoy this classic with lemon wedges and tartar sauce instead. Scrod is the official term for the smallest of the Atlantic cods. If it is unavailable, you may substitute any white fish with medium-firm flesh, such as cod, pollock, or haddock; however, be sure to avoid their more delicate-fleshed relatives, such as flounder, sole, whiting, or hake.

1 Pour the corn oil into a deep-fat fryer or deep, heavy saucepan to a depth of about 3 inches (7.5 cm) and heat over medium-high heat to 375°F (190°C).

2 Meanwhile, prepare the potatoes: Have ready a large bowl of cold water. Cut the potatoes into strips 2½ inches (6 cm) long by ⅜ inch (1 cm) wide by ⅜ inch (1 cm) thick. As they are cut, immerse them in the water. Leave the potatoes to soak while the oil heats. Preheat the oven to 225°F (110°C). Line a large baking sheet with paper towels.

3 When the oil is almost up to temperature, drain the potatoes and dry well with paper towels. It is important to dry thoroughly, or the oil will spatter. Add one-third of the potatoes to the hot oil and cook until golden brown, about 4 minutes. Using a slotted spoon, transfer the potatoes to the prepared baking sheet and sprinkle generously with salt. Place in the oven to keep warm. Repeat with the remaining potatoes in 2 batches, allowing the oil to regain its correct frying temperature between the batches.

4 While the potatoes are cooking, in a bowl, sift together the flour, the baking powder, 1 teaspoon salt, and the pepper. Once the potatoes are cooked, whisk the water, milk, and egg into the dry ingredients until smooth and well blended.

5 Pat the fish strips dry. Dip a strip into the batter and carefully slip into the hot oil. Repeat with a few more pieces, dipping only 1 strip at a time. Do not crowd the pan or the fish will not brown. Cook, carefully turning the fish as needed with the slotted spoon, until golden brown, about 4 minutes. Transfer to the baking sheet, sprinkle with salt, and keep warm in the oven. Repeat with the remaining fish in batches, allowing the oil to regain its correct frying temperature between the batches.

6 Serve the fish and chips at once in napkin-lined bowls with lemon wedges, malt vinegar, or tartar sauce, if you like.

Corn oil for deep-frying

4 large russet potatoes, unpeeled

Salt to taste, plus 1 teaspoon

1 cup (5 oz/155 g) all-purpose (plain) flour

1½ teaspoons baking powder

½ teaspoon freshly ground pepper

½ cup (4 fl oz/125 ml) water

½ cup (4 fl oz/125 ml) milk

1 egg, lightly beaten

2½ lb (1.25 kg) scrod or other firm white-fleshed fish fillets, cut into strips 4 inches (10 cm) long by 2 inches (5 cm) wide

Lemon wedges, malt vinegar, or tartar sauce (optional)

Serves 6

Trout in Herb Sauce

Trucha en Salsa de Hierbas • Michoacán • Mexico

Once abundant with fish, the streams and lakes of Mexico's high tablelands are now quite polluted. In Michoacán, whose name translates to "the place of fish," the scarcity has forced the locals to turn to fish farming to satisfy the demand. This recipe comes from Señora Livier de Suarez, one of Morelia's outstanding cooks. Garlic bread is a great accompaniment.

SAUCE

1 cup (1½ oz/45 g) chopped fresh cilantro (fresh coriander)

1 cup (1½ oz/45 g) chopped fresh flat-leaf (Italian) parsley

1 cup (8 fl oz/250 ml) dry white wine

3 cloves garlic, chopped

1 teaspoon Worcestershire sauce

1 teaspoon chopped fresh oregano or ½ teaspoon dried, preferably Mexican

¼ teaspoon Tabasco sauce or other hot-pepper sauce

3 tablespoons extra-virgin olive oil

Sea salt to taste

½ teaspoon freshly ground pepper

TROUT

4 rainbow trout, cleaned with heads intact, 6–8 oz (185–250 g) each

Sea salt to taste, plus 1 teaspoon

1 teaspoon freshly ground pepper

1 cup (5 oz/155 g) all-purpose (plain) flour

½ cup (2½ oz/75 g) *masa harina* for tortillas (page 224)

1 cup (8 fl oz/250 ml) milk

6 tablespoons (3 oz/90 g) unsalted butter

1 teaspoon safflower or canola oil

2 limes or lemons, cut into wedges

Serves 4

1 To make the sauce, put the cilantro, parsley, wine, garlic, Worcestershire sauce, oregano, and Tabasco sauce in a blender and process briefly. Slowly pour in the oil, blending until just absorbed. Season with salt and the pepper. Pour the sauce into a saucepan and bring to a simmer. Keep warm over low heat.

2 Rinse the fish and pat dry. Season the cavities with salt to taste and ½ teaspoon of the pepper. In a shallow dish, mix together the flour, *masa harina*, 1 teaspoon salt, and the remaining ½ teaspoon pepper. Pour the milk into a shallow bowl.

3 In a large frying pan over medium heat, melt the butter with the oil. Dip each trout into the milk and then into the seasoned flour. When the butter is just bubbly but not yet browned, gently slide in the fish. Fry, turning once, until lightly golden and the flesh is just becoming opaque, 4–5 minutes per side.

4 Transfer the fried trout to warmed individual plates. Pour the warmed sauce over the top, arrange the lime or lemon wedges on the side, and serve.

Dungeness Crab Boil with Shallot Butter

Pacific Northwest • America

Most Northwest crab recipes are devoid of too many additional flavorings, all the better to let the sweet flavor of the crab shine through. This is true of the region's crab boil dinners, which focus on piles of steaming crabs in the middle of a big table covered by newspapers. Accompaniments include melted butter, lemon wedges, and maybe cocktail sauce. Here, that basic idea has been embellished, with some lemon and herbs added to the cooking water, and the butter blended with the sweetness of roasted shallot.

SHALLOT BUTTER

1 shallot, peeled but left whole

1 teaspoon olive oil

¾ cup (6 oz/185 g) unsalted butter, melted

Pinch of salt

Salt

1 lemon, sliced

Handful of fresh herb sprigs such as flat-leaf (Italian) parsley, chervil, tarragon, and/or chives

2 live Dungeness crabs, about 2½ lb (1.5 kg) each

Serves 2–4

1 To make the shallot butter, preheat an oven to 400°F (200°C). Set the shallot on a piece of aluminum foil, drizzle the olive oil over the shallot, and wrap the foil around it to seal securely. Roast the shallot until aromatic and tender when squeezed, about 30 minutes. Remove from the oven, unwrap, and let cool.

2 Coarsely chop the shallot and place in a food processor or blender. Add the melted butter and process until the shallot is puréed. Add the pinch of salt and continue to process until the mixture is very smooth. Pour into a small saucepan and set aside.

3 Fill a large pot three-fourths full of water, salt generously, and add the lemon slices and herbs. Bring to a boil over high heat. (If you don't have a pot large enough to cook both crabs at the same time, cook them one at a time.) When the water is at a full rolling boil, grab each of the crabs securely at the back of the carapace (top shell) and gently drop them headfirst into the boiling water. Cover the pot, return to a boil, and then reduce the heat to medium-high. Cook the crabs for 20 minutes, counting from the time that the water returns to a boil. Watch the pot during cooking; the liquid may bubble up and over the edge, so you might want to set the lid askew to allow steam to escape.

4 Drain the crabs well. When they are just cool enough to handle, and working with 1 crab at a time, lift off and discard the carapace. Turn the crab over and lift off the "apron," or small, narrow triangular shell flap. Pull or scrape out the dark gray intestines and the liver from the body section and discard. The crab "butter," a yellowish amber mass, can be scooped out and saved for eating along with the crabmeat. Also lift off and discard the feathery gills on either side of the cavity. Use a large, heavy knife to cut the body in half where it narrows at the center.

5 Arrange the hot crabs on a large platter and serve with crab crackers for cracking the shells and with seafood forks for picking the meat from the shells. Gently reheat the shallot butter and pour it into individual bowls for dipping the sweet crabmeat. Place an empty bowl on the table for discarded shells.

Petrale Sole Doré with Lemon-Caper Butter

California • America

A specialty of San Francisco's oldest seafood restaurants, sole doré is coated with egg before frying to give it a gilded (*doré*) appearance. Many knowledgeable diners consider the petrale—which is technically flounder, not sole—one of the best West Coast fish because of its fine texture and delicate flavor, but any small flatfish fillets will work in this preparation. You can also make the recipe with whole petrale sole or sand dabs, although the fish will take longer to cook.

1 Season the fillets on both sides with salt and pepper. Spread the flour on a sheet of waxed paper. Crack the eggs into a large, shallow bowl and beat until well blended. Place a large nonstick frying pan over medium-high heat. When it is hot, add the olive oil. When the oil is hot, add the 2 teaspoons butter. Do not allow it to burn.

2 Working quickly, dip the fillets in the flour, coating both sides lightly and shaking off any excess. One at a time, dip the floured fillets in the beaten egg. Coat them thoroughly, allowing excess egg to drip back into the bowl. Place the fillets in the hot pan. Reduce the heat to medium-low.

3 Cook until the underside is nicely browned, about 5 minutes. Turn carefully with an offset spatula. Season the browned side with paprika. Continue cooking until the fish is opaque throughout when tested with a knife, 3–4 minutes longer.

4 Transfer the fish to a warmed platter. Wipe the frying pan with paper towels and return to low heat. Add the remaining 3 tablespoons butter, and the capers, parsley, and lemon juice. Swirl the pan until the butter melts. Pour the pan sauce over the fish. Garnish with lemon wedges and serve immediately.

2 petrale sole fillets, about ¾ lb (375 g) total weight

Salt and freshly ground pepper to taste

About ¼ cup (1½ oz/45 g) unbleached all-purpose (plain) flour

2 eggs

2 teaspoons olive oil

2 teaspoons plus 3 tablespoons unsalted butter

Sweet paprika

2 tablespoons capers, coarsely chopped

1 tablespoon chopped fresh flat-leaf (Italian) parsley

1 tablespoon fresh Meyer lemon juice

2 Meyer lemon wedges

Serves 2

Shrimp with Orange and Tequila

Camarones con Naranja y Tequila • Jalísco • Mexico

This coastal dish from María Dolores Torres Yzábal has an orange-and-chile sauce for a tangy accent. Serve it over steamed white rice, if you like.

1 orange

6 tablespoons (3 oz/90 g) unsalted butter

2 tablespoons finely chopped white onion

2 cloves garlic

16 large shrimp (prawns), peeled with final tail segment intact and deveined

1 *chile chipotle en adobo* or 2 serrano chiles, finely chopped

¼ cup (2 fl oz/60 ml) *tequila reposado*

3 tablespoons minced fresh cilantro (fresh coriander)

Sea salt to taste

Serves 4

1 With a zester or vegetable peeler, cut the zest from the orange in very narrow strips, being careful to avoid any of the white pith. Bring a saucepan of water to boil. Place the strips in a small sieve or slotted spoon, plunge them into the boiling water, remove immediately, and rinse under running cold water. Repeat three times to remove the bitter taste. Pat the orange strips dry with paper towels.

2 In a frying pan over medium heat, melt the butter. Add the onion and sauté until translucent, 3–4 minutes. Add the garlic and shrimp and cook, stirring frequently, until the shrimp turn pink and begin to curl, 4–5 minutes. Do not overcook the shrimp; they should be tender, not rubbery.

3 Add the chipotle chile or serrano chiles and the orange strips. Stir briefly to mix. Pour the tequila over the shrimp, carefully ignite with a long match, and let the flames burn out. Add the minced cilantro, season with salt, and serve on a warmed platter.

Fish Tacos

Tacos de Salpicón de Pescado · Veracruz · Mexico

Up and down the long coastline of Veracruz are weather-ravaged, palm-thatched stands selling tacos made of shredded fish, as well as all kinds of seafood cocktails. Frosty bottles of Mexican beer are set up on the counter along with guacamole, and everyone forgets their troubles, relaxes, and enjoys the day.

1½ lb (750 g) red snapper or other firm white-fleshed fish fillets

1 teaspoon sea salt

Freshly ground pepper to taste

¾ cup (4 oz/125 g) all-purpose (plain) flour

¼ cup (2 fl oz/60 ml) corn or safflower oil

2 cups (16 fl oz/500 ml) fresh tomato salsa

10 corn tortillas, warmed

1 cup (3 oz/90 g) chopped cabbage

2 limes, quartered

Makes 10 tacos; serves 4

1 Season both sides of each fish fillet with the salt and a generous amount of pepper. Spread the flour on a plate and dip the fish in it, coating evenly and shaking off any excess.

2 In a large frying pan over medium-high heat, warm the oil until it is rippling hot but not smoking. Add the fish fillets and fry, turning once, until golden on both sides, just over 1 minute total. Using a slotted spatula, transfer the fillets to paper towels to drain briefly. While the fillets are still hot, shred them with a fork. Put the salsa in a bowl and stir in the fish.

3 To assemble the tacos, place some fish into each tortilla and add a bit of the crunchy cabbage. Serve with the limes on the side.

Fritto Misto of Squid, Artichokes, and Lemon

California · America

California fishermen find squid all along the state's coast, but the catch is most abundant in Southern and Central California. Local restaurant-goers like to launch a meal with fried calamari or, in the Italian tradition, a mixed fry (*fritto misto*) with artichokes and paper-thin lemon slices. Onion rings and shrimp (prawns) are other possible additions. Be sure to use plenty of oil when you fry and to maintain the oil temperature at 375°F (190°C). A deep-frying thermometer is critical.

1 First, clean the squid: Working with 1 squid at a time, pull the head from the body. Cut off and reserve the tentacles; discard the head. Squeeze out and discard the small, hard "beak" at the base of the tentacles; leave the tentacles whole. Using your fingers, pull out any internal matter from the body, including the quill-like cartilage, and discard. Peel off the mottled skin that covers the body. Rinse the body well. Cut the body crosswise into rings ½ inch (12 mm) wide. Put the rings and tentacles in a bowl and add enough of the buttermilk to coat the squid. Set aside.

2 Working with 1 artichoke at a time, pull back and snap off the outer leaves until you reach the pale heart. Trim the base of any brown parts and cut about ½ inch off the top. Cut each artichoke into 4 lengthwise slices, each with some stem attached. Put the sliced artichokes in a bowl and add enough buttermilk to coat the slices.

3 Slice the lemon into very thin rounds, discarding the end pieces. Put the lemon slices in a bowl and add buttermilk to coat the slices.

4 Pour the oil into a deep saucepan to a depth of about 3 inches (7.5 cm), and heat to 375°F (190°C). While the oil heats, combine the flour, 2 teaspoons sea salt, cayenne pepper, and black pepper in a pie dish and stir to blend.

5 Drain the artichokes well in a sieve, then transfer to the pie dish. Toss to coat evenly with the flour mixture. Transfer to another sieve and shake to remove any excess coating.

6 Fry the artichokes in batches until golden brown outside and tender within, about 1½ minutes. Using a wire skimmer or slotted spoon, transfer the artichokes to paper towels to drain. Repeat the process with the squid, then with the lemon slices. Be sure to let the oil return to 375°F (190°C) before frying each new batch. Each squid batch will take about 1 minute, and the lemon slices about 30 seconds. Drain on paper towels.

7 Season the artichokes, squid, and lemon slices with salt. Combine in a basket or on a platter, or divide among individual plates, and serve.

1 lb (500 g) squid

About 2 cups (16 fl oz/500 ml) buttermilk

12 baby artichokes

1 lemon

Olive oil for deep-frying

2 cups (10 oz/315 g) unbleached all-purpose (plain) flour

2 teaspoons sea salt, plus salt to taste

1 teaspoon cayenne pepper

Several grinds of black pepper

Serves 4

Steamed Thai Red Curry Mussels

Pacific Northwest · America

Mussels are among the most prolific wild seafoods of the Northwest, but virtually all of those sold in the area are farm-raised and are primarily blue mussels, with shells that are deep blue-black on the outside and pearlescent on the inside. The abundant seafood melds well with the Asian influences that have become part of Northwest cooking. Here, Thai flavors dress up the plump shellfish.

1 tablespoon olive oil

½ cup (1½ oz/45 g) chopped green (spring) onion, including tender green tops

2 teaspoons Thai red curry paste

¾ cup (6 fl oz/180 ml) unsweetened coconut milk

¾ cup (6 fl oz/180 ml) dry white wine

3 lb (1.5 kg) mussels, scrubbed and debearded

Coarse country bread

Serves 4

1 In a large pot over medium heat, warm the olive oil. Add the green onion and sauté until tender, 2–3 minutes.

2 Add the curry paste and cook, stirring, until aromatic and softened, about 1 minute. Stir in the coconut milk and wine and raise the heat to medium-high. Bring just to a boil, stirring to blend the ingredients evenly.

3 Add the mussels, discarding any that do not close to the touch, and cover the pot. Cook, occasionally shaking the pot gently for even cooking, until the mussels open, 3–5 minutes.

4 Using a slotted spoon, divide the mussels evenly among individual bowls, discarding any that failed to open. Spoon the cooking liquid over the mussels, again dividing evenly.

5 Serve immediately, and pass the bread at the table. Place an empty bowl or two on the table for discarded shells.

Grilled Salmon with Shaved Fennel Salad

California · America

Commercially fished in waters from Central to Northern California, wild salmon arrives in markets in late spring and summer, conveniently coinciding with barbecue season.

2 fennel bulbs, plus ¼ cup (⅓ oz/10 g) chopped leaves

2 large shallots, halved and very thinly sliced

8 tablespoons (4 fl oz/125 ml) extra-virgin olive oil

1½–2 tablespoons fresh lemon juice

Salt and freshly ground pepper to taste

1 side of salmon, about 3½ lb (1.75 kg), with skin intact

1 lemon, very thinly sliced

Serves 8

1 Cut the fennel bulbs in half through the core, then slice crosswise as thinly as possible. Put the fennel slices in a bowl along with the fennel leaves, the shallots, and 6 tablespoons (3 fl oz/80 ml) olive oil. Add 1½ tablespoons lemon juice, and salt and pepper. Toss well, taste, and add more lemon juice if desired. Let stand at room temperature for 45 minutes.

2 Rub your fingers along the surface of the salmon, and then use needle-nose pliers or tweezers to remove any fine pin bones. Rub the flesh side with the remaining 2 tablespoons olive oil. Season generously with salt and pepper. Arrange the lemon slices down the center of the flesh side of the salmon, overlapping them.

3 Prepare a hot fire in a charcoal grill. When the coals are gray, arrange them in 2 piles on either side of the grill bed, leaving a space between them large enough for the salmon. Put the salmon on the grill, skin side down. Cover the grill, leaving the vents wide open. Cook until the salmon is firm to the touch, 20–25 minutes.

4 Serve the fish directly from the grill. Use a long offset spatula to lift portions of the salmon from the skin, leaving the skin on the grill and dividing the fish evenly among individual plates. With a slotted spoon, put some of the fennel salad alongside the salmon, dividing it evenly. Serve at once.

PACIFIC KING SALMON

The salmon, with its distinctive orange-pink flesh, is a West Coast icon—a fish that seduces both the eye and the palate. From Alaska to California, salmon fishermen maintain an age-old way of life, going out into Pacific Coast waters to retrieve the glistening, silvery fish for salmon lovers across the country. Five species are native to the Pacific Coast: king (Chinook), sockeye (red), coho (silver), pink (humpback), and chum (keta). But the king is easily the most sought after, with anglers and eaters quick to praise its natural richness—thanks to a high fat content—and its impressive size—an average weight between twenty and twenty-five pounds (10 and 12.5 kg) each.

The most prized kings are those caught in the wild runs that begin in late spring and continue into early autumn. Lucky West Coast residents can buy the salmon directly from fishing boats at key docks, including San Francisco's Fishermen's Wharf, the port of Astoria in Oregon, and Seattle's Fishermen's Terminal. This celebrated fish needs only the simplest treatment. Locals like to grill or panfry king salmon and serve it with fresh salsa or a scattering of herbs. Because of their richness, kings are also ideal for the smoker: typically, the fillets are brined and then are set over smoldering wood chips that infuse them with flavor and gently cook the flesh.

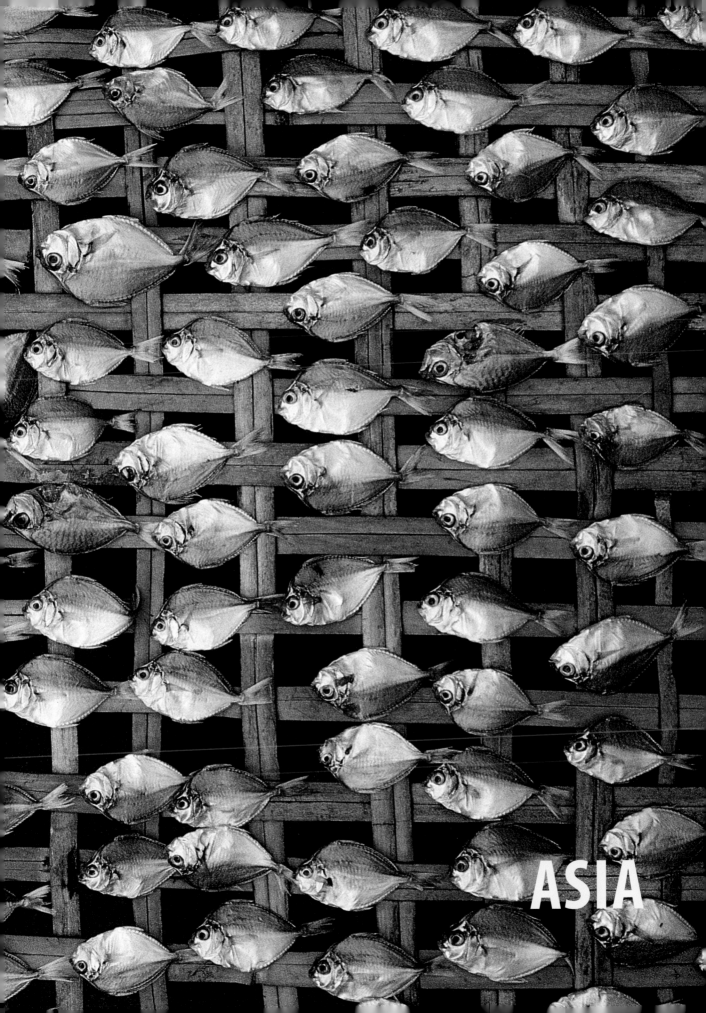

ASIA

Preceding pages: Small silver fish dry on a simple rack in the steady heat of a Manila afternoon. **Top:** China's longest river, the Changjiang (Yangtze), flows between the towering skyscrapers of Chongqing, deep in the heart of China. **Above:** Fish heads are commonly sold at Asian markets for making stock and clay pot dishes. **Right:** On the waterways of China's scenic Li River, cormorant fishing has been practiced for centuries.

*F*ish and seafood are highly regarded in Asia. China's vast inland rivers, lakes, dams, and ponds provides an impressive variety of fish, shellfish, eels, turtles, water-grown vegetables, and edible mosses. Offshore waters teem with deep-sea fish, shellfish, and peculiar sea creatures treasured by Chinese cooks and epicures, while estuaries supply crustaceans and shrimp (prawns). Those too small for the cooking pot are dried and fermented into a pungent paste. Symbolism plays a significant role in formal Chinese dining. The word for fish is yu, a homonym for abundance. So, to serve a whole fish is to wish guests abundance and prosperity.

In Guangdong, whole fish is served steamed with ginger, to highlight and intensify its fresh, natural flavor. The famous West Lake fish of Hangzhou features a freshwater fish poached and served beneath a glossy coating, with the mild tang of rice vinegar. In Sichuan, a whole carp would be shallow-fried with a potent chile sauce, and in Beijing it would be deep-fried and bathed in a complex, wine-based sauce. These seasoning preferences briefly show the cooking styles of the major regions of China: mild with the emphasis on natural flavors in the south; intense yet elegant for the east; fiery and pungent in Sichuan and the central west; and refined and well honed in the north.

While Indian meat and vegetable dishes have become international favorites, the country's considerable seafood repertoire is less well known. Many Indians, such as those of West Bengal, Orissa, and Tamil Nadu who live along the waterways of the east coast, prefer freshwater fish to saltwater varieties, even though India is bound by the sea on two sides. Fish caught in local rivers and streams are used in local specialties, such as the Bengali *machor jhal*, usually made with a silvery green-and-purple fish known as *hilsa*. Prized for its meatiness, it also comes bristling with bones, which can make eating it treacherous. Bengalis don't seem to mind, but other Indians often substitute a different fish when preparing these braised fish steaks with potatoes, eggplant, and the spice blend *panch phoron*. The people of the Konkan region and Kerala on the west coast

traditionally fish in bays. Their most popular catches are pomfret, a delicate fish similar to Dover sole, and large, succulent, stripe-shelled tiger prawns. Both of these can be flash-roasted in the intense, dry heat of the tandoor, tall, barrel-shaped clay ovens. Although many Indian fish species are unavailable fresh in the West, salmon, sea bass, flounder, sole, haddock, and monkfish make excellent substitutes.

A defining element of the Southeast Asian table is fresh- and saltwater fish and shellfish, which appear in some form at nearly every meal. The mighty Mekong River starts in China and meanders through the rice paddies of Laos, Thailand, and Cambodia until it finally empties into the South China Sea at the southern tip of Vietnam. Everyone who lives along its path depends on the river's bounty for food. With the exception of Laos, each Southeast Asian country has a border on the sea, with the Philippines and Indonesia home to particularly fertile fishing grounds. Pomfret, mackerel, snapper, catfish, perch, lobster, crab, shrimp, clams, and cockles are plentiful in the region, and cooks toss them into blazing hot woks. Grilled fish is an everyday preparation, too. Pulled from nearby waters, the fish are quickly cleaned, seasoned with aromatic herbs and spices, and then, either left naked or wrapped in banana leaves, placed atop wood-fired grills. They are cooked until the flesh is perfectly

succulent—and not a moment longer. Also popular is steamed whole fish, a preparation borrowed from the southern Chinese kitchen. A staple dish on the streets of Singapore is chile crab, served straight from the hawker's wok. Quickly boiled, then cleaned and chopped, crabs are wok-fried in a pungent, spicy sauce of ginger, fresh red chiles, garlic, fish sauce, and sugar, then glazed with egg and served with French bread to mop up the sauce.

Fish and shellfish are central to Southeast Asian cooking in other ways, too. Extracted from salted anchovies packed into barrels and left to ferment, the amber, nutrient-rich liquid known as fish sauce is an indispensable item in the kitchens of Thailand, Vietnam, Laos, and Cambodia, and shares cupboard space with soy sauce in Malaysia, Singapore, Indonesia, Myanmar, and the Philippines. It is a key ingredient in *nuoc cham*, the ubiquitous sweet-sour-salty dipping sauce of Vietnam, in which the pungency of the fish sauce is tempered with sugar, lime juice, garlic, and hot chiles. Dried shrimp paste is another condiment without which no Southeast Asian kitchen would be complete. It comes in two basic forms, a hard, sliceable cake and a very thick, spoonable mass sold in a plastic tub. Although the types of shrimp paste are different, they both deliver the sharp, pungent flavor that many Southeast Asians have grown to expect on the dinner table.

Left: According to a local saying, there are more coconut palms in southern India than there are stars in the sky. Coconut is an integral part of Indian food, with coconut milk often replacing cow's milk. **Above, left:** The waters of the Arabian Sea, off India's southwestern coast, yield an abundance of shellfish, sardines, and mackerel, resulting in a local cuisine that is rich in seafood. **Above, right:** Dried starfish, snakeskins, and frogs make striking wall decorations as they hang in a stall in China's Qing Ping Market, which is located in central Guangzhou, Guangdong province.

Scallops and Snow Peas with Crabmeat Sauce

Bai Zhi Xian Bei Pang Xie • Eastern • China

Ginger wine is a seasoning and marinade made by combining 1 part ginger juice with 2–3 parts Chinese rice wine. To make ginger juice, peel and finely grate fresh ginger root onto a piece of muslin (cheesecloth), gather the cloth into a tight ball, and squeeze to extract the juice from the ginger. Keep in mind that one tablespoon of grated ginger will produce approximately 1½ teaspoons of ginger juice.

9 oz (280 g) sea scallops

½ teaspoon salt

2 teaspoons ginger wine (see note)

CRABMEAT SAUCE

1 tablespoon vegetable oil

½ cup (2½ oz/75 g) crabmeat, flaked, or finely chopped shrimp (prawn) meat

2 green (spring) onions, white part only, chopped

2 teaspoons rice wine

1 teaspoon light soy sauce

1½ teaspoons cornstarch (cornflour) dissolved in ½ cup (4 fl oz/125 ml) fish stock or chicken stock

Salt and ground white pepper to taste

1 egg white, lightly beaten

2 tablespoons vegetable oil

3 oz (90 g) small snow peas (mangetouts), trimmed

2 oz (60 g) small fresh oyster mushrooms, brushed clean

5 thin fresh ginger slices, peeled and finely julienned

Serves 4

1 Place the scallops in a bowl, add the salt and ginger wine, and mix gently. Let stand for 10 minutes.

2 To prepare the sauce, in a small saucepan over high heat, warm the oil. When it is medium-hot, add the crabmeat or shrimp and green onion and stir until warmed through, about 30 seconds. Add the rice wine and soy sauce and stir briefly. Add the cornstarch mixture and stir slowly until the sauce thickens and becomes clear, about 40 seconds. Season with salt, if needed, and generously season with white pepper.

3 Remove from the heat and slowly pour in the egg white in a fine stream. Allow to set without stirring, returning to low heat if the heat is insufficient to set the egg white.

4 In a wok over high heat, warm the oil. Add the scallops and stir-fry for 30 seconds. Be sure the heat is as high as possible, or the juices will run from the scallops, making them tough and chewy. Add the snow peas and stir-fry briefly, then add the mushrooms and ginger and stir-fry until the scallops are firm and white, about 40 seconds longer.

5 Add the sauce to the scallops and heat over high heat for about 20 seconds. Transfer to a serving plate and serve at once.

Spice-Rubbed Grilled Shrimp

Richeiado • Goa • India

Richeiado is a popular, simple preparation celebrating the shrimp harvest along the shores of Goa. Serve these hot-and-spicy shrimp with tropical cocktails made with Goa's *fenni*.

1 lb (500 g) jumbo or large shrimp (prawns), peeled with the last shell segment and tail fin intact and deveined

SPICE PASTE

1 tablespoon minced garlic

1 tablespoon peeled and grated fresh ginger

2 teaspoons cayenne pepper

1 teaspoon ground black pepper

1 teaspoon ground cumin

½ teaspoon ground cinnamon

¼ teaspoon *each* ground cloves and ground turmeric

2 tablespoons *fenni* (see sidebar, below) or gin

1 teaspoon dark brown sugar

2 tablespoons mustard oil or olive oil

1 tablespoon fresh lemon juice

Salad greens

Serves 2

1 Place the shrimp in a dish. To make the spice paste, combine the garlic, ginger, cayenne pepper, black pepper, cumin, cinnamon, cloves, turmeric, *fenni* or gin, and dark brown sugar. Rub the paste evenly over the shrimp. Set aside for 30 minutes at room temperature.

2 In a large frying pan over high heat, warm the oil. When very hot, add the shrimp and cook, tossing, until they turn pink and curl, about 5 minutes. Sprinkle with the lemon juice. Serve immediately over a bed of salad greens.

CASHEW FRUIT LIQUOR

Mention Goa to an Indian, and palm-fringed beaches, fiery vindaloos, haunting *mando* music, and sipping *fenni* come to mind. One seldom hears of *fenni* outside the state, however, because the Goans love the liquor so much that none is left for export.

There are two varieties of *fenni*: coconut and cashew. Centuries ago the Konkan people of Goa tapped and fermented coconut, turning it into mild-tasting coconut *fenni*. Cashew *fenni*, however, is relatively new. The Portuguese, who colonized Goa in 1510,

introduced the cashew plant. Pear-shaped and juicy, the orange-yellow fruits were plucked when fully ripe and the nuts were separated. The fruit was processed in a manner similar to that for coconut *fenni*. Today, the strong and assertive cashew *fenni* (an acquired taste for some) is the favorite.

Purists prefer to sip *fenni* straight, like cognac, but the most popular way to serve it is with lime soda over ice. The cashew liquor is also the secret ingredient in many Goan marinades for seafood.

Balinese Fish with Lemongrass and Lime

Ikan Goreng Sambal Bawang • Indonesia

Bali is an island of fishing villages: the local diet is rich in catches pulled from the sea and from the interior lakes. Whole or cut-up fish is typically grilled, deep-fried, steamed, or curried and served with a *sambal*. This particular dish is perfect for festive occasions. The *sambal* that is served spooned over the fish is nicely tart and wonderfully refreshing.

1 Rinse each fish and pat dry with paper towels. With kitchen shears, carefully cut off the top dorsal fins, the bottom ventral fins, and the side fins. Working with 1 fish at a time, make 3 diagonal cuts almost to the bone in the thickest part on each side of the body. Rub the entire fish with some of the lime juice and the turmeric. Season both sides with salt and pepper. Cover and refrigerate for a few hours.

2 To make the *sambal*, wrap the dried shrimp paste in aluminum foil and place the packet directly on a stove-top burner turned on to medium-high heat. Toast it, turning twice, until fragrant, 1–2 minutes. Remove the packet and open it; if the shrimp paste crumbles, it is ready. Let cool. Put the cooled shrimp paste into a bowl and add the lemongrass, shallots, chiles, garlic, lime leaves, salt, lime juice, and canola oil. Stir well and set aside.

3 Pour peanut oil to a depth of about 1 inch (2.5 cm) in a large frying pan and heat to 365°F (185°C) on a deep-frying thermometer. Sprinkle the fish on both sides with salt.

4 When the oil is ready, slip the fish into the oil in a single layer without touching (you may need to fry them in 2 batches) and deep-fry, undisturbed, until browned and crusty, about 3 minutes. Turn the fish over and fry on the second side until browned, crusty, and cooked through, about 3 minutes longer, depending upon the thickness of the fish. (Calculate 10 minutes cooking time per 1 inch/2.5 cm, measured at the thickest section of the fish.)

5 Using a slotted utensil, carefully transfer the fish to paper towels to drain. Arrange on a platter, spoon the *sambal* over the fish, and serve at once.

4 whole small rock cod, pomfret, red snapper, bream, striped bass, or perch, each about 1 lb (500 g), cleaned, with head and tail intact

Juice of 1 lime

1 teaspoon ground turmeric

Salt and freshly ground pepper to taste

SAMBAL

1 slice dried shrimp paste, ⅛ inch (3 mm) thick

2 lemongrass stalks, tender midsection only, finely slivered (about 2 tablespoons)

3 small shallots, halved lengthwise, then finely slivered crosswise

4 red Thai, jalapeño, or serrano chiles, seeded and finely slivered

2 cloves garlic, finely slivered

2 kaffir lime leaves, spines removed and leaves finely slivered

½ teaspoon salt

Juice of 1 lime

2 tablespoons vegetable oil

Vegetable oil for deep-frying

Serves 4

Scallops in Thick Red Curry Sauce

Choo Chee Hoy Phat · Thailand

Unlike the more well-known Thai curry, or *gaeng*, which generally has a consistency similar to that of soup and is served in a bowl, *choo chee* curry uses less coconut milk, resulting in a thicker sauce and a dish that can easily be served on a plate.

½ cup (4 fl oz/125 ml) coconut cream (page 222)

1 tablespoon red curry paste

1 tablespoon palm sugar or brown sugar

1–2 tablespoons fish sauce

1 cup (8 fl oz/250 ml) coconut milk (page 222)

10 kaffir lime leaves, spines removed

1 tablespoon vegetable oil

¾ lb (375 g) sea scallops

Handful of fresh Thai basil leaves, plus sprigs for garnish

1 fresh red chile, seeded and finely sliced

Serves 4

1 In a wok or saucepan over medium-high heat, bring the coconut cream to a gentle boil. Adjust the heat to maintain a gentle boil and cook, stirring continuously, until tiny beads of oil appear on the surface, 5–8 minutes. Add the curry paste and fry gently, stirring constantly, for about 2 minutes. Add the palm or brown sugar and fish sauce and stir for a few seconds. Add the coconut milk and lime leaves and bring to a boil. Reduce the heat to medium-low and simmer, stirring occasionally, for 5 minutes.

2 Meanwhile, in a frying pan over medium-high heat, warm the vegetable oil. While the oil is heating, pat the scallops dry with paper towels. When the oil is hot, add as many of the scallops as will fit in a single layer. Let brown, undisturbed, for about 1 minute. Using tongs, turn the scallops over and brown on the second side, about 1 minute. Transfer to a plate. Repeat with the remaining scallops.

3 When the sauce thickens to a creamy consistency, taste and adjust with curry paste, palm or brown sugar, and fish sauce. Add the scallops and basil leaves and stir to heat through. Transfer to a serving platter and garnish with the chile slices and basil sprigs.

FLOATING MARKETS

In and around Bangkok, many of the local people spend much of their lives on a *klong*, or canal. Along these byways travels every kind of water conveyance, from small paddled boats to midsized taxis to long rice barges, the last often so fully loaded that their prows barely rise above the water. The Chao Phraya River, which flows from Thailand's northern hills and winds through the heart of the country like a sinuous snake, fans out into a huge network of canals that extends to almost every village in the central plains. For locals whose homes are perched on stilts along the banks, this floating world is both the source of their livelihood and their shopping center.

Every morning, women in brightly colored dress and straw hats load up their homegrown vegetables, fruits, coconuts, and flowers in long, narrow boats. For them, these boats are the family car. Some are pushed along with a bamboo pole or paddles, while more fortunate sellers switch on gasoline-driven motors. Their daily destination is the central floating market at Thonburi, Bangkok's sister city across the river, or to such smaller—and less touristed—markets as Khu Wiang or Damnoen Saduak. They will peddle goods straight from their boats, chanting promises of bargains.

In true entrepreneurial spirit, some boat owners have installed small kitchen burners in their crafts so that they might sell ready-to-eat foods. Not surprisingly, noodle dishes are at the top of most menus. In the twentieth century, Bangkok, once called the Venice of the East because of its many canals, saw its waterways slowly filled in to accommodate the growing number of cars. With the arrival of the car has come the sacrifice of much of the city's traditional *klong* life. Yet the floating market is likely to remain a vital part of the landscape.

Flaked Pomelo and Shrimp Salad

Yam Som • Thailand

The pomelo, a winter fruit native to Southeast Asia, looks like an enormous yellow grape-fruit with a slightly pointed top. Pomelo segments are not as juicy as those of grapefruit, but they have a snappier texture.

Vegetable oil for frying

1 tablespoon thinly sliced garlic

½ lb (250 g) large shrimp (prawns), peeled and deveined

1 large pomelo or 2 sweet grapefruits

DRESSING

2 teaspoons roasted chile paste (optional; page 221)

2 tablespoons fresh lime juice

1 tablespoon fish sauce

2 teaspoons sugar

1 red jalapeño chile, seeded and thinly sliced

1 tablespoon chopped fresh mint

2 tablespoons fried shallots

2 tablespoons roasted peanuts, crushed

¼ cup (¼ oz/7 g) fresh cilantro (fresh coriander) leaves

Serves 4–6

1 Pour vegetable oil to a depth of about 1 inch (2.5 cm) in a small frying pan, place over medium heat, and heat to 325°F (165°C) on a deep-frying thermometer. Add the garlic slices and fry until they turn light golden brown, about 5 minutes, reducing the heat if they color too quickly. Scoop them out with a slotted spoon, drain on a paper bag, and let cool.

2 Bring a large saucepan three-fourths full of salted water to a boil. Add the shrimp and boil until they turn orange-pink, 1–2 minutes. Drain and set aside to let cool. Peel the pomelo and divide it into segments. Remove the membrane from each segment and, using your fingers, break the flesh apart into smaller pieces, dropping them into a bowl. If using grapefruits, treat them in the same way, but place the pieces in a sieve to drain.

3 To make the dressing, in a large bowl, combine the roasted chile paste (if using), lime juice, fish sauce, sugar, and chile. Stir until the sugar dissolves. Add the shrimp, pomelo or grapefruit, mint, fried shallots, fried garlic, and peanuts and toss to mix. Turn out onto a serving plate, garnish with the cilantro, and serve.

West Lake Fish

Xihu Yu • Eastern • China

Life in the city of Hangzhou is a constant interaction with its famous scenic landmark, West Lake. Artists and poets are inspired by the lake's beauty, and chefs by the extraordinary variety of its harvest. For *xihu yu*, perhaps Hangzhou's most famous dish, plump carp from the lake are seasoned with local Shaoxing rice wine, black vinegar, and *lajiangyou*, a thin, pungent sauce rather like Worcestershire sauce.

1 large or 2 smaller freshwater fish such as trout or carp, about 1½ lb (750 g), cleaned

2 teaspoons peeled and grated fresh ginger

1 tablespoon rice wine

2 green (spring) onions, white part only, finely chopped

Large pinch of salt

SAUCE

¼ cup (2 fl oz/60 ml) light soy sauce

2 tablespoons vegetable oil

2 tablespoons Worcestershire sauce or 2 teaspoons tamarind concentrate

3–4 teaspoons black vinegar

1 tablespoon superfine (caster) sugar

Large pinch of ground white pepper

2 teaspoons cornstarch (cornflour)

Salt to taste

2 tablespoons peeled and finely julienned fresh ginger

2 green (spring) onions, tender green tops only, finely julienned

1 small, hot red chile, seeded and finely julienned

Serves 4–6

1 Rinse the fish well and drain thoroughly. Using a cleaver or large, sharp knife, and working from the cavity, make a deep cut to one side of the backbone of the fish and open the fish out flat. Carefully slide the blade of the knife beneath the breastbone of the side without the backbone, releasing the bones. One side of the fish will be boneless, while the other side will retain the backbone and breastbone. Turn the fish skin side up and make several deep, diagonal slashes across the thicker side, cutting almost down to the bone.

2 Set the fish on a plate and spread the grated ginger, rice wine, and chopped green onion evenly over the fish. Let stand for 15–20 minutes, turning once.

3 Pour water to a depth of about ¾ inch (2 cm) into a wide, shallow frying pan large enough to hold the fish flat. Add the salt and bring to a gentle boil over medium-high heat. Carefully slide in the fish and the marinade ingredients, skin side up. As soon as the water returns to a boil, remove the pan from the heat, cover, and leave the fish to poach gently in the hot liquid for about 10 minutes. Using 2 spatulas or slotted spoons, lift the fish onto a serving plate and scrape off any remaining marinade ingredients. The fish should be opaque near the bone when pierced with a knife. Keep warm.

4 To make the sauce, strain ⅓ cup (3 fl oz/80 ml) of the poaching liquid into a small saucepan and stir in the soy sauce, oil, Worcestershire sauce or tamarind concentrate, 3 teaspoons vinegar, and the sugar, pepper, and cornstarch. Place the pan over high heat and bring quickly to a boil, stirring continuously. Reduce the heat to low and simmer, stirring often, for about 2 minutes to blend the flavors. Taste and adjust the seasoning with salt and additional vinegar. It should be reasonably tart.

5 Spread the julienned ginger, the julienned green onion, and the chile evenly over the fish and spoon on the hot sauce. Serve at once.

CLAY POT COOKING

Clay pot cooking is widespread in China. For everyday cooking, unglazed "sand pots" made of sand and clay are designed to be used directly on top of the wood, charcoal, and gas ovens in most homes. The pots have a shiny interior glaze to make cleaning easier, and to hold in moisture and conduct heat. They come with a tight-fitting lid that makes them perfect for cooking rice, simmering soups, and long, slow braising and poaching.

Clay pots are lightweight, inexpensive, and hard-wearing. However, to avoid cracking, they should never be heated without liquid inside, used directly on electric rings or hotplates, or placed when hot on a cold surface. The wire cage on some clay pots makes them more resistant to breakage.

Yunnan clay steam pots have a unique function. Made from the same hard, dark clay that makes a perfect Chinese teapot, these pots have a tapering funnel inside. They are used in a steamer, and the funnel directs a flow of steam into the closed pot so the contents are steamed from both the inside and outside, lending an unsurpassed tenderness to the food.

Seafood Clay Pot

Hai Xian Geng • Eastern • China

Seafood soups and stews cooked in clay pots are a welcome dish in a home-cooked Chinese meal, particularly in the winter. With steamed rice and a plate of steamed greens, a seafood clay pot is a meal in itself. Timing is everything when cooking fresh seafood, and even more so when cooking several different varieties together. Shrimp (prawns) should retain a palatable crunch and fish should be tender enough to separate in moist flakes without crumbling dryly. Oysters and crabmeat require no more than a gentle warming.

½ lb (250 g) large shrimp (prawns) in the shell

¼ lb (125 g) squid

½ lb (250 g) firm white fish fillet

2-inch (5-cm) piece carrot

2 tablespoons vegetable oil

1 celery stalk, thinly sliced on the diagonal

½ yellow onion, cut into narrow wedges and layers separated

8 very thin slices fresh ginger, peeled

1¼ cups (10 fl oz/310 ml) chicken or fish stock

2 teaspoons rice wine

2 tablespoons oyster sauce

¼ cup (1¼ oz/40 g) thinly sliced bamboo shoot

¼ cup (1¼ oz/40 g) canned small straw mushrooms

1½ tablespoons cornstarch (cornflour) dissolved in 2 tablespoons water

2–3 oz (60–90 g) shucked oysters (optional)

3 oz (90 g) peeled small shrimp (prawns)

3 oz (90 g) crabmeat or 2 egg whites, lightly beaten

Salt and ground white pepper to taste

2 tablespoons thinly sliced green (spring) onion tops

Serves 4–8

1 If you have a large, flameproof Chinese clay pot, fill it with hot water and set it aside to warm up. If not, have ready a heavy saucepan.

2 To prepare the large shrimp, peel each shrimp, leaving the last segment of the shell and the tail in place. Cut deeply down the back, devein, and rinse in cold water. Pat dry with paper towels. Then, clean the squid: pull the head from the body. Cut off and reserve the tentacles; discard the head. Squeeze out and discard the small, hard "beak" at the base of the tentacles; leave the tentacles whole. Using your fingers, pull out any internal matter from the body, including the quill-like cartilage, and discard. Peel off the mottled skin that covers the body. Rinse and thoroughly dry the squid bodies. To prepare the squid, using a sharp knife, slit each body lengthwise to open it flat. Using the knife, score a ⅛-inch (3-mm) crosshatch pattern over the inside surface. Cut into 1-inch (2.5-cm) squares and set aside. Cut the fish into 1-inch (2.5-cm) cubes.

3 Peel the carrot and, using a carving tool or sharp knife, remove 5 or 6 V-shaped strips along the length. Slice the carrot crosswise to create flower-shaped pieces. Set aside.

4 Drain the water from the clay pot, if using. In the clay pot or saucepan over high heat, warm the oil. When it is hot, add the carrot, celery, yellow onion, and ginger and stir-fry until beginning to soften, about 1 minute. Pour in the stock and bring to a boil. Add the rice wine and oyster sauce and simmer for about 30 seconds to blend the flavors.

5 Add the large shrimp, squid, fish, bamboo shoot, and mushrooms and cook until the stock returns to a boil, about 2 minutes. Stir in the cornstarch mixture and cook, stirring, until the mixture returns to a boil, about 40 seconds.

6 Stir in the oysters, if using, the small shrimp, and the crabmeat, if using. If using the egg whites, pour them through a fine-mesh sieve held above the clay pot or saucepan, so they fall in fine streams. Remove from the heat and do not stir the dish for at least 2 minutes.

7 Season with salt and pepper and stir to distribute the seafood evenly. Leave in the clay pot, or tip into a deep serving dish. Scatter on the green onion tops and serve at once.

Hanoi-Style Fried Fish

Cha Ca Hanoi · Vietnam

This dish is virtually the only one served at Cha Ca La Vong, a famous rustic eatery in Hanoi. A waiter brings a table-top charcoal brazier topped with a small sauté pan. Inside the pan are a few crisp cubes of fish sizzling in golden oil, looking something like fondue. As you take pieces of fish and various fresh greens—basil, cilantro, green onions, dill—from the pan and dunk them into a bowl of rice noodles, the waiter promptly replenishes the pan with more cubes of light, sweet fish such as rock cod, bass, or catfish.

1 To make the *nuoc cham* dipping sauce, in a mortar, using a pestle, pound together the garlic and fresh red chile until the mixture is puréed. Stir in the lime juice, fish sauce, sugar, and water. Add the carrot, stir, and divide the dipping sauce among 6 small saucers

2 In a bowl, toss the fish cubes with the fish sauce, salt, and pepper and set aside.

3 Bring a large saucepan three-fourths full of water to a boil. Add the drained noodles and cook for 1 minute. Pour into a colander, rinse with cold water, and drain well. Divide the noodles among 6 bowls.

4 In a small saucepan over medium-high heat, warm the vegetable oil. Add the turmeric and ginger and heat until the oil turns yellow and is fragrant, about 1 minute. Remove from the heat.

5 Arrange the green onions, basil, cilantro, mint, dill, and peanuts on a platter and place on the table with the lime wedges and the saucers of dipping sauce.

6 Place a table-top burner on the table. Preheat an 8-inch (20-cm) frying pan on a stove top over medium-high heat. Pour the turmeric-flavored oil to a depth of about ¼ inch (6 mm) into the pan and heat to 325°F (165°C) on a deep-frying thermometer. Add a small batch of the fish (about one-third) to the oil and, using chopsticks, turn the fish pieces as necessary to brown them lightly and cook them through, 2–3 minutes. Add a handful of the green onions, basil, cilantro, dill, mint, and peanuts (about one-third of each) to the pan and stir with the chopsticks for a few seconds. When the herbs have wilted, spoon some of the fish mixture and some seasoned oil into each bowl of rice noodles. Start the next batch of fish frying and repeat until all the fish, green onions, basil, cilantro, dill, mint, and peanuts are used up.

7 Each diner squeezes a little lime juice or drizzles a little of the dipping sauce on the fish and vegetables, mixing them with the noodles.

NUOC CHAM DIPPING SAUCE

1 large clove garilc

1 fresh red chile, seeded

¼ cup (2 fl oz/60 ml) fresh lime juice

5 tablespoons (2½ fl oz/75 ml) fish sauce

3 tablespoons sugar

6 tablespoons (3 fl oz/80 ml) water

2 tablespoons grated carrot

1½ lb (750 g) firm white-fleshed fish fillets, cut into ¾-inch (2-cm) cubes

2 tablespoons fish sauce

1½ teaspoons salt

½ teaspoon ground pepper

1 lb (500 g) dried rice vermicelli, soaked in warm water for 15 minutes, drained

½ cup (4 fl oz/125 ml) vegetable oil

¼ teaspoon ground turmeric

6 thin slices fresh ginger

9 green (spring) onions, halved and cut into 1½-inch (4-cm) lengths

Leaves from 1 bunch *each* fresh Thai basil, fresh cilantro (fresh coriander), and mint

12 fresh dill sprigs, long stems removed

1 cup (6 oz/185 g) crushed unsalted roasted peanuts

2 limes, cut into wedges

Serves 6

Steamed Fish with Ginger and Green Onions

Zheng Cong Jiang Yu • Southern • China

To make the carrot flowers, using the point of a small, sharp knife, make 5 or 6 deep angled incisions into the narrow end of a carrot, about 1 inch from the tip. The cuts should meet in the center of the carrot. Twist off the tip of the carrot to give a flower-bud shape.

1 whole fish such as snapper, porgy, or sea bass, 1¾–2 lb (750 g–1 kg), cleaned

2-inch (5-cm) piece fresh ginger, peeled, thinly sliced, and then finely julienned

3 green (spring) onions, white part only, cut into 2-inch (5-cm) lengths and finely julienned lengthwise

3 tablespoons light soy sauce

2 tablespoons rice wine

1 tablespoon vegetable oil

Fresh cilantro (fresh coriander) sprigs

Carrot flowers (see note)

Serves 4–6

1 Hold the fish under running cold water to rinse the cavity thoroughly. Drain and pat dry with paper towels. Place on a cutting board and, using a sharp knife, cut deep slashes on the diagonal across both sides, spacing them about 1¼ inches (3 cm) apart.

2 Place the fish on a large, heatproof plate. Place about one-third of the ginger and green onions inside the cavity of the fish, and spread the remainder over the top. Pour the soy sauce, rice wine, and vegetable oil evenly over the fish.

3 Bring water to a boil in the base of a steamer. (If you do not have a large steamer or a covered wok, a double thickness of aluminum foil to cover the wok will work as well.) Set the plate in the steamer, cover tightly, reduce the heat so the water continues to simmer, and steam for 15–18 minutes. To test for doneness, insert the tip of a knife into the thickest part of the fish below the head. If it penetrates easily and no pink shows, the fish is done.

4 Using oven gloves to protect your hands from the steam, carefully remove the plate from the steamer. Garnish the plate with the cilantro and carrot flowers and serve at once.

Shrimp with Cashew Nuts

Qing Chao Xiaren • Southern • China

In Chinese cuisine, no other seafood ingredient enjoys as much popularity as shrimp (prawns). Their sweet taste offers a perfect background for myriad Chinese flavors—salty black beans, tangy sweet-and-sour, and pungent *kung pao* sauces redolent of chile and Sichuan pepper. Shrimp taste superb after they are simmered in sweet wines or with *Longjing* tea leaves and rich, deep soy seasonings. And what can compare with a pile of the freshest shrimp straight from the steamer?

18 shrimp (prawns) in the shells, about 7 oz (220 g) total weight

½ cup (4 fl oz/125 ml) vegetable oil

½ cup (2½ oz/75 g) raw cashew nuts

6 thin carrot slices, halved

1 small yellow onion, cut into wedges ⅓ inch (9 mm) thick and layers separated

8 pieces red bell pepper (capsicum), each ¾ inch (2 cm) square

Pinch of salt, plus salt to taste

6 small, very thin fresh ginger slices

2 asparagus, tough ends removed and sliced on the diagonal ½ inch (12 mm) thick, or 8 small snow peas (mangetouts)

2 heads baby bok choy, quartered lengthwise

2 tablespoons water

2 teaspoons rice wine

1 tablespoon light soy sauce

6 canned straw mushrooms or button mushrooms (champignons), halved

1 tablespoon cornstarch (cornflour) dissolved in ¾ cup (6 fl oz/180 ml) chicken stock

Ground white pepper to taste

2 tablespoons chopped green (spring) onion tops

Serves 2–4

1 Peel each shrimp, leaving the last segment of the shell and the tail in place. Using a sharp knife, cut down the back, devein, and rinse in cold water. Pat dry with paper towels.

2 In a wok over high heat, warm the oil. When it is hot, add the cashews and fry until golden, 45–90 seconds. Using a slotted spoon, transfer to paper towels to drain.

3 Add the shrimp to the hot oil and stir-fry until they curl, turn pink, and are firm, about 1 minute. Using the slotted spoon, transfer the shrimp to a plate and set aside.

4 Pour off the oil into a small, heatproof bowl, wipe the wok, and return 2 tablespoons of the oil to the wok. Place the wok over high heat. When it is hot, add the carrot, yellow onion, bell pepper, and a pinch of salt and stir-fry for 40 seconds, until the vegetables begin to soften. Add the ginger, asparagus or snow peas, and bok choy and stir-fry for 20 seconds. Add the water and stir-fry until the water has evaporated, about 1 minute. Season with the rice wine and soy sauce, add the mushrooms, and toss and stir to mix.

5 Reduce the heat to medium, add the cornstarch mixture, and cook, stirring slowly, until lightly thickened, about 1½ minutes. Season with salt and white pepper.

6 Return the shrimp to the wok and heat through, turning to coat evenly with the sauce. Fold in the cashews and the green onion tops, then transfer to a serving plate and serve.

Spicy Fish Cakes

Tod Mun Pla • Thailand

This snack food is readily available from street hawkers in Thailand. Many versions exist, but this one, made with kaffir lime leaves, is a favorite. You can substitute the zest of 1 lime for the leaves, but the unique perfumed character of the kaffir lime will be missing.

1 lb (500 g) white fish fillets, such as cod or halibut, finely ground

1 tablespoon roasted chile paste (page 221) or red curry paste

1 tablespoon fish sauce

1 tablespoon cornstarch (cornflour)

½ teaspoon salt

2 oz (60 g) green beans, ends trimmed and beans thinly sliced

6 kaffir lime leaves, spines removed and leaves finely slivered

Peanut oil for deep-frying

Sriracha sauce (page 225)

Serves 6

1 In a bowl, combine the fish, chile paste or curry paste, fish sauce, cornstarch, salt, green beans, and lime leaves. Knead the mixture for 1 minute. Moisten your hands with water and divide the mixture into 20 balls. Flatten each ball into a patty about 2 inches (5 cm) in diameter and ½ inch (12 mm) thick.

2 Preheat a frying pan over medium-high heat. Add peanut oil to a depth of about 1 inch (2.5 cm) and heat to 375°F (190°C) on a deep-frying thermometer. Slip a few patties into the hot oil and fry on the first side until golden brown, about 2 minutes. Turn the patties over and fry on the second side until golden, about 2 minutes longer. Using a slotted spatula or tongs, transfer to paper towels to drain.

3 Arrange the fish cakes on a platter and serve at once, passing the Sriracha sauce at the table.

SOUTHEAST ASIAN STREET FOOD

The best way to experience true Southeast Asian cooking is to eat hawker fare, authentic dishes served in plain stalls at bargain prices. Made according to recipes passed down through generations, these street foods are the labor of entrepreneurial cooks, many of whom turn out wonderful plates despite makeshift workplaces.

Old-timers in Singapore recall the days when hawkers commuted to work each day by negotiating the busy streets at the helm of their portable restaurants, wood-and-tin structures on bicycle wheels with small stools hanging from the sides and a faded canopy covering the "kitchen." Some even wore their places of business across their shoulders, balancing bamboo poles with pots and woks, bowls and plates dangling from each end. They would come right to your door in the morning, hawking a breakfast soup of rice or noodles. Those itinerant hawkers are gone now, replaced by the government's admirably efficient, perfectly sanitary, highly convenient food centers, populated with large numbers of permanent stalls—literally hundreds in Chinatown's Kreta Ayer center—and tables gathered together under a single roof. Some locals lament the loss of the old-style traveling hawker, but many others appreciate the orderliness that the city-state's stringent regulations have delivered.

Singapore has the most organized system of food stalls in Southeast Asia, but every community boasts clusters of talented street-based cooks. In the night markets of Chiang Mai, many of them stretched out along the banks of the river that winds through the city, locals fuel up on *khao soi* (curry noodles), *khanom jiin* (noodles with spicy fish), and other dishes. In Hanoi, not far from the train station, in alleyways off Hang Bong Street, bureaucrats and students, families and pensioners perch on stools to consume bowls of herbal chicken soup and plates of fish cakes and *cha gio* (spring rolls). And just beyond central Yangon's (Rangoon's) cavernous Bogyoke Market, with its stalls selling lacquerware, Shan bags, and *longyis* (Burmese sarongs), stands an open-air market thick with steam rising from pots of *mohingha*, the typical breakfast of the Burmese workingman.

Tandoori Grilled Fish

Tandoori Machi • Maharashta • India

Tandoori fish, a star item on the menus of a number of Indian restaurants, is associated with light and healthy cooking. This delicate marinade, infused with ginger, garlic, and ajowan, adds wonderful flavor to salmon. Using sour cream instead of the more traditional yogurt lends a buttery taste and an appealing sheen as well. Serve the fish with a salad, rice dish, or bread on the side.

2 salmon fillets, 12–14 oz (375–440 g) total weight

1 teaspoon fresh lemon juice

1 teaspoon minced garlic

1 teaspoon peeled and minced fresh ginger

½ teaspoon garam masala (page 222)

½ teaspoon ajowan seeds (page 221), bruised

¼ teaspoon cayenne pepper

½ teaspoon salt

1 tablespoon sour cream

1 tablespoon *usli ghee* (page 222) or olive oil

Serves 2

1 Lay the fish in a shallow dish. In a cup, combine the lemon juice, garlic, ginger, garam masala, ajowan, cayenne pepper, and salt. Rub this mixture all over the fish. Coat the fillets with the sour cream, cover, and set aside to marinate for 30 minutes at room temperature or 3 hours in the refrigerator.

2 The fish may be grilled or broiled. If using a charcoal grill, prepare a fire for direct-heat cooking. Position the grill rack about 5 inches (13 cm) from the fire. Allow the coals to burn until white ash covers them and the heat is moderate. Liberally brush the fillets with the *usli ghee* or oil and place them on the grill rack. Grill, turning once and basting from time to time with more ghee or oil, until the fish is just cooked, about 6 minutes total.

3 If using a broiler (griller), preheat it, positioning the broiler pan at least 5 inches (13 cm) from the heat. Brush the fillets with the *usli ghee* or oil and place them on the broiler pan in a single layer. Broil, turning once, until the fish is barely opaque, about 7 minutes total.

4 Transfer to a warmed platter and serve.

Stir-Fried Crab with Black Beans

Chao Pangxie Heidou • Southern • China

China's most prized crab is the small, box-shaped hairy crab. The most delicious of these freshwater crustaceans are harvested from the lakes around Shanghai and have become popularly known as Shanghai hairy crabs. Enthusiasts from all over the country flock eastward during the season to enjoy this treat, while Hong Kong gourmets anxiously await the first air shipments. To balance the succulence and sublime sweetness of the roe and pincer meat, tiny cups of ginger tea are served with a crab feast.

1 live hard-shelled saltwater crab, about 1½ lb (750 g)

1 tablespoon rice wine

1 tablespoon cornstarch (cornflour)

1½-inch (4-cm) piece fresh ginger, peeled

SAUCE
½ cup (4 fl oz/125 ml) water or chicken stock

1½ tablespoons light soy sauce

2 teaspoons cornstarch (cornflour)

¾ teaspoon superfine (caster) sugar

2 cups (16 fl oz/500 ml) vegetable oil

1 green bell pepper (capsicum), seeded and cut into ¾-inch (2-cm) squares

Pinch of salt dissolved in 1 tablespoon water

1 green (spring) onion, including tender green tops, sliced on the diagonal

1½ tablespoons salted black beans, rinsed, drained, and chopped

1½ teaspoons finely chopped garlic

Serves 2–6

1 Bring a large pot three-fourths full of water to a boil. Rinse the crab well under running cold water, then slip the crab into the boiling water and leave for 20 to 30 seconds. Lift the crab from the boiling water and immediately place under running cold water to halt the cooking. Drain well.

2 Place the crab upside down on a cutting board. Using a cleaver or heavy knife, cut the body into 4 pieces, cutting straight through the shell. Pull off the carapace (top shell) and scrape out the inedible parts, including the dark gray intestines, the liver, and the spongy, feathery gills. Rinse under gently running cold water and drain well. Break off the claws, and crack the hard shells with a meat mallet or heavy pestle.

3 In a large, shallow dish, stir together the rice wine and cornstarch. Grate the ginger onto a clean cloth, gather up the cloth, and squeeze to release the ginger juice into the wine mixture. Dip the cut edges of the crab pieces into this mixture to coat, and let stand for 5 minutes. Reserve the squeezed ginger flesh.

4 To prepare the sauce, in a small bowl, stir together the water or stock, soy sauce, cornstarch, and sugar. Set aside.

5 In a wok over high heat, warm the oil to about 360°F (182°C), or until it begins to shimmer and is smoky. Add the crab pieces and fry, stirring and turning frequently, until the shells are bright red and the cut edges are lightly browned, about 1½ minutes. Lift out with tongs and set on a plate. Pour the oil into a heatproof container.

6 Return 1 tablespoon of the oil to the wok and reheat over high heat. Add the bell pepper and stir-fry until beginning to soften, about 30 seconds. Add the salted water and stir over high heat until the pepper is almost softened, about 1 minute. Transfer to a plate.

7 Return the pan to the heat and add 1 tablespoon of the reserved oil. Warm over high heat until it shimmers and is smoky, then add the crab pieces. Stir-fry until warmed through and coated with the oil, about 40 seconds. Return the bell pepper to the wok and add the green onion, black beans, reserved ginger pulp, and garlic. Stir-fry until the dish is aromatic and the ingredients are well mixed, about 40 seconds.

8 Pour the sauce into the wok and cook over high heat, stirring and turning, until the sauce thickens and clings to the crab and bell pepper, about 30 seconds.

9 Transfer to a serving platter and serve at once.

CHINESE WINE

When the Chinese accidentally discovered a palatable wine made from fermented rice some four thousand years ago, they embraced the new beverage with such gusto that the emperor of the day had to introduce hastily four decrees that are still followed today: wine must only be drunk from small cups; "wine-accompanying dishes" (hot and cold hors d'oeuvres) must be eaten to absorb the alcohol; wine should not be served during the main part of the banquet menu; and, lastly, drinkers must indulge in mild forms of physical and mental exercise. The "drinking games" devised in those far-off days—scissors-paper-stone and the fingers game—are still played with noisy enthusiasm in Chinese restaurants around the world. Toasts usually accompany drinks. At a signal from the toast maker, the tiny cups are filled and raised and the wine is tossed back in one gulp with shouts of *gan bai* (bottoms up).

Shaoxing, southwest of Shanghai, in Zhejiang province, is where China's finest amber rice wines are made and marketed under that name. The best rice wines, which are mild in taste, have an alcohol content of around 20 percent, and sometimes flowers are steeped in them to make elegant dessert and aperitif beverages. However, as the wines are usually served warm, their effect can be instant and invigorating. Flavors range from mellow and slightly sweet to sharp and scorching, depending on the quality and alcohol content. Unwary travelers should accept a glass of "white wine" with caution—it may be local millet brew as potent as vodka, or fiery *maotai*, eighty to one hundred proof rice wine. Chinese-distilled rice wines are different and far more potent than the sakes brewed in Japan.

Rice wine is used in stir-fries and marinades and is a primary seasoning in hot and cold wine sauces, particularly in seafood and chicken dishes. It imparts a distinct flavor and aroma reminiscent of dry sherry, which can be used if rice wine is not available. Japanese *mirin* may be substituted if the dish demands a sweet flavor.

Sweet fruit wines from plums and grapes have been made on a small scale in China since early times, but the grape wine industry began in the nineteenth century, when Germans resident in Shandong decided their Alsace-style wines were perfect with Chinese food. Grape wine production continues today in the Yangtai and Tianjin wineries in the north.

Shrimp with Chile and Garlic in Wine Sauce

Jiu Suan La Jiao Xiaren • Northern • China

In recipes such as this Beijing classic, using rice wine, such as the mellow Shaoxing rice wine, is best, but Japanese *mirin* is a worthy substitute.

12 peeled shrimp (prawns), about 7 oz (220 g) total weight (about 1 lb/500 g unpeeled)

1 tablespoon salt, plus salt to taste

2 egg whites

⅓ cup (1½ oz/45 g) cornstarch (cornflour)

2½ cups (20 fl oz/625 ml) vegetable oil

1 large, hot red chile, seeded and sliced

3 cloves garlic, sliced

¾ cup (6 fl oz/180 ml) rice wine

2 teaspoons light soy sauce

1½ teaspoons superfine (caster) sugar

2 teaspoons cornstarch (cornflour) dissolved in ½ cup (4 fl oz/125 ml) fish or chicken stock

Few drops of chile oil

1½ tablespoons chopped green (spring) onion tops

Serves 8–10

1 Cut each shrimp in half lengthwise and remove and discard the dark vein. Sprinkle the shrimp with the 1 tablespoon salt and let stand for 10 minutes. Rinse under running cold water and drain well. Pat dry with paper towels.

2 In a bowl, beat the egg whites until blended, then whisk in the cornstarch until the mixture becomes a thin batter.

3 In a wok over high heat, warm the vegetable oil. When it is hot, dip about half of the shrimp in the batter and slip into the oil. Fry until lightly golden, about 1 minute. Using a slotted spoon, transfer to a rack placed over paper towels to drain. Repeat with the remaining shrimp.

4 Pour off the oil into a small, heatproof bowl, wipe out the wok, and return 1 tablespoon of the oil to the wok. Place the wok over high heat. When it is hot, add the chile and garlic and stir-fry for 20 seconds. Add the rice wine, soy sauce, and sugar and simmer until partially reduced, about 40 seconds. Add the cornstarch mixture and cook, stirring slowly, until lightly thickened, about 1½ minutes. Season with salt.

5 Return the shrimp to the wok and heat through, turning to coat evenly with the sauce. Transfer to a serving dish, sprinkle with the chile oil and green onion tops, and serve.

Braised Fish with Eggplant and Potato

Machor Jhal • West Bengal • India

Machor jhal is an everyday classic in West Bengal, where it is traditionally made with the fish *hilsa*, available frozen in Indian grocery stores. Any oily fish, such as shad, carp, or mackerel, however, will make a fine substitute. Nonoily fish can be used, too.

¾ teaspoon ground turmeric

1½ teaspoons salt

1½ lb (750 g) fish steaks such as *hilsa*, sea bass, flounder, or haddock

4 tablespoons (2 fl oz/60 ml) mustard oil or vegetable oil

2 dried red chiles

2 cassia leaves (page 221)

2 teaspoons *panch phoron* (page 224)

1 tablespoon prepared mustard

1 baking potato, cut into 8 pieces

1 small eggplant (aubergine), about ¾ lb (375 g), cut into 16 pieces

3 cups (24 fl oz/750 ml) water

12 large spinach leaves, fresh or thawed frozen

¼ cup (⅓ oz/10 g) fresh cilantro (fresh coriander) (optional)

Serves 8–10

1 In a small bowl, combine the turmeric and ½ teaspoon of the salt. Place the fish on a plate and rub each steak all over with the turmeric-salt mixture.

2 In a large nonstick frying pan over high heat, warm 2 tablespoons of the oil. When the oil is very hot, add the fish and fry, turning once, until just lightly browned, about 1 minute total. Do not cook the fish all the way through. Transfer to a plate.

3 Add the remaining 2 tablespoons oil to the pan. When very hot, add the dried chiles and fry, stirring, until they turn black, about 1 minute. Reduce the heat to medium-low, add the cassia leaves and *panch phoron*, and fry, stirring, until the spices turn several shades darker, about 20 seconds. Add the mustard, the potato pieces, the eggplant pieces, the remaining 1 teaspoon salt, and the water. Mix well and bring to a boil, then reduce the heat to low, cover, and cook until the vegetables are tender, about 20 minutes.

4 Add the fish and the spinach leaves and carefully stir to submerge them in the sauce and vegetables. Cook briefly over medium heat until the fish is heated through, about 2 minutes. Taste and correct the seasonings. Transfer to a warmed serving dish, sprinkle with the cilantro, if desired, and serve at once.

Mussels with Garlic and Basil

Hoi Ma Laeng Poo • Thailand

When you visit one of Bangkok's enormous seafood garden restaurants, be careful you are not bumped by one of the waiters whizzing by on roller skates. The skates give them a fast start out of the kitchen as they deliver hot dishes to the tables.

½ teaspoon peppercorns

2 red jalapeño or serrano chiles, seeded and coarsely chopped

2 cloves garlic, quartered

1 tablespoon chopped fresh cilantro (fresh coriander) roots or stems

3 tablespoons vegetable oil

1½ tablespoons oyster sauce

1 tablespoon fish sauce

2 lb (1 kg) mussels, scrubbed and debearded

¼ cup (2 fl oz/60 ml) chicken stock

½ teaspoon sugar

½ cup (½ oz/15 g) fresh Thai basil leaves

Fresh cilantro (fresh coriander) leaves

Serves 4–6

1 In a mortar, pound the peppercorns until crushed, then add the chiles, garlic, and cilantro roots or stems and pound or grind until a rough paste forms.

2 Preheat a wok or frying pan over medium-high heat. When hot, add the oil and swirl to coat the pan. When the oil is hot, add the chile paste and fry until fragrant, about 30 seconds. Stir in the oyster sauce and fish sauce. Add the mussels, discarding any that fail to close to the touch, and stir and toss with the sauce to mix. Add the stock and sugar, then cover and cook until the mussels open, about 2 minutes. Taste and adjust the seasoning with fish sauce.

3 Toss in the basil leaves and cook only until they begin to wilt. Transfer the mussels to a platter, discarding any that failed to open, and garnish with the cilantro leaves.

Sichuan Chile and Garlic Fish

Sichuan Douban Yu • Western • China

The landlocked province of Sichuan has never wanted for fresh fish and shellfish in its cuisine. Its many lakes, rivers, ponds, and streams are the habitat of an impressive variety of freshwater fish, from carp, perch, and catfish to eels, frogs, turtles, and deliciously sweet shellfish. With such a large variety available, it is the Sichuanese penchant for vibrant flavors and powerful, peppery seasoning, rather than the need to disguise inferior quality, that has resulted in some of their most delicious fish and shellfish dishes.

10 oz (315 g) white-fleshed fish fillets

1½ teaspoons rice wine

2 tablespoons light soy sauce

1–4 teaspoons hot bean sauce

1 teaspoon superfine (caster) sugar

1 cup (8 fl oz/250 ml) vegetable oil

1 celery stalk, thinly sliced on the diagonal

5 thin slices fresh ginger, peeled and finely julienned

2 large cloves garlic, very thinly sliced

½–1 hot red chile, seeded and finely sliced

⅓ cup (1½ oz/45 g) thinly sliced bamboo shoot

2 teaspoons cornstarch (cornflour) dissolved in ½ cup (4 fl oz/125 ml) fish stock or water

Salt to taste

1 green (spring) onion, including tender green top, chopped

Serves 4–6

1 To prepare the fish, working from the tail end of a fillet, and holding a sharp knife or cleaver at a 45-degree angle, cut the fillet crosswise into slices ½ inch (12 mm) thick. Cut each slice into 2 or 3 pieces. Place the fish in a bowl, and season with the rice wine and 1 tablespoon of the soy sauce. Set aside for 10 minutes.

2 In a small bowl, stir together the remaining 1 tablespoon soy sauce, the hot bean sauce to taste, and the sugar. Set aside.

3 Drain the marinade from the fish into the bowl holding the soy mixture, and pat the fish dry with paper towels. Pour the oil into a wok or large frying pan and place over high heat until the oil begins to shimmer and is nearly smoking. Carefully slide half the fish into the hot oil and fry until lightly cooked, 1½–2 minutes. Using a slotted spoon, transfer the fish to paper towels to drain. Fry the remaining fish in the same way. Pour the oil through a fine-mesh sieve into a heatproof container and reserve.

4 Wipe out the wok or frying pan and place over high heat. Add 2 tablespoons of the strained oil and heat over high heat until smoking. Add the celery, ginger, garlic, and chile and stir-fry until slightly softened, about 40 seconds. Still on high heat, add the bamboo shoot and the soy–bean sauce mixture and cook for about 30 seconds, stirring slowly. Pour in the cornstarch mixture and stir over high heat until the sauce is lightly thickened, about 40 seconds. Season with salt.

5 Reduce the heat to low, return the fish to the sauce, and add the green onion. Allow the fish to reheat gently, without stirring, for about 1 minute. Carefully transfer the fish and sauce to a serving dish and serve at once.

Masala Shrimp Stir-Fry

Yera Varuval • Kerala • India

Varuval literally means "pan-fried" or "crisped." In Kerala, the dish is made with succulent small shrimp that have an oyster-like aroma and texture. For variety, bay and sea scallops may be used in place of the shrimp.

1½ lb (750 g) medium-sized shrimp (prawns)

1 tablespoon fresh lime juice

2 teaspoons peeled and grated fresh ginger

1 teaspoon minced garlic

1 teaspoon ground cumin

½ teaspoon cayenne pepper

¼ teaspoon ground turmeric

Pinch of ground cloves

3 tablespoons vegetable oil

1 small yellow onion, thinly sliced

¼ cup (¼ oz/7 g) fresh kari leaves (page 223) or a combination of fresh basil and fresh cilantro (fresh coriander) leaves

Serves 6

1 Peel the shrimp, leaving the last shell segment with the tail fin intact, and devein. Rinse, pat dry on paper towels, and place in a bowl. Add the lime juice, ginger, garlic, cumin, cayenne pepper, turmeric, and cloves. Toss to combine and set aside to marinate for 30 minutes at room temperature.

2 In a shallow frying pan over high heat, warm 2 tablespoons of the oil. Add the onion and cook, stirring occasionally, until it is light caramel brown, about 5 minutes. Stir in the kari leaves or basil and cilantro. Transfer the onion mixture to a plate.

3 Add the remaining 1 tablespoon oil to the pan over high heat. When it is smoking hot, add the shrimp and cook, turning and tossing, until they turn pink and curl, about 3 minutes. Transfer the shrimp to a platter. Scatter the onion mixture on top and serve.

TIFFIN

Indians have a custom of greeting even unexpected visitors with beverages and food. This tradition began when sages (holy Hindu Brahmin priests), who regularly traveled long distances, stopped along the way to ask for a little water and food. Today the visitor is equated with the sage, and the offering is more a courtesy and tradition than a duty. Such snacks are known as tiffin. The gesture of serving them is a literal one as well as symbolic, and so the venerable snack-time endures.

In southern India, tiffin can be as simple as a handful of roasted peanuts or as elaborate as a fried dish of rice noodles with sauces and sambals. Most common are spicy savories like *ompadi* (fried noodles), *masala vada* (fried dumplings), and *bajjia* (fritters), and sweets such as *laddoo* (sweet balls), *halwa* (puddings), and *jangari* (candied twists). Recently, cut-up fruits, sliced fresh coconut, and legume salads have become popular. The beverage of choice is coffee prepared in the southern Indian style, with milk and sugar, much like caffe latte.

Spicy Fish

Denji Fry • Karnataka • India

This dish is a specialty of the Mangalorians who live along the Konkan coast. It is usually made with soft-shell crabs—those caught just after molting, when their new shells are still soft enough to be eaten. If they are out of season, fish fillets make a fine substitute.

1-inch (2.5-cm) piece tamarind

½ cup (4 fl oz/125 ml) boiling water

¼ teaspoon salt

1 lb (500 g) skinless thin white-fleshed fish fillets, such as sole or flounder, or 4 very fresh soft-shell crabs, about ¼ lb (125 g) each

⅓ cup (2 oz/60 g) rice flour

2 teaspoons garam masala (page 222)

2 teaspoons cayenne pepper

½ teaspoon ground turmeric

3 tablespoons mustard oil or *usli ghee* (page 222)

Serves 2

1 In a small bowl, soak the tamarind in the boiling water for 30 minutes. Squeeze and press to extract as much pulp as possible. Strain the liquid into a medium bowl. Discard the fibrous residue. Add the salt and mix. Add the fish fillets or crabs, gently mixing and turning to coat them with the tamarind water. Set aside to marinate for 30 minutes.

2 When you are ready to cook the fish or crabs, combine the rice flour, garam masala, cayenne pepper, and turmeric on a plate. In a large frying pan over high heat, warm the oil or *usli ghee* until it begins to smoke. Remove from the heat and let the oil cool for about 30 seconds. Reheat it and, when it is hot, dip each fillet or crab in the seasoned flour to coat it completely. Add (shell side down, in the case of the crabs) to the oil. Cook, shaking the pan, until the underside is browned, about 3 minutes. Using tongs, turn and cook the second side to the same light brown crispness, about 3 minutes longer. Transfer to warmed serving plates and serve at once.

Fried Shrimp in the Shell with Tamarind

Udang Goreng Asam • Malaysia

The intense flavor of shrimp fried in the shell is popular in Asian cooking, and the crispy shells are usually edible. If you can find them, whole shrimp with the heads attached are preferred, but headless shrimp are delicious as well. *Udang goreng asam* is delicious served with *chin chow*, an iced black jelly beverage that is especially good with rich, spicy foods.

¾ lb (375 g) shrimp (prawns) in the shell

½ cup (4 fl oz/125 ml) tamarind water (see sidebar, page 92)

3 tablespoons peanut oil or vegetable oil, or as needed

½ teaspoon salt

1 teaspoon sugar

3 green (spring) onions, including tender green tops, cut into 1½-inch (4-cm) lengths

Serves 6

1 To prepare the shrimp, rinse well and pat dry with paper towels. Cut into the shell with a sharp knife to devein. Put the shrimp into a bowl and add the tamarind water. Let stand for 30 minutes at room temperature, turning occasionally.

2 Preheat a wok or large frying pan over medium-high heat. Add the oil and salt and swirl to coat the pan. When the oil starts to smoke, remove the shrimp from the tamarind water, reserving the liquid, and place as many as will fit in a single layer in the pan. Fry in the hot oil, undisturbed, until the bottoms are browned and crusty, about 1 minute. Turn the shrimp over and fry on the second side until browned and a bright orange-pink, about 1 minute longer. Using a slotted utensil, transfer to paper towels to drain. Keep warm. Fry the remaining shrimp in the same manner, using more oil if needed.

3 Pour the reserved tamarind water into the hot pan and add the sugar. Boil briskly until it forms a glaze, about 1 minute. Return the shrimp to the pan along with the green onions and cook, stirring constantly, until the shrimp are coated with the glaze. Transfer to a serving dish and serve at once.

Malabar Braised Fish in Sour Gravy

Meen Pollichathu • Kerala • India

Throughout Kerala, *karimeen*, a carp-like fish; *seer*, a mackerel-like fish; and *bahmeen*, the Indian salmon, are served in various ways: lightly braised in sauce, steamed in banana leaves, batter-fried, or stir-fried. There is also abundant use of coconut milk and fried onions. A uniquely Keralan flavoring is *kodampoli*, a smoky-sour tasting fruit that is used in many fish preparations. In *meen pollichathu*, pieces of *karimeen* are braised in a spicy-sour *kodampoli* sauce. Carp or salmon are good substitutes, but gray sole is particularly good.

1½ lb (750 g) skinless fish fillets such as gray or lemon sole, flounder, salmon, or haddock, cut into large serving portions

½ teaspoon ground turmeric

½ teaspoon cayenne pepper

½ teaspoon ground black pepper

½ teaspoon salt

4 tablespoons (2 fl oz/60 ml) vegetable oil

1 teaspoon brown mustard seeds

1 cup (3½ oz/105 g) thinly sliced yellow onion

1 teaspoon minced garlic

4 fresh hot green chiles such as serrano, seeded and slivered

18 fresh or 36 dried kari leaves or 8 kaffir lime leaves (page 223)

2 teaspoons ground coriander

1 *kodampoli* (see note) or unripe star fruit, sliced, or 1 teaspoon fresh lime juice

¾ cup (6 fl oz/180 ml) coconut milk

Fresh kari sprigs (optional; page 223)

Hot steamed basmati rice

Serves 4

1 Place the fish on a plate. Combine the turmeric, cayenne pepper, black pepper, and salt. Rub each piece of fish thoroughly with the spices. Let the fish marinate for 10 minutes at room temperature.

2 In a large frying pan over high heat, warm 2 tablespoons of the oil. When hot, add the fish and fry on one side until lightly browned, about 30 seconds. Using a spatula, turn and fry the other side for about 30 seconds. Do not fully cook the fish. Transfer to a plate and set aside.

3 To the same pan over high heat, add the remaining 2 tablespoons oil and the mustard seeds and cover the pan. When the seeds stop sputtering, after about 30 seconds, uncover and add the onion, garlic, chiles, kari or kaffir lime leaves, and coriander. Reduce the heat to low and cook, stirring occasionally, until the onion is lightly colored, about 7 minutes.

4 Return the fish to the pan. Add the *kodampoli*, star fruit, or lime juice and the coconut milk. Stir carefully to submerge the fish in the sauce. Cook briefly until the fish is just done, about 4 minutes. Check and correct the seasonings. Transfer to a warmed platter, garnish with the kari sprigs, if using, and serve at once accompanied with rice.

FRESH FROM THE WATER

The Chinese word for fish is *yu*. When pronounced with a different inflection it means abundance, so the presence of seafood at a banquet carries great symbolic importance. The Chinese are so fastidious about the freshness of their seafood that, whenever possible, they purchase fish still live and flapping. From gargantuan fresh food markets to the tiniest shopfront, fish sellers display their wares in tubs of bubbling fresh water, to be carried home wriggling in a plastic bag. Garoupa, rock cod, silver and black pomfret, dory, golden thread, hairtail, dace, and red snapper are the favored saltwater fish, while China's wide rivers and lotus-covered lakes yield eels, turtles, bearded catfish, many varieties of carp, and freshwater shrimp. Good seafood restaurants stock their fish and shellfish in aquariums. Your choice is brought live to your table for inspection, and the restaurateur offers advice on how it should be cooked.

Huge, oceangoing junks head away from the coast to ply the far reaches of the sea. They pursue the exotics so prized in Chinese cuisine: shark's fins, jellyfish, sea slugs, and drifts of sea laver, a type of seaweed, to compress into papery sheets. In river estuaries from rocky shorelines, fishermen harvest shellfish, including scallops, mussels, oysters, winkles, clams and cockles, shrimp (prawns) and crayfish, and the now scarce abalone.

Hundreds of thousands of the Chinese who work on the water seldom leave it. Generations of junk- and sampan-dwelling Hoklo fishermen rarely step on land, and the cormorant fisherman and his birds have a partnership that may span a lifetime.

Not everyone relies on the fish markets. Give a man a fishing pole and a pond of water and you have a very contented man, and not just in rural China. The pensive fisherman watching for the tug on his line has been the subject of paintings for thousands of years, and an artist today in the heart of any major city can still easily find a subject on a bridge over a river, on a wooden boat on a lake, or on a rock beside a stream.

"Broken Tile" Fish with Sweet-and-Sour Sauce

Cuipi Wakuai Yu · Southern · China

A fanciful chef named the result "broken tiles" after an apprentice's unskillful slicing of a fish. The apprentice improved, but the name stayed.

FISH "TILES"

10 oz (315 g) firm white-fleshed fish fillets

½ teaspoon salt

1½ teaspoons rice wine

SWEET-AND-SOUR SAUCE

¼ cup (2 fl oz/60 ml) chicken stock or water

⅓ cup (3 fl oz/80 ml) rice vinegar

1 tablespoon light soy sauce

⅓ cup (1½ oz/45 g) superfine (caster) sugar

½ teaspoon salt

2 tablespoons vegetable oil

1–3 teaspoons peeled and finely julienned fresh ginger

½ teaspoon crushed garlic (optional)

½ cup (2 oz/60 g) diced red bell pepper (capsicum)

½ cup (2 oz/60 g) diced, unpeeled English (hothouse) cucumber

2 green (spring) onions, including tender green tops, chopped

3 or 4 drops red food coloring (optional)

1 tablespoon cornstarch (cornflour) dissolved in 1 tablespoon water

⅔ cup (2½ oz/75 g) cornstarch (cornflour) or tapioca starch

Vegetable oil for deep-frying

1 tablespoon sesame oil (optional)

Serves 8–10

1 To prepare the fish "tiles," working from the tail end of a fillet, and holding a sharp knife or cleaver at a 45-degree angle, cut the fillet crosswise into slices ⅓ inch (9 mm) thick. Sprinkle with the salt and rice wine and set aside.

2 To prepare the sauce, in a small bowl, combine the stock or water, vinegar, soy sauce, sugar, and salt and stir until the sugar dissolves. In a saucepan over medium heat, warm the vegetable oil until the surface shimmers. Add the ginger to taste, garlic (if using), bell pepper, cucumber, and green onions and stir-fry until slightly softened, about 1 minute. Raise the heat to medium-high, pour in the vinegar mixture, bring quickly to a boil, and simmer for 1 minute, stirring constantly. If using the food coloring, first stir it into the cornstarch mixture and then stir the mixture into the sauce. Simmer over medium-high heat, stirring slowly, until the sauce is lightly thickened and becomes clear, about 1 minute. Remove from the heat and set aside.

3 Place the cornstarch or tapioca starch in a plastic or sturdy paper bag. Add the fish slices to the bag, hold the bag top firmly closed, and shake vigorously to coat the fish slices thickly. Tip into a colander and shake off the excess cornstarch or tapioca starch.

4 Pour the vegetable oil into a wok to a depth of 1¾ inches (4 cm) and heat to 360°F (182°C), or until a small cube of bread dropped into it begins to turn golden within a few seconds. Add the sesame oil, if using, then carefully slide half the fish into the hot oil. Fry until lightly browned, about 1½ minutes. Using a wire skimmer or slotted spoon, lift out the fish, holding it over the oil for a few moments to drain, and spread on a large serving plate. Cook and drain the remaining fish slices.

5 If the sauce has cooled, return it to high heat and reheat, stirring constantly. Pour the sauce evenly over the fish. Serve at once.

Chile Crab

Kepiting Pedas • Singapore

In Singapore, chile crab is customarily brought to the table with no plates but lots of small paper napkins. People help themselves to the communal pot of crab, which is served with cucumber chunks and French bread or toast. Just as you have used up the very last corner of a dozen napkins, a finger bowl arrives. If you are reluctant to kill a live crab, buy a cooked crab and ask the fishmonger to clean and crack it.

2 live Dungeness or other large crabs, each about 1½ lb (750 g)

6 fresh red chiles

1-inch (2.5-cm) piece fresh ginger, peeled and quartered

3 cloves garlic, quartered

⅓ cup (3 fl oz/80 ml) vegetable oil

1 teaspoon salt

⅓ cup (3½ oz/105 g) tomato ketchup

¼ cup (2 oz/60 g) firmly packed dark brown sugar

1 tablespoon fish sauce

½ cup (4 fl oz/125 ml) chicken stock or water

2 green (spring) onions, including 1 inch (2.5 cm) of the tender green tops, cut into 1½-inch (4-cm) lengths

1 egg

Fresh cilantro (fresh coriander) sprigs

1 English (hothouse) cucumber, cut into irregular ¾-inch (2-cm) chunks or wedges

French bread slices or hot steamed long-grain white rice

Serves 4

1 To prepare the crabs, bring a large stockpot three-fourths full of water to a boil. Using long-handled tongs, drop 1 crab into the boiling water. Quickly add the second crab and boil them both for 2 minutes. Transfer the crabs to a large colander and rinse with cold water until cool. Working with 1 crab at a time, pull off the top shell. If desired, scrub the shell with a brush, rinse it with cold water, pat dry, and save it for a garnish. Lift the tip of the triangular apron on the underside of the body and twist it off and discard. Remove the mandibles at the face end. Pull off the feathery gills and the gray intestinal matter from the body and discard. Spoon out the creamy yellow tomalley from the middle of the chest and reserve for another use, if desired. Rinse the body under cold running water and pat dry with paper towels. Using a cleaver or chef's knife, chop the body in half lengthwise, leaving the legs and claws attached. Then cut each half crosswise into thirds to make a total of 6 pieces. Each half will have 1 piece with a claw attached, and the other 2 pieces will each have 2 legs attached. Repeat with the remaining crab. With a mallet, crack the claw and leg shells at the joints and in the middle.

2 In a mortar or mini food processor, combine the chiles, ginger, and garlic and pound or process until a rough paste forms.

3 Preheat a wok or large, heavy pan over high heat. When the pan is hot, add the oil, salt, and chile paste and cook, stirring continuously so that the mixture does not brown, until fragrant, about 30 seconds. Toss in the crab and stir-fry with the mixture for 1–2 minutes. Add the ketchup, brown sugar, fish sauce, and stock or water and stir together. Cover, reduce the heat to a gentle boil, and cook, stirring once or twice, until the crab is bright orange and cooked through, 5–6 minutes. (If using precooked crab, cook for 2 minutes only to heat through.)

4 Uncover the pan, raise the heat to high, and toss in the green onions. Crack the egg into the pan and toss quickly, breaking up the egg to incorporate it into the sauce. When the sauce thickens to a loose glaze, the crab is ready to serve.

5 Transfer the crab to a large platter and garnish with the fresh cilantro sprigs. Serve hot with the cucumber and the French bread or rice.

Shrimp in Spiced Cream Sauce

Jheenga Masala • West Bengal • India

Serve this flavorful dish from Calcutta with rice for a truly Indian-style meal. Or, for an elegant first course, plate the shrimp on a bed of salad greens.

¼ cup (2 fl oz/60 ml) vegetable oil

½ cup (2½ oz/75 g) finely chopped yellow onion

2 fresh hot green chiles such as serrano, thinly sliced

2 teaspoons paprika

1 teaspoon garam masala (page 222)

1 teaspoon minced garlic

¼ teaspoon ground turmeric

1 lb (500 g) medium-sized shrimp (prawns), peeled with the last shell segment and tail fin intact and deveined

½ cup (4 fl oz/125 ml) half-and-half (half cream)

2 tablespoons minced fresh cilantro (fresh coriander)

Coarse salt to taste

Serves 6

1 In a large frying pan over medium-high heat, warm the oil. When hot, add the onion and cook, stirring often, until it begins to brown, about 4 minutes. Stir in the chiles, paprika, garam masala, garlic, and turmeric.

2 Add the shrimp and toss to coat with the spices. Cook, stirring, until the shrimp turn pink and begin to curl, 2–3 minutes. Stir in the half-and-half, cilantro, and salt. Cook until the sauce is bubbling, about 1 minute more. Check and adjust the seasonings. Transfer to a warmed platter and serve at once.

Catfish Simmered in a Clay Pot

Ca Kho To • Vietnam

This dish calls for caramel syrup, a simple seasoning that Vietnamese cooks adapted from the French and use to enrich the flavors of savory dishes. The recipe, cooked in a small clay pot, serves one as a main course or four as part of a multicourse meal.

3 catfish steaks, each about 1 inch (2.5 cm) thick (6 oz/185 g total weight)

Ground pepper to taste

2 tablespoons fish sauce

2 teaspoons sugar

1 tablespoon vegetable oil

3 cloves garlic, chopped

6 shallots, sliced

2 tablespoons caramel syrup

2 green (spring) onions, including the tender green tops, cut into 2-inch (5-cm) lengths

Serves 1

1 Rinse the fish and pat dry with paper towels. Sprinkle on both sides with pepper. Place in a shallow bowl and add the fish sauce and sugar. Turn to coat, then marinate for about 10 minutes.

2 Meanwhile, in a 2-cup (16–fl oz/500-ml) clay pot or saucepan over medium heat, warm the vegetable oil. Add the garlic and shallots and cook, stirring, until they start to turn golden, 1–2 minutes. Raise the heat to high; remove the catfish from the marinade, reserving the marinade; and put the fish into the clay pot or pan. Quickly sear on both sides, then add the caramel syrup, the reserved marinade, and the green onions. Reduce the heat to medium-low, cover, and simmer for 8 minutes.

3 Uncover and check to see if the fish is done. If it is, transfer it to a plate. If not, you can leave it in the cooking vessel while you reduce the sauce. Raise the heat to high and boil to reduce the sauce by half. When the sauce is thick, return the fish to reheat.

4 Serve the catfish directly from the clay pot, or transfer to a plate, and serve at once.

Stir-Fried Okra and Shrimp with Sambal

Sambal Bhindi Udang • Malaysia

Here, okra is cooked just until tender with a little crunch and infused with a multidimensional flavoring typical of a Malaysian *sambal*. Use small, tender okra for the best results.

SPICE PASTE

2 tablespoons dried shrimp, soaked in warm water for 15 minutes

2 shallots, quartered

3 cloves garlic

2 red jalapeño chiles, seeded

1 slice dried shrimp paste (page 225), ⅛ inch (3 mm) thick

3 tablespoons vegetable oil

1 lb (500 g) okra, ends trimmed and cut into 1-inch (2.5-cm) pieces

¼ cup (2 fl oz/60 ml) tamarind water (see sidebar, below)

½ lb (250 g) large shrimp (prawns), peeled and deveined

1 small head pickled garlic, coarsely chopped (optional)

Serves 6

1 To prepare the spice paste, drain the soaked dried shrimp, reserving 2 tablespoons of the water. In a blender, combine the shrimp, the 2 tablespoons water, and the shallots, garlic, chiles, and dried shrimp paste. Process to a fine-grained paste. Set aside.

2 Preheat a wok or frying pan over medium-high heat. When the pan is hot, add the oil and swirl to coat the pan. When the oil is hot, add the spice paste and fry, stirring frequently, until the mixture is emulsified, about 2 minutes. Reduce the heat to medium and cook, stirring occasionally, until beads of oil appear on the surface of the paste, about 8 minutes.

3 Raise the heat to high and add the okra. Fry for 1 minute, tossing frequently. Stir in the tamarind water. If the mixture seems too dry, add a tablespoon or so of water to moisten it and continue cooking until the okra is tender but still crisp, 3–5 minutes. Add the shrimp and toss and stir until they turn bright orange-pink, about 1 minute.

4 Transfer the okra and shrimp to a platter, top with the pickled garlic, if using, and serve.

TAMARIND

In the searing heat of a Ho Chi Minh City afternoon, residents sometimes take refuge under the spreading tamarind trees that line many of the streets. The sickle-shaped, thin-skinned fruit pods that hang from the branches are an invaluable ingredient throughout Southeast Asia. The pods contain a fruity, slightly citric sour pulp that is pressed into a liquid that is used in soups, salads, curries, meats, and fish dishes.

Tamarind water is easy to make and store. Look for tamarind pulp sold in blocks in Asian markets. To make about 1½ cups (12 fl oz/375 ml) tamarind water, cut up ½ pound

(250 g) of the pulp into small pieces, place in a bowl, and add 2 cups (16 fl oz/500 ml) boiling water. Mash the pulp to separate the fibers and seeds, then let stand for 15 minutes, stirring two or three times. Pour the liquid through a fine-mesh sieve placed over a bowl, pushing against the pulp with the back of a spoon and scraping the underside of the sieve to dislodge the clinging purée. Transfer to a jar and refrigerate for up to 4 days or freeze in an ice-cube tray for up to 1 month. A tamarind concentrate, which dissolves instantly in hot water, is also available in some Asian markets and can be used in a pinch.

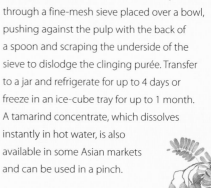

Fried Cuttlefish "Pinecones" with Pepper-Salt

Songshu Yuanzhuiti Youyu • Southern • China

Creative Chinese chefs have developed many imaginative ways of presenting seafood. Scoring the firm, snow-white flesh of cuttlefish or squid makes it exquisitely tender, and, once cooked, the pieces curl up to resemble miniature pinecones. The finished dish, with its crisp-fried parsley leaves, becomes a bonsai on a plate.

7 oz (220 g) cleaned cuttlefish or large squid bodies (about 10½ oz/330 g before cleaning)

2 teaspoons fresh lemon juice

½ teaspoon salt

½ teaspoon crushed garlic

PEPPER-SALT

2 tablespoons salt

2 teaspoons ground Sichuan pepper

¼ cup (1 oz/30 g) cornstarch (cornflour)

Vegetable or peanut oil for deep-frying

Leaves from 1 bunch fresh parsley

Serves 4

1 First, clean the cuttlefish or squid: Working with 1 at a time, pull the head from the body. Cut off and reserve the tentacles; discard the head. Squeeze out and discard the small, hard "beak" at the base of the tentacles; leave the tentacles whole. Using your fingers, pull out any internal matter from the body, including the quill-like cartilage, and discard. Peel off the mottled skin that covers the body. Rinse and thoroughly dry the cuttlefish (or squid) bodies. Using a sharp knife, slit each body lengthwise to open it flat. Using the sharp knife, score a $\frac{1}{16}$-inch (2-mm) crosshatch pattern over the inside surface. Cut into pieces 1 by 1¾ inches (2.5 by 4.5 cm).

2 In a bowl large enough to hold the cuttlefish, stir together the lemon juice, salt, and garlic. Add the cuttlefish and stir to coat. Marinate for 20 minutes, stirring occasionally.

3 To prepare the pepper-salt, place a dry wok over medium-high heat. When it is hot, add the salt and warm for about 40 seconds, stirring constantly. Add the pepper and remove immediately from the heat. Stir to mix, then pour into a shallow dish to cool.

4 Drain the cuttlefish and dry on paper towels. Put the cornstarch into a shallow dish and lightly coat the cuttlefish pieces with the cornstarch, tapping off the excess.

5 Pour the oil into a wok to a depth of 2 inches (5 cm) and heat to 375°F (190°C), or until a piece of the cuttlefish dropped into it sizzles immediately. Working in batches, add the cuttlefish and fry for only about 15 seconds. It will remain white and should be very tender. Do not overcook, or it will toughen. Using a wire skimmer or slotted spoon, transfer to a rack placed over paper towels to drain.

6 Add the parsley to the hot oil and fry until it is crisp and bright green and you hear a rustling sound, about 1½ minutes. Be careful that the oil does not spatter onto you. Using a wire skimmer, transfer to paper towels to drain.

7 Arrange the cuttlefish on a platter, sprinkle with about one-third of the pepper-salt, and surround with the fried parsley. Serve at once with the remaining pepper-salt in small dishes for dipping.

Steamed Whole Fish with Pickled Plums

Pla Nurng • Thailand

Originally from China, pickled plums are a variety of green plum preserved in a sour-salty brine and sold in jars. Despite the name, the tiny fruit, the size of a kumquat, is actually a type of apricot. It adds a salty and tart finish to the sauce.

1 whole pomfret, sea bass, or flounder, about 1¼ lb (625 g), cleaned, with head and tail intact

Salt and ground white pepper to taste

2 green (spring) onions, including 1 inch (2.5 cm) of greentops, bruised and cut into 1½-inch (4-cm) lengths

2 oz (60 g) pork fat, cut into fine, thin strips (optional)

2 pickled plums (see note), pitted and coarsely chopped

1 tablespoon fish sauce

¼ teaspoon sugar

1 tablespoon peeled and finely slivered fresh ginger

1 red serrano or jalapeño chile, sliced

Fresh cilantro (fresh coriander) sprigs

Serves 4

1 Rinse the fish and pat dry. Cut 3 diagonal slashes on each side almost to the bone. Sprinkle with salt and white pepper.

2 Place half of the green onions on a heat-resistant shallow plate that will fit in a bamboo steamer or other steamer rack. Lay the fish on top of the green onions. In a small bowl, mix the pork fat (if using), plums, fish sauce, and sugar and pour over the fish. Scatter the ginger, the remaining green onions, and the chile slices over the top.

3 Pour water into a wok or other pan and bring to a boil. Place the steamer over the water, cover, and steam until the fish is opaque throughout, about 15 minutes. (Plan on 10 minutes per 1 inch/2.5 cm, measured at the thickest section of the fish.)

4 Remove the plate from the steamer and garnish the fish with the cilantro. Spoon some of the juices that accumulated on the plate bottom over the fish and serve at once.

Steamed Pork and Shrimp Dumplings

Shao Mai · Southern · China

The acknowledged master chefs of dim sum usually come from Guangzhou, in Guangdong province, training in restaurants like the Pan Xi Jiujia. At this famous restaurant, you can order direct from the chefs, then watch them prepare the mounds of fresh dumplings that will be lined up in gigantic bamboo baskets and stacked to steam over huge woks of simmering water. One of the restaurant's specialties is *shao mai*, the tender dumplings of moist pork and succulent shellfish, seasoned with green (spring) onions and oyster sauce.

1 To prepare the filling, remove and discard the stems from the mushrooms if necessary and very finely chop the caps. Place in a bowl and add the pork, shrimp or crab, and green onions and mix well. Mix in the sugar and oyster sauce, then stir in the cornstarch, pepper, and oil. Let stand for 20 minutes.

2 To shape each dumpling, make a circle with the thumb and first finger of one hand and position a dumpling wrapper centrally over the circle. Place about 2 teaspoons of the filling in the center of the wrapper, and gently push the dumpling through the circle so that the wrapper becomes pleated around the sides of the dumpling filling. You should have a cup-shaped dumpling with the top of the filling exposed.

3 Brush the rack of a steamer basket with the vegetable oil and place the dumplings in the basket, leaving some space between them. Bring water to a simmer in a steamer base. Set the steamer basket in the steamer, cover tightly, and steam the dumplings until the filling is firm, 7–8 minutes.

4 Serve the dumplings in the steamer basket or transfer to a plate. Accompany with soy sauce, mustard, or chile sauce in small dishes for dipping.

FILLING

4 large dried black mushrooms, soaked in hot water to cover for 25 minutes and drained

½ lb (250 g) coarsely ground (minced) fatty pork such as pork butt

6 oz (185 g) shrimp (prawn) meat or crabmeat, finely chopped

2 green (spring) onions, including tender green tops, finely chopped

1 teaspoon superfine (caster) sugar

4 teaspoons oyster sauce

1 tablespoon cornstarch (cornflour)

½ teaspoon ground white pepper

1 tablespoon vegetable or peanut oil or 1½ teaspoons *each* vegetable oil and sesame oil

24 round wheat-flour dumpling wrappers

2–3 teaspoons vegetable oil

Light soy sauce, mild mustard, or chile sauce

Makes 24

DIM SUM

Dim sum restaurants are the daily precinct of millions of enthusiastic diners in many parts of China, and in particular the southern provinces of Guangdong and Guangxi. But it wasn't always that way. During the Ming dynasty, *yum cha*, or "taking tea," was a privilege of the wealthy, leisured classes, who lingered for hours in ornate teahouses exchanging social and business gossip while they sipped tea and nibbled exquisite snacks. Many of the delicious snacks had originated in the kitchens of the royal households, where they were served as palate refreshers between the ostentatious courses of imperial banquets.

As the teahouse became accessible to everyone, the food came to be known as *dim sum*, meaning "dot-hearts" or "heart's delight." These names poetically describe the diminutive portions of a panoply of dumplings, buns, meaty tidbits, cakes, and pastries, which collectively offer an unmatched spectrum of tastes, aromas, and textures. Elegant teahouses were replaced by gargantuan, multistoried canteens, some accommodating over a thousand at a seating, and speed of service became as vital to commercial success as variety and quality were to customer satisfaction. The ingenious dim sum cart solved the problem, and the tradition was exported. Steamer baskets and plates of steaming hot snacks are piled high on the carts, which hostesses push between the tables advertising their fare in singsong voices. The diner takes a peek beneath the lids, makes a selection, and the plates are transferred to the table with dipping sauces of chile and soy, mustard and red vinegar.

A pot of steaming-hot Chinese tea, which is never allowed to run empty, accompanies dim sum. A wave of the hand or the lid laid askew on top of the teapot is the signal for a roving water carrier to top it up. *Pu er* (black tea) is preferred in the south, while jasmine tea has universal appeal.

When it's time to pay, the waiter simply adds up the number of serving plates on the table or tots up the entries made by the serving staff on a paper chit.

FRANCE

*F*rance's long coastline and many rivers play an important role in French cooking and are celebrated in a wide variety of ways, each region adding its unique elements of the terroir. Shellfish are a wonderful way to start a meal, especially near the sea. Many restaurants are known for their fresh coquillage, displayed near the entrance on banks of crushed ice decorated with fresh lemons and seaweed to tempt the customer into ordering a grand plateau de mer, a multi-tiered platter of raw and cooked delicacies served with lemon, a simple mignonette sauce of champagne vinegar and chopped shallots, and thinly sliced bread and butter.

Oysters, crayfish, shrimp, whole cracked crab, tiny clams, sea urchins, and whelks all figure in the choices, depending upon the season. But then, it's difficult to pass up such specialties as oyster soup in Brittany, a bowl of mussels steamed in Muscadet and scattered with minced garlic and fresh parsley savored along the Atlantic coast, grilled anchovies with sweet Banyuls vinegar eaten under the bright sunshine of the Mediterranean, or spicy salt-cod fritters nibbled in Languedoc.

In Normandy, you'll find salmon with a bit of cream, in the Loire with a little local white wine. In Savoy, fresh mountain trout are paired with walnuts, in Haute Provence with local almonds. Monkfish, meaty and lobsterlike in both flavor and texture, is a favorite throughout the country and may be served roasted whole or sliced into thick medaillons, garnished with local herbs or vegetables. Stews are made of fish as well; two of the most famous are bouillabaisse from Provence and cotriade from Brittany. In the inland regions of the Loire, the Berry, the Dordogne, and the Garonne, and in the freshwater marshlands where the rivers meet the sea, small eels are served grilled or poached, in sauces or with a vinaigrette, depending on the region. When near the Spanish borders of Spain, and around Perpignan and Biarritz, be sure to look for salads made with fish and seasoned with saffron and peppers, while fish salads of the northern coasts are likely to be full of *coquillage*, local shellfish.

Preceding pages: The port of Collioure, in the Roussillon, is renowned for its anchovies. **Top:** The inhabitants of Cancale are devoted to the cultivation and consumption of France's most prized oysters. **Above:** At Provençal fish markets, cooks can purchase such delicacies as sea snails, sea urchins, and oysterlike shellfish called *vioulets*. **Right:** Le Vieux Port, the Old Port of Marseilles, is aptly named—ships still dock here after twenty-six centuries.

In Provence, one finds fishing communities all along the Mediterranean shore, and the fishermen who live there are descended from men who for centuries pulled their living from the sea. Once a haven for small rockfish and larger, oilier fish farther from shore, the Mediterranean is now largely overfished. What is caught is expensive, especially the prized fish like *rascasse* (scorpion fish), *loup de mer* (sea bass), and *rouget barbet* (red rock mullet). Still, the Provençaux love their seafood, and their most renowned dishes are a celebration of this fact.

On the tables of a local open-air fish market may be the ugly, spiny *rascasse*—rare now, but without it the cooks of Marseilles would not even contemplate making their famed bouillabaisse—and its cousin, the red chapon. The *baudroie* (monkfish), the giant-headed stargazer, the John Dory, and the little red mullets, *rougets grondins* (sea robins), and other rockfish that add complexity to bouillabaisse are also much loved grilled. The affordable sardine is grilled; deep-fried; sautéed; boned, stuffed with spinach and walnuts, and rolled; or prepared *en escabèche*, that is, served cold in a spiced vinegary marinade.

Anchovies, too, are inexpensive and plentiful, particularly around Nice, where in spring they rise in hordes to spawn. Apart from being grilled or fried, they are preserved between layers of sea salt, the intense result ideal for hors d'oeuvres. Away from the coast, one sees market displays of trout caught in the freshwater torrents that flow from the Alps, displays of perch, or the rare *omble chevalier* from mountain lakes.

If bouillabaisse is the most famous Provençal soup, it is not the only one. The beautiful *bourride*, a broth made from white-fleshed fish and served creamy and rich with an emulsion of garlicky aioli, is nearly as renowned. Home cooks use the local fish varieties, simmering them with tomatoes, saffron, leeks, and other vegetables, to make the family's *soupe de poissons*.

Although the fish soups are models of sophistication, with fish, as with most of Provençal cookery, the motto *faites simple* (make it simple) prevails. Two common threads run through this tradition: a respect for the integrity of each ingredient and the use of local produce to dress the centerpiece of any dish. As always, olive oil is the cooking medium, and herbs and garlic the major additions, whether fish is panfried, broiled, grilled over an outdoor fire, or baked.

Also adhering to the *faites simple* premise is the tradition of poaching seafood. Water is used rather than stock and the flavorings here, too, are local. Fennel or coriander seed and the ubiquitous orange peel give the liquid its flavor, and the fish or shellfish is more than likely served in a little of the reduced liquid rather than with a *velouté* (thickened stock-enriched sauce) or a butter or cream sauce as it would be farther north.

Left: The hardworking fishermen of Marseilles bring in a steady harvest for seafood-loving Provençaux. **Above, left:** Plump and fresh from the market, these *rougets barbets*, or red mullets, are ideal for preparing *en papillotes*, in paper packets that are a delight to open at the table. **Above, right:** Fish occupies a sizeable niche in the French menu, whether simmered in bouillabaisse or *soupe aux poissons*, baked in *cabillaud à la bordelaise* (cod with tomato and onion), or grilled in *loup flambé au fenouil* (sea bass and fennel flamed with Pernod).

Vegetables and Salt Cod with Mayonnaise

Le Grand Aïoli • Provence • France

In Provence, *un grand aïoli* might be prepared for a Sunday afternoon summertime gathering of family and friends, with the feast enjoyed outdoors in the shade of a spreading mulberry tree. Or the occasion might be a village celebration, with every local shopkeeper and schoolchild sitting down to a bountiful meal at long tables set up in the main square. In both cases, red wine or a chilled rosé flows freely, and lots of fresh bread is served.

12–14 pieces salt cod, about 6 oz (185 g) each, soaked (page 225)

AIOLI

6–10 cloves garlic, minced

½ teaspoon salt

6 egg yolks

2½ cups (20 fl oz/625 ml) extra-virgin olive oil

Scant ½ teaspoon freshly ground pepper

24 boiling potatoes such as Yellow Finn, White Rose, or Yukon gold

6 teaspoons salt

36 carrots

5–6 lb (2.5–3 kg) young, tender green beans, trimmed

36 beets

24 eggs

Serves 12–14

1 Place the fish in a shallow saucepan or frying pan and add water to cover. Bring to a simmer over low heat and poach the fish just until it flakes when poked with a fork, 3–4 minutes. Using a slotted spatula, transfer to a platter and let cool.

2 To make the aioli, in a mortar or bowl, pound the garlic cloves and salt together with a pestle until a paste forms. Set aside. In a large bowl, whisk together the egg yolks until blended. Very slowly drizzle in about ½ teaspoon of the olive oil, gently whisking it into the egg yolks. Repeat until a thick emulsion forms, usually after about 2 tablespoons have been added. Then whisk in 1 teaspoon olive oil at a time until all the oil is used. Gently stir in the garlic-salt mixture and season with the pepper. You should have about 2½ cups (20 fl oz/625 ml). Cover and refrigerate until needed.

3 In a large saucepan, combine the potatoes, 2 teaspoons of the salt, and water to cover. Bring to a boil over medium-high heat, reduce the heat to medium, and cook until easily pierced with the tip of a sharp knife, about 25 minutes. Drain and set aside.

4 Peel or scrub the carrots. Cook them as you cooked the potatoes, using 2 teaspoons salt and cooking for only 20 minutes. Drain and set aside. Cook the beans in the same way, using the remaining 2 teaspoons salt and cooking for only 5–8 minutes or until tender-crisp. Drain and set aside. Cut off any beet leaves to within ½ inch (12 mm) of the top. Cook them in the same manner but without any salt. The cooking time will be longer, about 1 hour. Drain and set aside. Keep the beets separate from the other vegetables. Serve them peeled or unpeeled and cut into wedges.

5 Place the eggs in a large saucepan and add water to cover. Bring to a boil, reduce the heat to a simmer, and cook for 12 minutes. Pour off the hot water, then fill the pan with cold water to stop the eggs from cooking. Peel and quarter the eggs.

6 Arrange the vegetables, eggs, and salt cod on serving platters and set them on the table along with several bowls of the aioli. Serve warm or at room temperature.

Warm Oysters with Tomato Vinaigrette

Huîtres Tièdes à la Vinaigrette aux Tomates • Brittany • France

The majority of French oysters are raised in the numerous oyster *parcs* in the coastal waters of Brittany and Normandy. As you pass through the seaside villages, signs point you to the *parcs*, where you can buy freshly harvested oysters of different varieties and sizes. For this dish, you must use the *creuse*, a deep-shelled oyster, or a similar type, rather than the flat *belon* variety, because the well of the shell is needed to hold the sauce.

Rock salt

4 tomatoes, peeled, seeded, and minced

2 cups (16 fl oz/500 ml) Champagne vinegar

2 shallots, minced

1 tablespoon minced fresh chives

1 teaspoon freshly ground pepper

½ teaspoon salt

4 dozen oysters in their shells (see note)

Serves 4

1 Preheat the oven to 500°F (260°C).

2 Pour rock salt into 1 large or 2 smaller baking dishes to a depth of 1 inch (2.5 cm). Place in the oven to heat for 15 minutes.

3 In a bowl, stir together the tomatoes, vinegar, shallots, chives, pepper, and salt to form a vinaigrette. Set aside.

4 Remove the baking dish(es) from the oven and place the oysters, rounded side down, on the salt. Return to the oven and bake until the oysters open, 7–8 minutes. Remove from the oven and let cool until the shells can be handled, 3–4 minutes.

5 Discard any oysters that failed to open. Using a small, sharp knife, cut through the muscle near the hinge that attaches the shells together on each oyster, being careful not to spill any juices. Discard the flat upper shells and place the lower ones on a platter or 4 individual plates.

6 Spoon a tablespoon of the vinaigrette onto each oyster. Serve at once.

OYSTERS

Always buy oysters from reputable merchants who can vouch that they come from safe, clean, unpolluted waters. Fresh live oysters in the shell have a mild, sweet smell. Their shells should be closed tightly and they should feel heavy with water. Do not buy any oysters that remain open when touched. A strong fishy or ammonium odor indicates that the oysters are no longer fresh, so pass them by. While oysters are spawning during the summer months, their flesh becomes soft, milky, and less sweet. They are not toxic, but they do taste unpleasant. Generally, in both the United States and Europe, oysters are in season during the months that have the letter *r* in them—that is, from September to April. (One exception is the Kumamoto, which spawns in the autumn.) However, with the cultivation of sterile varieties, oysters are increasingly available all year long, which makes them perfect for serving for almost any occasion. The perennial accompaniment for oysters is, of course, chilled Champagne.

Sardines with Olive Oil and Tomatoes

Sardines Marinées aux Tomates et Huile d'Olive • Provence • France

Sardines are considered a delicacy along the Mediterranean, where they are often fried, then dressed in a sauce and served at room temperature, as with this dish. Sardines have long been plentiful in these waters, and many local dishes, including bouillabaisse, are made with them. When choosing sardines, look for those with bright, clear eyes and slippery skin. A dull-eyed, dry-skinned fish is not a fresh one. Allow at least four sardines per person if they are served fried or grilled without a sauce.

1 In a frying pan over medium heat, warm the olive oil. While the oil is heating, spread the flour on a plate and roll the sardines in it to coat lightly.

2 When the oil is hot, place the sardines, a few at a time, into the pan and fry on the first side until the skin is crispy and golden, 2–3 minutes. Turn and fry on the second side until the skin is crispy and golden and the meat pulls easily away from the bone, another minute or so. Using a slotted spatula, transfer to paper towels to drain. Repeat until all the sardines are cooked. Sprinkle them with the salt and pepper and arrange on a platter.

3 Pour off all but 2 tablespoons of the oil from the pan and return to medium heat. Add the vinegar and deglaze the pan, stirring with a wooden spoon to dislodge any browned bits from the pan bottom. Remove from the heat and carefully pour the vinegar mixture over the sardines.

4 To make the marinade, in another frying pan over medium heat, warm the olive oil. When it is hot, add the minced onion, fennel, garlic, and bay leaf. Sauté until the onion is translucent, 1–2 minutes. Add the tomatoes, raise the heat to high, and cook for 2–3 minutes to reduce some of the liquid.

5 Pour the hot marinade over the sardines. Let cool to room temperature, 10–15 minutes, then cover and refrigerate for 12–24 hours before serving.

6 Serve slightly chilled or at room temperature.

¼ cup (2 fl oz/60 ml) olive oil

½ cup (2½ oz/75 g) all-purpose (plain) flour

12 fresh sardines, about 3 lb (1.5 kg) total weight, cleaned

½ teaspoon salt

1 teaspoon freshly ground pepper

¼ cup (2 fl oz/60 ml) red wine vinegar

MARINADE

2 tablespoons olive oil

1 yellow or white onion, minced

1 fennel stalk, about 6 inches (15 cm) long

1 clove garlic

1 fresh bay leaf or ½ dried bay leaf

2 ripe tomatoes, peeled, seeded, and chopped

Serves 4

Lingcod with a Black Olive Crust

Mostelle Croutée aux Olives Noires • Provence • France

If you have time, top the fish with the olive mixture about 3 hours before cooking. This allows the crust to dry and adhere better to the fish. If you can't find lingcod fillets, keep in mind that porgy, sea bass, turbot, and halibut can be similarly prepared.

BLACK-OLIVE OIL

½ cup (4 fl oz/125 ml) extra-virgin olive oil

1 tablespoon very finely minced brine-cured black olives

¾ cup (4 oz/125 g) diced black olives

¼ cup (2 fl oz/60 ml) olive oil

3 shallots, finely chopped

½ cup (1 oz/30 g) fine white bread crumbs from day-old bread

2 teaspoons fresh thyme leaves

Salt and freshly ground pepper to taste

4 thick lingcod fillets, each 6 oz (185 g) and about 4 by 3 by 1 inch (10 by 7.5 by 2.5 cm)

Serves 4

1 To make the black-olive oil, in a bowl, combine the oil and minced olives. Let stand for 1–2 hours.

2 Preheat the oven to 425°F (220°C). Oil a baking dish large enough to hold the fish in a single layer. Place the diced olives in a bowl. In a small frying pan over medium heat, warm the olive oil. Add the shallots and sauté for about 45 seconds. Raise the heat to high and add the bread crumbs, stirring until the crumbs crisp, 45–60 seconds. Add the crumbs to the olives in the bowl, mix well, and then stir in the thyme. Season with salt and pepper.

3 Place the fish in the prepared baking dish. Coat the top of each fillet with the olive mixture, dividing evenly. Bake until the fish is opaque throughout, 8–10 minutes. Transfer to warmed individual plates. Drizzle a circle of the black-olive oil around each piece of fish and serve at once.

Lobster in the Style of Cherbourg

Demoiselles de Cherbourg à la Crème • Normandy • France

This is a luxurious dish, but one that is well worth making. *Demoiselle* is considered the traditional name for a small lobster. The "lobster butter" and the roe, if any, combine to make a rich, complexly flavored sauce that you will want to scoop up every last bit of with shards of bread. Serve with brut Champagne or Meursault.

2 live lobsters, 1½–1¾ lb (750–875 g) each

½ teaspoon salt

¾ teaspoon freshly ground black pepper

3 tablespoons unsalted butter

3 tablespoons Calvados

3 tablespoons Lillet, sweet vermouth, or dry white wine

2 cups (16 fl oz/500 ml) crème fraîche

3 egg yolks

2 teaspoons minced fresh tarragon

⅛ teaspoon cayenne pepper

⅛ teaspoon paprika

Serves 4

1 Bring a large pot three-fourths full of water to a boil over high heat. Immerse the live lobsters in the water and cook them for 2 minutes, just long enough to kill them. Lift out with tongs and set on a work surface. When cool enough to handle, using kitchen shears, cut the lobsters in half lengthwise, and separate the halves. Remove the head sac and the small intestine in the center of the tail and discard. Using a small spoon, scoop out the yellowish green tomalley (the "butter") and the reddish black coral, or roe, if present, and reserve them in a bowl. Break the claws with a mallet or nutcracker just enough to crack them, being careful not to crush the meat.

2 Sprinkle the lobster halves with the salt and black pepper. In a large frying pan over medium-high heat, melt the butter. When it foams, add the lobster halves, shell side down, and cook them for about 2 minutes, turning so that all sides of the shell are exposed to the butter. Turn the halves and cook, meat side down, for another 2 minutes, moving them around in the pan. Add the Calvados, carefully ignite it with a long match to burn off the alcohol, and let the flames subside. Add the Lillet, vermouth, or white wine and raise the heat to high. Boil until reduced by half, about 1 minute. Reduce the heat to medium, add the crème fraîche, and continue to cook until the lobster meat is cooked through and pulls away from the shell when lifted with a fork and the cream has thickened, 2–3 minutes.

3 Meanwhile, add the egg yolks and the tarragon to the bowl containing the tomalley and the roe, if using, and whisk well.

4 Using tongs, remove the lobster halves, letting the juices drain back into the frying pan. Arrange on a warmed platter or individual plates.

5 Reduce the heat to low and whisk the egg yolk mixture into the pan juices. Whisk until thickened, being careful not to allow the mixture to boil, just a minute or two. Add the cayenne and the paprika.

6 Spoon the sauce evenly over the lobster halves and serve at once.

Salmon in Cream and Muscadet Sauce

Saumon à la Crème au Muscadet • Loire Valley • France

Muscadet, a very dry white wine, is produced in a relatively small area in the westernmost point of the Loire Valley, where the Loire River reaches the Atlantic at Nantes. The salmon, of course, comes from the river.

4 tomatoes, peeled, seeded, and diced

2 shallots, diced

1½ cups (12 fl oz/375 ml) Muscadet or other dry white wine

1 teaspoon salt, plus more to taste

1 teaspoon freshly ground pepper, plus more to taste

3 tablespoons unsalted butter

6 center-cut salmon fillets, about 1½ lb (750 g) total weight, skin removed

⅔ cup (5 fl oz/160 ml) crème fraîche

1 teaspoon minced fresh chervil

1 teaspoon minced fresh chives

1 teaspoon minced fresh tarragon

Serves 6

1 In a saucepan over medium heat, combine the tomatoes, shallots, wine, and ½ teaspoon *each* salt and pepper. Cook, stirring occasionally, until reduced by one-third, about 10 minutes. Remove from the heat and set aside.

2 In a large frying pan over medium-high heat, melt the butter. When it foams, add the salmon fillets. Sear until golden, about 2 minutes, then turn and sear on the second side until golden and just opaque throughout, about 2 minutes longer. Sprinkle with the remaining ½ teaspoon *each* salt and pepper and transfer to warmed individual plates.

3 Strain the tomato mixture through a fine-mesh sieve placed over a bowl, pressing against the pulp to extract all the juice. Stir in the crème fraîche, then taste and adjust the seasonings. Return to the saucepan over medium heat and cook, stirring, until the sauce thickens a bit, 2–3 minutes.

4 Pour the sauce over the salmon and sprinkle with the chervil, chives, and tarragon. Serve at once.

CREAM

It is well-known that some of the finest, richest cream in the world is produced in France, and the French use it generously, especially in their most traditional cooking. The dairy regions, where local cows graze and feed on lush green pastures, are found in virtually every French province except Provence, and the national table reflects the regional bounty. Nowhere, though, is the influence of cream as evident as it is in the dishes of Normandy, where you will find everything from soups and salad dressings to sauces, tarts, and breads made with the highly valued cream and crème fraîche.

Crème fraîche is especially beguiling to cook with because it is thickened and slightly acidulated, giving it ready-made texture and flavor. It is particularly good for making sauces that are reduced, because it doesn't separate when it is boiled. To make crème fraîche at home, add 2 tablespoons whole buttermilk to ½ cup (4 fl oz/125 ml) heavy (double) cream, cover the container, and let it stand overnight at room temperature. If time is short, 2 tablespoons cider vinegar added to 1 cup (8 fl oz/250 ml) heavy cream at room temperature will thicken the cream within the hour.

Spicy Salt Cod Fritters

Beignets de Morue • Languedoc • France

The windows of *traiteurs* in Perpignan, like those of other towns throughout southwestern France, typically display mounds of freshly fried salt cod fritters, delicious and ready to be taken home for a snack or enjoyed on a picnic. Although they can be made with salt cod chunks, if the cod is shredded and folded into the batter, the result is a lighter puff. The squeeze of lime juice and the lemon quarters heighten the flavor.

1 To cook the salt cod, fill a saucepan half full with water, add the bay leaf, and place over medium heat. Bring to just below a boil, reduce the heat to low, and add the salt cod. Cook until the fish easily flakes with a fork, about 10 minutes.

2 Using a slotted spoon, transfer the fish to a plate. Discard the cooking water. When the fish is cool enough to handle, remove any errant bones or pieces of skin. Put the fish in a mortar and crush to a purée with a pestle, or purée the cod in a food processor along with the 1 teaspoon olive oil.

3 In a mortar or small food processor, crush together the garlic and whole chile or cayenne pepper. Add the garlic mixture to the puréed cod and mix well. Set aside.

4 In a bowl, stir together the flour, the baking powder, the water, and the 1 tablespoon olive oil, mixing well to make a thick cream. Add the cod mixture, onion, parsley, and lime juice and mix well.

5 Pour in vegetable oil into a deep-fryer or a deep, heavy saucepan to a depth of 4 inches (10 cm) and heat to 375°F (190°C), or until a small spoonful of the batter dropped into it puffs and sizzles upon contact. Working in batches, drop the cod mixture by the heaping tablespoonful into the hot oil. Cook until they are puffed and golden, 3–4 minutes. Using a slotted spoon, transfer to paper towels to drain; keep warm. Repeat until all the cod mixture is used.

6 Arrange the fritters on a warmed platter and serve at once with the lemon quarters.

½ lb (250 g) salt cod, soaked (page 225)

1 bay leaf

1 teaspoon extra-virgin olive oil, if needed, plus 1 tablespoon

1 clove garlic

1 small dried red chile or ¼ teaspoon cayenne pepper

1 cup (5 oz/155 g) all-purpose (plain) flour

1 teaspoon baking powder

¾ cup (6 fl oz/180 ml) water

1 yellow onion, minced

1 tablespoon minced fresh flat-leaf (Italian) parsley

1 teaspoon fresh lime juice

Vegetable oil for deep-frying

2 lemons, quartered

Makes about 24 fritters; serves 4

Squid Braised with Peas

Calmars aux Petits Pois • Provence • France

This recipe is from Toulon, the great French naval military harbor, where cooks slowly braise squid and cuttlefish with excellent results.

2 lb (1 kg) medium to large squid

5 tablespoons (2½ fl oz/75 ml) olive oil

1 small yellow onion, chopped or thinly sliced

1 lb (500 g) tomatoes, peeled, seeded, and coarsely chopped

1 clove garlic, finely chopped

About 1 cup (8 fl oz/250 ml) water

2 fresh thyme sprigs

2 small bay leaves

Salt and freshly ground coarse pepper

2⅓ cups (12 oz/375 g) fresh or frozen shelled English peas (about 2½ lb/1.25 kg unshelled)

Tomato paste to taste (optional)

Serves 6

1 First, clean the squid: Working with 1 squid at a time, pull the head from the body. Cut off and reserve the tentacles; discard the head. Squeeze out and discard the small, hard "beak" at the base of the tentacles; leave the tentacles whole. Using your fingers, pull out any internal matter from the body, including the quill-like cartilage, and discard. Peel off the mottled skin that covers the body. Rinse the body well. Cut the small tubular parts of the body into rings. Cut the larger parts lengthwise into strips the width of fettuccine and 4–5 inches (10–13 cm) long. Cut the tentacles into similar lengths.

2 In a saucepan over medium heat, warm the olive oil. Add the onion and sauté for about 1 minute. Add the tomatoes and garlic, cover, and simmer for about 5 minutes. Add the squid and the water just to cover. Stir in the thyme sprigs and bay leaves. Season with salt and pepper. Bring to a boil, reduce the heat to low, cover, and simmer until the squid is tender, about 50 minutes.

3 Add the peas and simmer until tender, 15–20 minutes if using fresh peas and 5 minutes if using frozen peas. Taste and adjust the seasoning, adding a generous grinding of pepper. Add a little tomato paste to taste, if desired. Remove the thyme sprigs and bay leaves and discard. Ladle into warmed shallow bowls and serve at once.

Mussels in White Wine

Moules à la Marinière • Brittany • France

Mussels are an important part of local French fare along both the Mediterranean and Atlantic coastlines. There are myriad preparations and variations, but perhaps the most popular is *moules à la marinière*. It's hard to tell which is better: the tender mussels pried from the blue-black shells, or the broth of Muscadet, butter, and garlic that each diner can soak up every last drop of with a piece of warm, crusty bread.

1 tablespoon unsalted butter

1 tablespoon extra-virgin olive oil

½ yellow or white onion, chopped

1 clove garlic, minced

½ teaspoon freshly ground pepper

4–5 lb (2–2.5 kg) mussels, well scrubbed and debearded

2 cups (16 fl oz/500 ml) Muscadet or other dry white wine

1½ tablespoons minced fresh flat-leaf (Italian) parsley

Serves 4

1 In the bottom of a pot large enough to accommodate all the mussels, melt the butter with the olive oil over medium-high heat. When the butter foams, add the onion and sauté just until translucent, 2–3 minutes. Add the garlic, pepper, and mussels (discard any that do not close to the touch), pour over the wine, and sprinkle with the parsley.

2 Cover, reduce the heat to low, and cook just until the mussels open, 10–12 minutes. Uncover and turn the mussels in the broth.

3 Using a large slotted spoon, scoop the mussels into individual bowls, discarding any that failed to open. Ladle an equal amount of the broth into each bowl. Serve at once.

LA CRÊPERIE

All towns of any size in France have at least one *crêperie*. It might be a full-fledged restaurant or simply a storefront that is just big enough to house a large hot plate for cooking the paper-thin pancakes and to display an assortment of toppings for passersby. Prepared crepes can be purchased by the dozen in supermarkets, making it easy to serve them at home.

Chartres, dominated by its magnificent cathedral, stands out to most people for its beautiful *crêperies* as well. Many visitors choose to dine at a *crêperie* near the beautifully lit cathedral. Often, guests are presented with the option of a trio of crepes. The first is usually rather like a salad, filled with tomato, frisée, and bacon. The second may either contain ham or sausage. The third is often a simple *crêpe sucrée* with butter and sugar. A pitcher of white wine is the perfect thing to wash all three dishes down.

Red Mullet in Parchment

Rougets Barbets en Papillotes à l'Estragon • Provence • France

The French habit of wrapping fish fillets in little parchment parcels is a traditional one. Here, the favorite small rockfish of the Mediterranean, red mullet, is used, making the recipe indisputably Provençal in origin. Any rockfish fillets available would be the best choice for this classic preparation, but most white-fleshed fillets, such as whiting or garfish, would lend themselves to the method. The packages swell in the oven and they are always brought to the table at once, so diners can appreciate the aroma as the paper is slit open.

1 First, prepare the vegetables: In a small saucepan, combine the shallots, turnips, carrots, butter, and sugar, and season with salt and pepper. Add water just to cover (about 2 cups/16 fl oz/500 ml), bring to a boil over high heat, cover partially, and boil until the water evaporates, 6–8 minutes, adding the zucchini halfway through the cooking time. Do not allow the vegetables to scorch. Remove from the heat and set aside.

2 Preheat the oven to 350°F (180°C).

3 Cut out six 14-inch (35-cm) squares of parchment (baking) paper. Fold each one in half and then tear off the top and bottom corners of the folded edge to round these corners slightly. To form each parcel, lay a piece of paper on a work surface and open like a book. Put 2 fish fillets on the right half of the square. Drizzle 1 tablespoon olive oil over the fish. Season with salt and pepper. Top the fish with a tarragon sprig and 3 lemon slices, and drizzle 2 teaspoons lemon juice over all. Fold the left half of the paper over the fish to cover. Then, starting from the bottom edge near the fold, fold the edge of the paper over itself every 2 inches (5 cm), working your way around the package, to enclose the fish. Repeat to make 5 more airtight parcels.

4 Slide all the parcels onto a baking sheet and brush the tops with olive oil. Bake for 6 minutes.

5 Meanwhile, reheat the vegetables over medium heat, stirring them to prevent scorching and adding the sugar snap peas or snow peas, which require only 1 minute or so to cook.

6 Transfer the fish parcels to individual plates. Spoon the vegetables alongside the parcels, dividing them evenly. Serve at once.

VEGETABLES

6 shallots

6 baby turnips

1 bunch baby carrots, peeled

5 tablespoons (2½ oz/75 g) unsalted butter

1 teaspoon sugar

Salt and freshly ground pepper to taste

6 baby zucchini (courgettes), trimmed

12 red mullet fillets, each about 6 inches (15 cm) long and ⅜ inch (1 cm) thick

6 tablespoons (3 fl oz/90 ml) olive oil, plus extra for brushing on parcels

Salt and freshly ground pepper to taste

6 fresh tarragon sprigs

2 small lemons, unpeeled, thinly sliced to yield 18 slices

¼ cup (2 fl oz/60 ml) lemon juice

12 sugar snap peas or snow peas (mangetouts), trimmed

Serves 6

Baked Stuffed Sardines

Sardines Farcies au Four • Provence • France

Sardines are a favorite catch along the Côte d'Azur, where they are deep-fried or panfried or are prepared with a spicy marinade, *en escabèche*, and stored in the refrigerator to have on hand for a quick meal. For a special occasion, the fish are boned and stuffed with herbs. Walnuts, a common addition to the filling, are included in this version.

16 large fresh sardines

¼ cup (⅓ oz/10 g) chopped fresh flat-leaf (Italian) parsley

Leaves from 1 small fresh rosemary sprig, chopped

1 tablespoon chopped fresh thyme

4 cloves garlic, finely chopped

2 tablespoons ground walnuts

1 tablespoon grated Parmesan cheese

5 tablespoons (2½ fl oz/75 ml) olive oil

Serves 4

1 One at a time, hold the sardines under running cold water, squeezing the body slightly, and use your fingers to pull off the head and then pull downward to remove the backbone. Break the bone free at the tail end and discard the spine in one piece. Using a sharp knife, scrape off the scales. Rinse the fish well and place on a platter, opening the fish flat like a book. When all of the sardines are boned, set aside.

2 Preheat the oven to 425°F (220°C). Oil a baking dish large enough to accommodate the closed sardines in a single layer.

3 In a small bowl, stir together the parsley, rosemary, and thyme. In another small bowl, stir together the garlic, walnuts, and Parmesan. Add 2 tablespoons of the mixed herbs to the garlic mixture along with 1 tablespoon of the olive oil and mix well. Spread over the flattened sardines, then fold them closed and place in the prepared baking dish. Sprinkle evenly with the remaining mixed herbs and 4 tablespoons (2 fl oz/60 ml) olive oil.

4 Bake the sardines until opaque throughout, about 6 minutes. Transfer to a platter and serve at once.

Steamed Cod with Vegetables

Cabillaud Demoiselle d'Avignon · Vaucluse · France

This light recipe comes from an Avignon hostess more concerned with her figure than most French home cooks are reputed to be. Turbot, mahi-mahi, or even swordfish may be used in place of the cod, if you like. The fish is steamed, and the vegetables are only lightly cooked in oil, so there is a minimum of extra calories.

6 cod fillets, each 6 oz (185 g) and about 4 by 3 by 1 inch (10 by 7.5 by 2.5 cm)

5 tablespoons (2½ fl oz/75 ml) olive oil

1 small eggplant (aubergine), unpeeled, cut into neat ⅜-inch (1-cm) dice

1 small zucchini (courgette), trimmed and cut into neat ⅜-inch (1-cm) dice

4 large, firm tomatoes, peeled, seeded, and cut into neat ⅜-inch (1-cm) dice

Salt and freshly ground pepper to taste

6 tablespoons (3 fl oz/90 ml) extra-virgin olive oil

3 tablespoons fresh chive lengths (1 inch/2.5 cm)

Serves 6

1 Place the fish on a steamer rack and set aside. Pour water into the steamer pan and bring to a boil.

2 Meanwhile, in a small frying pan over medium heat, warm the olive oil. Add the eggplant and sauté quickly, adding the zucchini as the eggplant begins to soften. Finally, add the tomatoes just to heat through. Do not overcook, or they will lose their texture. The total cooking time should be about 4 minutes. The vegetables should be crisp-tender when served. Season with salt and pepper and keep warm.

3 Place the steamer rack over the boiling water, cover, and steam until the fish is opaque throughout, 4–6 minutes.

4 Using a slotted spoon, transfer the vegetables to warmed individual plates, arranging them in a ring. Place a steamed fillet in the center of each ring. Drizzle 1 tablespoon extra-virgin olive oil over each fillet, garnish with the chives, and serve.

LE REPAS DE MIDI

In Provence's small communities and large cities alike, the arrival of midday is announced with the sound of shopkeepers and school principals shuttering their windows and locking their doors and of townspeople flocking into the streets to return home to share the midday meal with their families. Breakfast has been simple—bread, *café au lait*, hot chocolate for the children—and *le repas de midi* is the main meal of the day.

The meal always begins with an appetizer, even if only sliced sausage, hard-boiled egg on a vegetable *macèdoine*, or a slice of pâté. The main dish is meat or fish with an accompanying vegetable, but rarely more than one. Salad and cheese commonly follow, then fresh fruit or, for the children, maybe a fresh cheese drizzled with honey is brought to the table.

On Sunday, lunch becomes a more elaborate affair, with the table expanded to include members of the extended family. The ritual aperitif is pastis or the local Suze, Vennoise, or Figuoun, accompanied with little biscuits, a bowl of nuts, and an assortment of olives. The meal itself may open with crudités and aioli or *tapenade*, shrimp and sardines fried or rolled over spinach or walnuts, or perhaps deep-fried zucchini flowers.

The week's largest piece of meat is served on this day, and the vegetable accompaniment is carefully chosen according to tradition and season, such as leg of lamb with flageolets, steak or lamb with ratatouille, fish with sliced leeks, or a roast and a decorative *tian*. Salad comes after the main dish, then is followed by one or two good-sized cheeses purchased especially for the occasion, served with a crusty loaf (never cracker or biscuits) and lingered over for a while before dessert is set in place. Wine is poured with every course, but after cheese the red is removed and the glasses changed for a sweet muscat, maybe one of the household *ratafias* (a rum-based liqueur), or a feisty local marc with the coffee.

Sunday lunch requires dessert. Accomplished cooks might make a *bavarois* or a *tarte maison* of the season's fruit. More likely, a family member will go to the local *pâtisserie*, believing that a professional will make something suitably special.

Crab with its Butter and Seaweed

Crabe à sa Beurre aux Algues • Loire Valley • France

At a brasserie in Angers, not far from the château that dominates the city, you might find this dish, served on a large oval platter lined with seaweed so fresh that it looks and smells as if it has just been pulled from the ocean. Often, the body of the crab is broken to expose the sweet, yellow butter inside, but the claws are left intact for the diner to crack open with a hinged tool delivered by the waiter. Serve it with a glass of cold, crisp Muscadet and warm bread.

¼ cup (2 oz/60 g) salt

1 lemon, halved, plus 1 lemon, quartered

1 dried bay leaf

2 live crabs, about 2 lb (1 kg) each

Several handfuls of fresh small-leaved seaweed, preferably dark amber kelp

Serves 2

1 Fill a big pot two-thirds full of water. Add the salt, two lemon halves, and the bay leaf and bring to a boil over high heat. Carefully drop in the crabs, bring to a boil again, and keep at a strong boil for about 20 minutes. Using tongs, remove the crabs and let cool.

2 To clean each crab, break off each leg by twisting it at the joint closest to the body; set the legs aside. Place the crab rounded-side down and, using the heels of your hands, press down on each side of the shell until it cracks down the middle. Pull off each half shell, being careful to reserve the juices, then pry up the tail flap, pull it back, and twist it off. Turn the crab over and remove the spongy gills—"dead man's fingers"—and discard. Leave the yellowish mass of crab butter intact for scooping out at the table. Pinch the mouth and mandibles, pull off, and discard. Crack each segment of the legs and claws at the joint with a crab cracker, being careful not to crush the meat.

3 Arrange the seaweed in beds on individual plates. Arrange a crab on top of each and serve with a crab cracker, crab forks, and the lemon quarters.

Grilled Anchovies with Banyuls Vinegar

Anchois Grillés au Vinaigre de Banyuls • Languedoc • France

Anchovies, packed in salt or oil, are a staple of the French table, but it is the Mediterranean port of Collioure, in the Roussillon near the Spanish border, that has claimed the anchovy as its own. During the May to October season, the fishing boats of Collioure arrive early in the morning, delivering some of their catch to the salting houses and the rest to the fresh market. The local restaurants offer fresh grilled or fried anchovies, frequently served with *vinaigre de Banyuls*, made from the sweet fortified wine of the region.

Vegetable oil for oiling grilling basket

45–48 whole fresh anchovies, about 3 lb (1.5 kg) total weight, cleaned

1 tablespoon fresh thyme leaves

2 teaspoons freshly ground pepper

1 teaspoon salt

½ cup (4 fl oz/125 ml) Banyuls vinegar or sherry vinegar, or 4 lemons, quartered

Serves 4

1 Prepare a fire in a charcoal grill, or preheat a gas grill. Generously oil the inside and outside of a hinged grilling basket with vegetable oil. Fill with as many anchovies as will fit in a single layer, spacing them ½ inch (12 mm) apart. Sprinkle with a little of the thyme, pepper, and salt. Fasten closed.

2 Grill over a hot fire, turning only once, until the flesh flakes easily away from the bone, 2–3 minutes on each side. Transfer to a platter. Repeat until all are cooked.

3 Serve accompanied with the vinegar or lemon quarters for sprinkling or squeezing over the fish.

Sole Cooked in Butter

Sole Meunière · Champagne and the North · France

Although delicate-fleshed petrale sole is not a true sole (it is actually a Pacific flounder), it is particularly well suited to this classic sole preparation with butter and lemon juice. A favorite accompaniment is boiled potatoes sprinkled with parsley.

½ cup (2½ oz/75 g) all-purpose (plain) flour

4 whole Dover sole or 2 petrale sole, cleaned and skin removed, or sole fillets, 1½–2 lb (750 g–1 kg) total weight, skin removed

5 tablespoons (2½ oz/75 g) unsalted butter

1 teaspoon salt

1 teaspoon freshly ground pepper

Juice of 1 lemon

2 tablespoons minced fresh flat-leaf (Italian) parsley

Serves 4

1 Spread the flour on a plate and dust the fish on both sides, tapping off the excess.

2 In a large frying pan over medium heat, melt 3 tablespoons of the butter. When it foams, add 2 of the whole sole, sprinkle them with ½ teaspoon each of the salt and pepper, and cook until the underside of the fish is lightly golden and the meat can be lifted from the bone with a fork, about 4 minutes. Turn and cook the other side until golden, about 4 minutes longer. Transfer to a warmed platter and cover loosely with aluminum foil. Cook the remaining 2 sole the same way, adding an additional tablespoon of butter to the pan. If using sole fillets, proceed as directed, but reduce the cooking time to 1½–2 minutes on each side.

3 Pour off all but 1 tablespoon of the butter in the pan and add the remaining 1 table-spoon butter and the lemon juice. When the butter melts, pour it over the fish and sprinkle with the parsley.

4 Serve at once, piping hot.

Shrimp with Fennel

Crevettes au Fenouil · Provence · France

Fennel and Pernod identify this dish as coming from France's sunny south. It calls for a simple method of cooking that is common to many other recipes of the region, which rely on garlic and parsley just as this one does. Leave out the fennel and Pernod and increase the garlic and you have *crevettes à l'ail*, the ubiquitous garlic shrimp. Change the shrimp to scallops and you have *coquilles Saint-Jacques à la provençal*. This dish, as well as the others, can also be offered as a first course, in which case it will serve six.

30–32 large shrimp (prawns), about 2 lb (1 kg) total weight, peeled and deveined

8½ tablespoons (4½ oz/140 g) unsalted butter

2 teaspoons fennel seed

1 clove garlic, finely chopped

3 tablespoons Pernod or pastis

Salt and freshly ground pepper to taste

2 heaping tablespoons chopped fresh flat-leaf (Italian) parsley mixed with 1 heaping tablespoon chopped fresh dill or fennel leaves

Serves 4

1 Pat the shrimp thoroughly dry with paper towels. In a frying pan over high heat, melt 2½ tablespoons of the butter until it is sizzling but has not browned. Add the shrimp, fennel seed, and garlic and sauté until the shrimp begin to change color, about 2 minutes, depending on size.

2 Add the Pernod or pastis and carefully ignite with a long match. Let the flames extinguish naturally.

3 Cut the remaining 6 tablespoons (3 oz/90 g) butter into small pieces and add to the pan. When it melts and forms a sauce, season with salt and pepper, then scatter the parsley and dill or fennel leaves in the pan. Mix in the herbs briefly.

4 Spoon the shrimp onto a warmed platter and serve at once.

THE FRENCH SEAFOOD PLATTER

The people of Marseilles are serious seafood eaters, and a *plateau de fruits de mer*—a "seafood platter"—is regarded as a special treat in restaurants and, on festive occasions, in the home. For decades, the Toinou family has been among the best-known seafood purveyors in the city, selling their exquisitely fresh inventory from refrigerated pavement kiosks and now at their five-hundred-table, five-story restaurant in the Cours Saint-Louis.

Here diners might partake of anything from a simple plate of six sea urchins and a glass of wine to giant *plateaux*, typically two-story, round, ice-covered metal platters, one resting above the other atop a chrome tripod, both laden with a variety of the day's catch, primarily raw. What ends up on the platters depends on the season, the preferences of the diners, and the sound guidance of the waiters. One day, diners might taste raw mussels from Carteau, compare them with Bouzigue oysters with Côtes Bleu, fish the roe from sea urchin shells, and try the famous *vioulet*, a yellow, oysterlike shellfish unique to this area—definitely an acquired taste. Cooked shrimp, langoustines, and super *gambas* (very large prawns) will complete the copious array.

Cuttlefish Stuffed with Tapenade

Encornets Farcis à la Tapenade • Provence • France

This recipe is from Saintes-Maries-de-la-Mer in the Camargue. The small seaside township is a lazy haven for tourists until the Gypsies come to town. The main church is the burial place of the Virgin Mary's two half sisters and their black maid, Sarah, the patron saint of Gypsies. In May, Gypsies from all over Europe make a pilgrimage to the church, and the ensuing celebration swells the population of the town. You will need only the cuttlefish bodies for this recipe, not the tentacles, so buy them already cleaned if you prefer.

SAUCE

2 tablespoons olive oil

1 yellow onion, finely chopped

1 clove garlic, finely chopped

12 fresh basil leaves

2 fresh thyme sprigs

1 bay leaf

Salt and freshly ground pepper to taste

1 lb (500 g) tomatoes, peeled, seeded, and coarsely chopped

Pinch of sugar

8 medium-large cuttlefish or squid, each 6–7 inches (15–18 cm) long

½ lb (250 g) ground (minced) veal

½ lb (250 g) ground (minced) pork

3 cloves garlic, finely chopped

1 red onion, finely chopped

¼ cup (2 oz/60 g) olive tapenade

4 tablespoons (2 fl oz/60 ml) olive oil

⅔ cup (5 fl oz/160 ml) dry white wine

About 1 cup (8 fl oz/250 ml) water, if needed

Serves 8

1 To make the sauce, in a wide, heavy saucepan over medium heat, warm the olive oil. Add the onion and sauté until it gains an oily sheen, about 30 seconds. Add the garlic, basil, thyme, bay leaf, salt, and pepper. Stir well, reduce the heat to low, and cook slowly until the mixture softens and the flavors blend, about 10 minutes.

2 Add the tomatoes and sugar, stir well, and continue to cook, mashing from time to time with a wooden spoon, until a chunky sauce forms, about 30 minutes longer. Remove the sauce from the heat and keep warm.

3 Preheat the oven to 325°F (165°C).

4 Clean the cuttlefish or squid: Working with 1 at a time, pull the head from the body. Cut off and reserve the tentacles; discard the head. Squeeze out and discard the small, hard "beak" at the base of the tentacles; leave the tentacles whole. Using your fingers, pull out any internal matter from the body, including the quill-like cartilage, and discard. Rinse the body well. Leave the bodies whole, and do not peel away the mottled membrane that covers each body, as it helps to color the sauce. Discard the tentacles.

5 In a bowl, combine the ground veal and pork and mix well. Mix in the garlic, onion, and tapenade, blending thoroughly. Add 2 tablespoons of the olive oil and 1 tablespoon of the white wine and mix again.

6 Spoon the stuffing into the cuttlefish or squid bodies, dividing it evenly and not packing it too tightly. Secure each with a toothpick.

7 Lay the stuffed cuttlefish or squid in a single layer in a baking dish. Spoon the sauce evenly over the top and drizzle with the remaining 2 tablespoons olive oil. Cover the dish with aluminum foil.

8 Bake until a skewer inserted into the stuffed cuttlefish or squid comes out clean, 50–60 minutes. Halfway through the cooking, remove from the oven, lift the foil carefully, and add the remaining white wine to the dish. If the sauce still looks dry, add the water, distributing it evenly around the dish.

9 Remove the dish from the oven and, using a slotted spatula, carefully lift out the stuffed cuttlefish or squid. Discard the toothpicks. Reheat the sauce, stirring, then taste and adjust the seasoning.

10 Serve the stuffed cuttlefish or squid whole, topped with the sauce. Alternatively, cut the bodies on the diagonal into ⅜-inch (1-cm) slices, fan them out on warmed individual plates, and spoon the sauce over the top.

LA CRIÉE

For centuries in Marseilles, everyone, merchants and consumers alike, went to la Criée, a great cavernous structure in le Vieux Port (Old Port), to buy their fish. The wonderfully expressive name—literally, "The Shout"—evokes the scene perfectly: the bustle, the jostling, the noise.

Brawny men with fish-filled boxes on carts would trundle them through the crowds, rolling them one by one into place on the podium to have their contents called by species, by merchant, by the origin of the catch. The auctioneer, eyes alert, pointing, negotiating, would gauge the cries of the crowd as prices were shouted from the floor. He would push the bids upward, raising the prospective buyers' voices to a fever pitch; then, the hammer would slam down as the deal was sealed, and the auctioneer would swiftly move on.

The fish are gone now from la Criée. Although the name is still etched into the facade of the building, the structure has become the Théâtre National de la Criée. Walking through it, one can see the original vaulted glass-paned ceiling and remnants of the old concrete floors. The nostalgic visitor can imagine the atmosphere of the onetime market, where wholesale vendors labored through the night, to be replaced by a retail trade of small market stalls during the day.

La Criée itself has moved to a much larger, highly modern complex in l'Estaque, a western coastal suburb of Marseilles, which it shares with the city's wholesale meat market. The market is now known as la Nouvelle Criée du Chalutage (the New Criée of the Fishing Fleet), but only the name retains the romance. Limited to professional buyers, and with high security, its large waterfront sheds are the portrait of efficiency, ensuring smooth dispersal of seafood from the coast of Provence to the rest of France.

One or two fishing boats continue to anchor daily among the pleasure cruisers in the Old Port, the skippers selling their catch directly to the public. The householder who fancies a greater variety will find plenty of choice from the decks of boats docked a little farther along the coast in the bays of Martigues, Carro, Sausset-les-Pins, or Carry-le-Rouet.

Scallops Gratin

Gratin de Coquilles Saint-Jacques • Provence • France

Try to find a fishmonger that sells scallops still in their shells for this eye-appealing dish. Ask him or her to open the shells and remove the scallop meats, since a large tough area must be discarded. If you can locate only already-shelled scallops, look for small ovenproof porcelain shells made by such French companies as Apilco and Pillivuyt.

16 sea scallops (see note)

4 green (spring) onions, including tender green tops, sliced

2 firm tomatoes, peeled, seeded, and cut into ⅓-inch (9-mm) dice

½ cup (2½ oz/75 g) diced mixed red and green bell pepper (capsicum)

2 tablespoons salt-packed capers, rinsed and drained

Salt and freshly ground coarse pepper to taste

1 cup (8 fl oz/250 ml) olive oil

2–3 tablespoons chopped fresh flat-leaf (Italian) parsley

Serves 4

1 Preheat the oven to 475°F (245°C).

2 Lay each scallop in the center of its bottom shell. Arrange 4 filled shells per person on ovenproof plates. Place the plates on baking sheets.

3 Scatter an equal amount of the green onions, tomatoes, bell pepper, and capers around each scallop. Sprinkle with salt and pepper. Drizzle evenly with the olive oil.

4 Bake until the scallops are opaque throughout, about 3 minutes. Remove from the oven, sprinkle with the parsley, and serve at once.

Sea Robin Monte Carlo

Rougets Grondins Monte Carlo • Provence • France

This unusual broiled (grilled) fish dish is made with the sea robin, sometimes known as *gurnard*, a ubiquitous rockfish of the Mediterranean. If choosing an equivalent fish, look for another fish that rests on its belly, such as red mullet.

1 To make the anchovy butter, in a bowl, whisk the butter until creamy. Finely chop the anchovies and add to the butter along with the pepper and lemon juice to taste. Mix well. Set aside until serving.

2 Preheat a broiler (griller). Oil a baking sheet.

3 To make the croutons, cut off the crusts from the bread loaf. Then cut the loaf lengthwise into 6 equal slices. Each slice should be long enough to hold a fish. Trim each slice to resemble the shape of the fish. Pour olive oil to a depth of ½ inch (12 mm) into a frying pan and heat until a small piece of bread dropped into the oil sizzles on contact. Add the bread slices, one at a time, and fry, turning once, until golden, about 45 seconds on each side. Using tongs, transfer to paper towels to drain.

4 Score the top of each fish, making 3 or 4 cuts on the diagonal along its length. Brush both sides of the fish lightly with the olive oil and set them, lying on their bellies, on the prepared baking sheet. Sprinkle with salt and pepper.

5 Slip the pan under the broiler about 5 inches (13 cm) from the heat source and broil (grill) until opaque throughout, about 8 minutes.

6 Lightly reheat the croutons in a low oven (200°F/95°C) if they have cooled completely, then spread them generously with the anchovy butter, dividing it evenly. Lay each crouton on a warmed individual plate and top with a fish.

7 In a small saucepan over medium heat, melt the butter. Add the shallots and sauté until translucent, about 1 minute. Season to taste with a little lemon juice and pepper, add the parsley, stir quickly, and spoon evenly over the fish. Serve at once.

ANCHOVY BUTTER

½ cup (4 oz/125 g) unsalted butter, at room temperature

3 salt-packed anchovies, filleted and rinsed, or 4–6 olive oil–packed anchovy fillets

Freshly ground pepper to taste

About 2 tablespoons fresh lemon juice

CROUTONS

1 day-old long white sandwich loaf, unsliced

Olive oil for frying

6 small sea robins, cleaned, with heads intact, about 6 oz (185 g) each (see note)

2 tablespoons olive oil

Salt and freshly ground pepper to taste

½ cup (4 oz/125 g) unsalted butter

2 shallots, finely chopped

About 1 teaspoon fresh lemon juice

3 tablespoons chopped fresh flat-leaf (Italian) parsley

Serves 6

Grilled Tuna with Herbs

Thon à la Méridionale · Provence · France

Tuna, with its firm red flesh and meaty texture, lends itself to grilling. Here, the flavor is highlighted with the fresh herbs of the south: rosemary, thyme, and fennel. Swordfish or marlin may be substituted.

6 tuna steaks, each 5 oz (155 g) and 1 inch (2.5 cm) thick

2–3 tablespoons olive oil, plus oil for brushing grill rack

¼ cup (¼ oz/7 g) fresh rosemary leaves, lightly chopped if desired

Leaves from 3 large fresh thyme sprigs (about 1 tablespoon)

1 tablespoon fennel seed, crushed

Salt and freshly ground pepper to taste

6 tablespoons (3 fl oz/90 ml) extra-virgin olive oil

Serves 6

1 Brush the tuna steaks with the 2–3 tablespoons olive oil. Combine the rosemary, thyme, and fennel seed on a sheet of parchment (baking) paper or a cutting board, mixing well, then spread in a thin layer. Press the tuna onto the herbs, coating both sides. Cover and allow the herbs to infuse the tuna for at least 30 minutes or up to 2 hours.

2 Prepare a fire in a grill.

3 Brush the grill rack with olive oil. Place the tuna steaks on the rack. Grill until the first side is nicely colored, 2½–3 minutes, rotating the fillets 45 degrees after about 1½ minutes to create grid marks on the surface. Turn the fillets, season with salt and pepper, and grill until done as desired, about 2 minutes longer for medium-rare. This is how the tuna steaks are preferred in Provence—seared on the outside and pink on the inside. (The tuna can also be cooked on a ridged cast-iron grill pan on the stove top, using similar timing.)

4 Transfer the tuna to warmed individual plates, drizzle each steak with 1 tablespoon of the extra-virgin olive oil, and serve at once.

Onion and Anchovy Tart

Pissaladière · Provence · France

The *pissaladière* is one of the most recognizable dishes of Nice, where squares of the warm, just-baked tart are often sold by street vendors.

1 cup (8 fl oz/250 ml) lukewarm water

1½ oz (45 g) fresh yeast, or 1 tablespoon active dry yeast

2¾ cups (13 oz/410 g) all-purpose (plain) flour

2 tablespoons olive oil, plus ⅓ cup (3 fl oz/80 ml)

Pinch of salt

3 lb (1.5 kg) yellow onions, sliced

Leaves from 3 or 4 fresh thyme sprigs

Salt to taste

20 olive oil–packed anchovy fillets

18–20 small black olives

Serves 8

1 Place the water in a cup, crumble in the yeast, and stir to dissolve. In a food processor, combine the flour and dissolved yeast and process for 15 seconds. Add the 2 tablespoons oil and pinch of salt. Process until the mixture forms a ball. If it is too dry, dribble in a little water; if it is too wet, add a little flour. Transfer to a floured work surface, knead briefly, and shape into a ball. Place in an oiled bowl, turn to coat with oil, cover with a damp kitchen towel, and let rise until doubled in bulk, about 1 hour.

2 Meanwhile, in a deep frying pan over medium heat, warm the ⅓ cup (3 fl oz/80 ml) olive oil. Add the onions and sauté for about 2 minutes. Add the thyme, reduce the heat to low, and cook, stirring occasionally, until the onions are soft, about 40 minutes.

3 Preheat the oven to 475°F (245°C). Have ready a 12-by-16-inch (30-by-40-cm) baking sheet. Turn the dough out onto a floured work surface and roll into a rectangle about 10 inches (25 cm) by 14 inches (35 cm). Transfer to the baking sheet. Salt the onions lightly and spread evenly over the dough. Arrange the anchovies in a grid pattern on top. Dot with the olives. Let stand in a warm place until the dough rises around the topping, about 15 minutes.

4 Bake until crisp and browned, 18–20 minutes. Remove from the oven and serve hot, warm, or at room temperature, cut into squares.

PROVENÇAL FLAT BREAD

A glance at the *pissaladière*, the traditional onion flat bread of Provence, often gives rise to comparison with the Italian pizza, which is not surprising in light of the similar-sounding names and the history of Nice as an Italian city-state. What few people realize is that the *pissaladière* takes its name from the fermented fish paste that originally served as the pungent base beneath the onion, a role now played by a few anchovies arranged on top. Called *le pissalat*, the fish paste was a direct descendant of the Roman fish paste *garum*, and was designed, as was *garum*, as a means of conserving the fishermen's harvest of anchovies and sardines.

The already strongly flavored fish were combined in roughly equal amounts, treated to a spicy blend of salt, ginger, peppercorns, chiles, cinnamon, and cloves, and then placed in an earthenware crock, or *toupin*. The mixture was turned daily but otherwise left to bubble and ferment like a witches' brew for a week or longer, at which point the partially decomposed mass was mashed and then sieved to produce the highly flavored paste. Finally, it was bottled and topped with oil to prevent oxidation. Some older folks still make *pissalat* at home and use it for picnics, at which it is relished spread thickly on crusty bread or croutons.

Sea Bass on a Bed of Vegetables

Loup Farci sur Son Lit de Légumes • Provence • France

This dish is a baked variation of *loup grillé au fenouil*, arguably the most famous whole-fish preparation in Provence. The grilled version is a simple dish, with the unscaled sea bass enveloped in dried fennel stalks and a little fresh fennel and placed in a fish-shaped wire grill basket that allows it to stand over the hot coals. The baked whole fish presented here is in the same vein but simpler to manage. Even in Provence, large sea bass is becoming increasingly hard to find, but the dish may also be made with snapper or porgy.

1 Preheat the oven to 400°F (200°C).

2 Rinse the fish, running your hands over it to remove any loose scales. Pat dry with paper towels and fill the cavity with the bay leaves, thyme sprigs, and fennel. Sprinkle the cavity with salt and pepper, then brush the exterior with olive oil and sprinkle with salt and pepper.

3 Oil a baking dish large enough to hold the fish. Scatter the lemons, tomatoes, zucchini, carrots, and onions to cover the bottom of the dish. Drizzle the ½ cup olive oil over the vegetables and distribute the garlic evenly throughout the vegetables. Season with salt and pepper and center the fish on top.

4 Bake for 15 minutes, then pour the wine and the Pernod or pastis, if using, evenly over the vegetables to moisten them. Bake for 15 minutes longer. Rotate the dish 180 degrees to ensure that the fish cooks evenly, and turn the vegetables with a spatula to keep them evenly moist. Continue to bake until the vegetables are tender and the fish is cooked through, 20–30 minutes longer. To test the fish for doneness, pierce with a sharp knife. The flesh should be opaque at the bone.

5 To serve, use 1 or 2 wide metal spatulas to lift the fish gently onto a cutting board. Using a slotted spoon, transfer the vegetables to a large warmed platter. Strain the liquid in the dish into a sauceboat to use as a sauce. With a sharp knife, sever the skin at the gills and tail, then lift it away from the fish. The scales will hold the skin together, so it should come away easily. Carefully turn the fish, skin-free side down, onto the vegetables on the platter. Remove the skin on the second side. Pour a little of the sauce over the fish and serve at once. Pass the remaining sauce at the table.

1 sea bass, 4½ lb (2.25 kg), cleaned but unscaled (see note)

2 bay leaves

4 large fresh thyme sprigs

5 fennel stalks with leaves attached

Salt and freshly ground pepper to taste

Olive oil for brushing fish, plus ½ cup (4 fl oz/125 ml)

2 large lemons, each cut into 6 wedges

4 tomatoes, each cut into 4 wedges or, if large, into 6 wedges

2 zucchini (courgettes), trimmed and sliced

3 thin carrots, peeled and cut crosswise into thirds

3 yellow onions, cut into small wedges

6 cloves garlic, sliced

¾ cup (6 fl oz/180 ml) dry white wine

2 tablespoons Pernod or pastis (optional)

Serves 6

Swordfish, Toulon Style

Espadon des Mémés Toulonnaises · Provence · France

Dishes cooked with mussels and laden with tomato are generally given the appellation *toulonnaise*. Tuna may be used in place of the swordfish.

¼ cup (2 fl oz/60 ml) olive oil

3 lb (1.5 kg) swordfish, in one piece

½ cup (4 fl oz/125 ml) dry white wine

3 large tomatoes, peeled, seeded, and coarsely chopped

½ lb (250 g) large fresh white mushrooms, brushed clean and quartered lengthwise

12 shallots

2 fresh thyme sprigs

12 fresh tarragon leaves, chopped

Salt and freshly ground pepper to taste

About 25 mussels, scrubbed and debearded

2 tablespoons chopped fresh flat-leaf (Italian) parsley

Serves 6

1 In a deep frying pan over medium heat, warm the olive oil. Add the swordfish and sauté until lightly colored on both sides, 6–8 minutes total. Raise the heat to medium-high, add the wine, and deglaze the pan, stirring to dislodge any browned bits on the pan bottom. Add the tomatoes, mushrooms, shallots, thyme, and tarragon. Season with salt and pepper. Bring to a boil, reduce the heat to low, cover, and cook until the fish is opaque, about 30 minutes.

2 Meanwhile, place the mussels in a saucepan, discarding any that fail to close to the touch. Cover, place over high heat, and cook, shaking the pan, for 3–5 minutes. Discard any that failed to open.

3 Transfer the fish to a platter. Add the mussels to the sauce. Taste and adjust the seasoning with salt and pepper. Stir the parsley into the sauce and spoon over the fish. Carve the swordfish at the table.

Deep-Fried Baby Fish

La Petite Friture • Provence • France

Small fish—baby sardines, baby anchovies, tiny red mullets, and other rockfish—are caught in nets while fishermen are harvesting larger specimens. These fish are nonetheless well appreciated and are grouped together in batches in the market, the price scrawled in pencil on the paper on which they lay. Although whitebait comes mainly from the Atlantic, many vendors add it to the mix. Often sold as "fish for the soup," they are also commonly deep-fried and served as a separate fish course, a single luncheon dish, or a light supper.

1¼ lb (625 g) mixed tiny fish or whitebait

About ¾ cup (6 fl oz/180 ml) milk, or as needed

1 cup (5 oz/155 g) all-purpose (plain) flour

Olive oil for deep-frying

Salt and freshly ground pepper to taste

1 cup (1 oz/30 g) fresh flat-leaf (Italian) parsley sprigs, well dried (optional)

2 lemons, cut into wedges

Serves 6

1 In a bowl, combine the fish with milk just to cover. Let stand for 30 minutes.

2 Place the flour in a bowl. Drain the fish well and add them to the flour. Toss to coat well with the flour, then transfer to a sieve and shake the sieve to rid the fish of excess flour. Set aside.

3 Pour olive oil into a deep saucepan to a depth of 1½ inches (4 cm) and heat to 325°F (165°C) on a deep-frying thermometer. When the oil is ready, carefully add one-third of the fish. Use a wire skimmer to move the fish around the pan to keep them separate, and turn them to ensure even cooking. When they are golden brown, after 1½–2 minutes, transfer to paper towels to drain. Repeat with the remaining fish in 2 batches.

4 Sprinkle the fish with salt and pepper. If desired, toss the parsley sprigs into the hot oil for a couple of seconds and scoop out onto paper towels to drain.

5 Arrange the fish on a large platter and toss the crisped parsley over them, if using. Serve at once with the lemon wedges.

LES NONATS

A specialty by decree of the Alpes-Maritimes, *nonats*, or *poutines*, are transparent, almost microscopic fish pulled from local waters. When the County of Nice became part of France in 1860, the government granted the fishermen between the Cap d'Antibes and Menton the right to keep the fingerlings and undersized fish that came up with the harvest in their nets. These tiny specimens, nowadays often mixed with *sardinettes* (baby sardines), tiny anchovies, and whitebait (though originally *nonats* were white fish only), can be bought in markets along the Riviera only during a forty-five-day period that falls between February and April.

When the fish are fresh, they cling together like a transparent gel. Cooks gather them into little patties, coat them in flour, and fry them to a crisp in a deep-fry basket. Another favorite use is in *sartagnade*, which calls for panfrying them in olive oil, pressed together and turned as one, to yield a crisp-fried cake of tiny fish that can be cut into wedges. In former times, the *nonats* were a staple of the fishermen's diet and helped extend the household budget. Although they are occasionally seen scrawled on a menu as a dish of the day in little bistros boasting local specialties, today they are prepared mainly as a curiosity.

Sea Bass with Vegetables

Le Blanc de Loup Belle Mouginoise • Provence • France

Roger Vergé has long been one of the most esteemed chefs in Provence. For many years, his Michelin-rated three-star restaurant, Le Moulin de Mougins, in the small town of Mougins, and its sister restaurant, L'Amandier, have attracted food-loving pilgrims from all over the world. His recipe for sea bass fillets is deceptively easy to prepare. Colorful and appetizing, it brings some of the legend of this great chef to the home dining table. Turbot, orange roughy, lingcod, or John Dory may be substituted for the bass.

1 Preheat the oven to 400°F (200°C). Generously butter a baking dish large enough to hold the fish fillets in a single layer.

2 Scatter the chopped shallot on the bottom of the prepared dish. Top with the fish fillets.

3 Put the tomatoes in a large heatproof bowl and pour boiling water over them. Let stand for 1 minute, then drain and immerse in cold water to cool. Carefully peel away the skin, keeping the surface as perfect as possible. Thinly slice the tomatoes. Thinly slice the mushrooms, to form slices as close as possible to the size of the tomato slices. Arrange the tomato, mushroom, and cucumber slices in three neat rows along the length of each fillet, overlapping them. Sprinkle with salt and pepper.

4 Pour the vermouth and white wine into the bottom of the dish. Bake until the fish is opaque throughout, about 4 minutes. Remove from the oven and, using a wide spatula, carefully transfer the fish fillets to a warmed large plate. Keep warm.

5 Pour the cooking juices from the baking dish into a saucepan and add the stock and cream. Bring to a boil over high heat and, whisking vigorously, reduce to the consistency of a sauce, about 1 minute. Remove from the heat, add the butter, and whisk to incorporate fully. Add the chopped chives, stir to combine, and season with salt and pepper.

6 Spoon some sauce onto the center of each warmed plate. Brush the vegetables with the sauce to give them a sheen. Gently transfer the fish fillets to the plates, placing them in the center of each pool of sauce. Serve at once.

3 tablespoons finely chopped shallot

6 sea bass fillets, each 6 oz (185 g) and about 1 inch (2.5 cm) thick

3 firm tomatoes

Boiling water, as needed

6 very large fresh white mushrooms, brushed clean

2 English (hothouse) cucumbers, unpeeled, thinly sliced

Salt and freshly ground pepper to taste

3 tablespoons red vermouth

5 tablespoons (2½ fl oz/75 ml) dry white wine

⅓ cup (3 fl oz/90 ml) chicken or fish stock

⅔ cup (5 fl oz/160 ml) heavy (double) cream

5 tablespoons (2½ oz/75 g) unsalted butter, cut into small pieces

2 tablespoons chopped fresh chives

Serves 6

Niçoise Sandwiches

Pan Bagnat • Provence • France

This specialty of the Côte d'Azur owes its unique flavor to the custom of making it well in advance and topping it with a weight to compress the ingredients in their own moisture.

1 baguette, halved crosswise, or 2 long, crusty bread rolls

1 clove garlic, halved lengthwise

About 6 tablespoons (3 fl oz/90 ml) olive oil

8 soft lettuce leaves such as butter (Boston) lettuce

1 tomato, sliced

1 hard-boiled egg, peeled and sliced

10 small black olives, pitted

10 English (hothouse) cucumber slices

4–6 green or red bell pepper (capsicum) strips

½ cup (4 oz/125 g) olive oil–packed canned tuna, flaked

4 olive oil–packed anchovy fillets, cut into pieces

Salt and freshly ground pepper to taste

Serves 2

1 Split the baguette halves or the bread rolls in half horizontally, without cutting all the way through. Remove a little of the soft crumb from the center of each portion to create a slight hollow. Rub the cut surfaces of the bread with the cut sides of the garlic clove. Drizzle 2 tablespoons of the olive oil over the cut surface of the bottom of each baguette half or roll and then drizzle 1 tablespoon of the oil over the cut surface of the top half.

2 Place 2 of the lettuce leaves on each bottom half. Top with the tomato and egg slices, olives, cucumber slices, and bell pepper strips, dividing them evenly. Scatter the tuna and anchovy pieces in among the layers. Season with salt and pepper and finish each sandwich with 2 lettuce leaves.

3 Close each sandwich and wrap in aluminum foil or plastic wrap, pressing together well. Weight the sandwiches lightly with a cutting board. Let stand in a cool place for up to 4 hours. Then, unwrap the sandwiches and serve.

Monkfish with Olives and Artichokes

Lotte de Mer aux Olives et Artichauts • Languedoc • France

In spring, one finds artichokes in this simple braise popular along the Mediterranean coast, but in summer and autumn it can also be prepared with sweet red peppers (capsicums), tomatoes, or eggplants (aubergines).

2 lemons, halved

16 small artichokes

3 tablespoons extra-virgin olive oil

1 clove garlic, minced

1¼ lb (625 g) monkfish fillet, cut into slices 1 inch (2.5 cm) thick

1 teaspoon minced fresh thyme

1 teaspoon minced fresh flat-leaf (Italian) parsley

Scant ½ teaspoon freshly ground pepper

¼ cup (2 fl oz/60 ml) chicken stock

3 tablespoons dry white wine

¼ cup (1¼ oz/37 g) Niçoise olives or other small Mediterranean-style black olives

Serves 8–10

1 Preheat the oven to 400°F (200°C).

2 Have ready a large bowl of water to which you have added the juice of 1 lemon. Working with 1 artichoke at a time, cut off the stem near the base. Snap off the first layer of leaves. Cut off the upper third of the artichoke. Rub the cut surfaces with a lemon half. Continue to peel back and snap off leaves until you reach the tender, pale inner yellow leaves. Cut off any remaining tough leaf tips. Rub with a lemon half. If the choke has developed prickly tips, scoop it out with the edge of a spoon. Cut the artichokes lengthwise into 4 or 6 pieces, and drop into the lemon water. When ready to cook, drain and pat dry.

3 In an ovenproof frying pan over medium heat, warm the olive oil. Add the garlic and artichokes and sauté until the artichokes begin to turn golden and soften, 5–6 minutes. Gently stir in the fish, thyme, parsley, pepper, stock, wine, and olives. Cover and bake until the artichoke bottoms are easily pierced and the fish is opaque throughout, 15–20 minutes.

4 Using a slotted spoon, transfer the fish to a warmed platter. Spoon the artichokes and olives around the fish, then spoon a little of the broth over all and serve.

OLIVE OIL

You know you're in southern France when you see olive trees. The visual border between the north and the south is the silvery gray orchards of olive trees that supply the thick, rich oil, *huile d'olive*, that perfumes the tables of the south. In the early-ripening regions around Arles and Avignon, the mills start pressing the fruit in November and the season continues until February, when the last milling ends at Entrevaux, in the nether regions of Haute Provence. But in every case, only the first cold pressing produces a fine-quality oil.

The flavors of these oils vary considerably, depending upon the variety and ripeness of the olives and how well they were handled after harvesting. The justly famous olive oil of Nyons is buttery yellow and very mild. It is used in baking and poured over warm vegetables. From the Moulin Jean-Marie Cornille at Maussane-les-Alpilles, near Les Baux, comes what many consider to be the finest olive oil in all of the south. Sweet, fruity, and a deep golden green, it makes an unctuous vinaigrette for salads of all kinds and a fine, rich aioli.

Mediterranean Fish Soup

Bouillabaisse • Provence • France

Commonly found in restaurants along France's Mediterranean coast, bouillabaisse has its origins in the fishermen's stews that were cooked after the day's catch was in and sold.

ROUILLE

2 dried red chiles, seeded

4 cloves garlic

1 tablespoon dried bread crumbs

2 egg yolks

½ teaspoon salt

½ cup (4 fl oz/125 ml) extra-virgin olive oil

SOUP

5 potatoes, 1½ lb (750 g) total weight

¼ cup (2 fl oz/60 ml) extra-virgin olive oil

1 yellow onion, chopped

2 leeks, white part only, chopped

2 tomatoes, peeled and coarsely chopped

2 cloves garlic, crushed

1 fresh bay leaf or ½ dried

2 fresh thyme sprigs

1 6-inch (15-cm) fennel stalk, chopped

1 fresh or dried orange zest strip, 2 inches (5 cm) long and 1 inch (2.5 cm) wide

½ teaspoon *each* salt and freshly ground pepper

2 cups (16 fl oz/500 ml) dry white wine

¼ teaspoon saffron threads

2 lb (1 kg) firm-fleshed fish steaks or fillets such as monkfish, halibut, or cod, cut into 1½-inch (4-cm) chunks

2 lb (1 kg) tender-fleshed whole fish such as red snapper, ocean perch, or rockfish, cut into 1½-inch (4-cm) chunks or filleted

1 lb (500 g) mussels, scrubbed and debearded

1 lb (500 g) small crabs

1 tablespoon minced fresh flat-leaf (Italian) parsley

8 slices country bread, each 1 inch (2.5 cm) thick, toasted and rubbed with garlic

Serves 8

1 To make the *rouille*, in a mortar, combine the chiles and garlic and crush them together with a pestle to make a paste. Add the bread crumbs and mash again. Mix in the egg yolks and the salt to make a smooth paste. Very slowly, drop by drop, whisk in the olive oil until the mixture thickens. Continue adding the oil in a thin stream, whisking constantly, until a mayonnaiselike mixture forms. (Alternatively, make the *rouille* in a blender.) Set aside.

2 To make the soup, peel the potatoes and cut into slices ½ inch (12 mm) thick. In a heavy-bottomed soup pot over medium-high heat, warm the olive oil. Add the onion and leeks and sauté until translucent, 2–3 minutes. Add the tomatoes, garlic, bay leaf, thyme, fennel, orange zest, salt, and pepper. Stir well and add the wine, 1 cup (8 fl oz/250 ml) water, and potatoes. Bring to a boil, reduce the heat to low, cover, and simmer until the potatoes are nearly tender, about 25 minutes.

3 Bring the mixture to a rolling boil. Stir in the saffron. Lay the firm-fleshed fish on top of the soup, pour over just enough boiling water to cover, and boil for about 7 minutes to half-cook the fish. Add the tender-fleshed fish, the mussels (discard any that do not close to the touch), and the crabs, adding more boiling water as needed to cover, and boil just until the tender-fleshed fish separates easily with a fork and the mussels open, 3–4 minutes. Using a spatula, transfer the fish and shellfish to a warmed platter, placing the tender-fleshed fish on one part, the firm-fleshed on another. Discard any mussels that failed to open. Using a slotted spoon, transfer the potatoes to the same plate. Ladle a few tablespoons of broth over them and garnish with the parsley. Stir 2–3 tablespoons of broth into the *rouille*. Ladle the remaining broth into a bowl.

4 Place a slice of bread in the bottom of each soup plate and ladle on some broth. Pass the fish, potatoes, and *rouille* for spooning into the plates.

ITALY

One of the five cliff-side Ligurian villages known collectively as the Cinque Terre, Manarola is a lively fishing port. **Top:** After bringing in their catch, fishermen turn to the task of mending their nets. **Above:** Mesh bags of clams are ready for the local market or *pescheria*. **Right:** Boats are the most convenient way to reach Portofino, an exclusive Italian Riviera town, because the village does not permit cars to enter its narrow streets.

*I*talians will eat fish only if it is absolutely fresh, and many fish restaurants are closed on Mondays for good reason: no fishing boats go out on Sundays. It is no surprise to hear of a woman in landlocked Umbria who, in order to buy the freshest seafood, drove to a distant town once a week to meet the fishmonger's van, rather than wait for him to arrive in her area late in the day. Even though the vendor kept the fish chilled, she feared that its quality suffered en route.

The kinds of fish available change from one region to the next, but Italian cooks agree on the two most popular ways to prepare them: grilled simply with olive oil and a squeeze of lemon juice or deep-fried in a light, crispy crust.

With the exception of a few inland restaurants specializing in seafood, as a general rule meat is eaten away from the coast, and fish and shellfish are enjoyed at the seaside. That said, Florence has two seafood recipes it can legitimately claim as its own: *baccalà coi porri* and *calamari in zimino*. The first is salt cod fried in olive oil and smothered with garlic-scented sautéed leeks, while the second is squid cooked in a spicy mixture of spinach or chard laced with wine and aromatic vegetables.

Shellfish also are often simply grilled or fried, although clams, mussels, squid, and cuttlefish frequently turn up in pasta sauces and risotti. Not surprisingly, the watery Veneto, fronting the Adriatic and crisscrossed with marshes and lagoons, is home to a wide array of rice and seafood dishes, from *risotto alla marinara* (with clams) to *risotto di pesse* (Venetian dialect for fish) to *risotto ai fruitti di mare* (with mixed seafood). Like most pastas, soups, and other dishes made with fish, these risotti are not served with grated cheese, which can overwhelm the delicate seafood flavor. Certain varieties of fish and shellfish flourish only in the lagoons of Venice and are sold with pride in the daily fish market along the Rialto.

Tiny *vongole veraci*, sweet thumbnail-sized clams, are prized for pasta sauces in Rome and throughout the south. As one descends farther south, the antipasti choices begin to focus more on seafood. Grilled

shrimp (prawns), stuffed clams, mussels steamed in white wine, and seafood salads made with octopus, calamari, and shrimp are just a few of the dishes on offer in Campania, Calabria, and Apulia.

The towns and villages scattered along the Tuscan coast are also known for their seafood *antipasti*, pasta sauces, and *secondi*. During the summer, Italian tourists race along the Firenze-Mare *autostrada* toward the enticing beaches of Viareggio or Livorno, or meander through the gorgeous country-side south of Siena on their way to the Maremma or the island of Elba or Giglio. Meals eaten *al mare* are tinged with that lovely carefree feeling of being *in vacanza*, of drinking a bottle of lightly chilled *vino bianco* at lunch with sizzling *cozze ripiene*, mussels stuffed with bread crumbs, garlic, shallots, and herbs served at a beachside restaurant in the beguiling 19th-century resort town of Viareggio. Farther south, at a modest trattoria along the strip of coast between the Marina di Pisa and Livorno, one might feast on a plate of exquisitely fresh, slim anchovy fillets marinated in lemon juice and sprinkled with garlic and parsley. Waiting for the ferry to Giglio, clusters of travelers might stop for lunch at one of the tiny restaurants overlooking a jumble of sailboats and *pescherecce* (fishing boats) in Porto Santo Stefano, ordering *carpaccio di polpo*, thinly sliced raw octopus scattered with crunchy slivers of celery and

cipolla di Tropea (a sweet onion grown in the south of Italy).

From the bustling port of Livorno to the manicured beaches of Versilia and the wild stretches of sand and sea of the Maremma, the emphasis is on freshness and simplicity. Certainly few pleasures can match that of a great seaside meal: your table steps away from the soft carpet of sand leading to the water, a glass of chilled wine in your hand, and on your plate some treasure from the sea. A bowl of *cacciucco* is itself worth the trip to Livorno. Part soup, part stew, it is thick, spicy, and never the same twice: its contents are less a reflection of a rigid recipe than of whatever fish and shellfish the *pescivendolo* (fishmonger) has on hand. (It is also a precursor to cioppino, San Francisco's famed seafood stew, made with Dungeness crab and local Pacific rockfish). North of Tuscany in Liguria, whole sea bass, rubbed with olive oil, lemon juice, and fresh marjoram and baked on a bed of sliced potatoes and black olives, is a particularly wonderful specialty.

The lagoon of Orbetello, which separates the rocky promontory of Mount Argentario from the mainland, is known for its nature reserve (home to extraordinary numbers of migratory birds) and its spectacular sunsets. However, it is equally famous for the abundance and quality of its eels, whose sweet, firm meat is roasted, stewed, braised, and even smoked.

Left: As they sip their drinks, young boys watch fishermen go about their work in the tiny village of Vernazza, the second link from the north in the chain of the Cinque Terre. **Above, left:** In Muggia, a small harbor town minutes away from Trieste on the northern Adriatic, a fishmonger's hand-painted sign—"Fish always fresh"—attracts both attention and customers. **Above, right:** Agreeable Italian fish vendors, or *pescivendoli*, will gladly clean their customer's purchases at the time of sale.

Grilled Sea Bream with Wild Fennel

Orata Grigliata con Finocchio Selvatico • Tuscany • Italy

Forte dei Marmi has the reputation of being Versilia's most elegant seaside town. The highlight of a meal here at Da Bruno might be a grilled sea bream. *Orata* comes from *oro*, or "gold," an allusion to the golden head of this beautiful fish. The meat is so tender and delicate that *orata* is nearly always prepared very simply, either roasted or grilled.

2 large tomatoes, cut into 1-inch (2.5-cm) wedges

¼ cup (2 fl oz/60 ml) extra-virgin olive oil

Juice of ½ lemon

1 tablespoon finely chopped fresh flat-leaf (Italian) parsley

2 large cloves garlic, crushed

Salt and freshly ground pepper to taste

2 sea bream, about 1½ lb (750 g) each, cleaned with heads and tails intact

Small handful of fresh fennel leaves, plus chopped fennel leaves for garnish

1 long fresh rosemary sprig

Serves 4

1 Prepare a medium-hot fire in a charcoal grill. Lightly oil the grill rack and arrange the tomato wedges on it. Grill, turning once, until they are dry but not leathery, 10–15 minutes on each side. Remove from the grill and set aside.

2 While the tomatoes are on the grill, in a bowl, stir together the olive oil, lemon juice, parsley, garlic, salt, and pepper. Set aside. Rinse the fish and pat dry. Sprinkle the cavity of each fish with salt and stuff loosely with the handful of fennel leaves. Drizzle half of the seasoned olive oil over the fennel.

3 Place the fish in 2 oiled grilling baskets. Grill, turning once, until opaque throughout, about 10 minutes on each side. Use the rosemary sprig to baste the fish with the remaining seasoned oil. Remove the fish from the basket and transfer to a warmed platter. Lay the grilled tomatoes over the fish. Scatter with the chopped fennel leaves and serve.

FISHMONGERS

It's possible to learn more about cooking fish from Tuscany's fishmongers than from all of the cookbooks lining your shelves. Livorno, Tuscany's largest city after Florence and Italy's second largest port after Genoa, is a treasure trove of seafood. Most of it is sold out of Livorno's beautiful nineteenth-century, cast-iron market, a replica of the Mercato Centrale in Florence. But unless you are lucky enough to live by the sea, buying fresh fish in Tuscany requires some forethought, since the nearest fish shop might be miles away. Many people, however, buy fresh fish from traveling fishmongers. On the same morning each week, a fishmonger drives his refrigerated truck into the small town of Impruneta, for example, where he sets up shop in the main square next to the church. His counter is filled with mesh bags of tiny, sweet clams; shrimp (prawns) of various sizes; squid and cuttlefish, their sacs still filled with black ink; small, flat *sogliola* (sole), which he expertly fillets; and an assortment of glorious, albeit expensive, catches like *orata* (sea bream) and *branzino* (sea bass). He never fails to ask how you plan to cook what you buy—and to offer his own very helpful advice.

Shrimp Salad with Tomatoes and Capers

Insalata di Gamberi alla Sarda • Sardinia • Italy

Until recently, most Sardinians did not eat much fish or shellfish, so not many traditional seafood recipes exist. Even though Sardinia is an island, the largest in the Mediterranean Sea, few people lived along the shore until malaria was eradicated in the 1950s.

1¼ lb (625 g) shrimp (prawns), peeled and deveined

1 teaspoon salt, plus salt to taste

2 tomatoes, chopped

3 green (spring) onions, including tender green tops, chopped

2 tender inner celery stalks, thinly sliced

¼ cup (2 oz/60 g) capers, chopped

2 tablespoons chopped fresh mint

¼ cup (2 fl oz/60 ml) extra-virgin olive oil

2 tablespoons fresh lemon juice

Lettuce leaves

Serves 4

1 Bring a large saucepan of water to a boil. Add the shrimp and the 1 teaspoon salt. Cook just until the shrimp turn pink and begin to curl, 1–2 minutes. Drain and rinse under cold water. Pat dry.

2 In a bowl, combine the shrimp, tomatoes, green onions, celery, capers, and mint. In a small bowl, whisk together the olive oil, the lemon juice, and salt to taste. Pour over the shrimp mixture and toss well. Let stand for 15 minutes, stirring once or twice.

3 Arrange the lettuce on a platter and spoon the salad on top. Serve at once.

Monkfish with Lemon and Capers

Coda di Rospo Piccata • Lazio • Italy

Lemon, capers, and parsley are frequently served as a sauce for thin veal cutlets, so you might be surprised to see this seafood dish on a menu in Rome. Firm, meaty monkfish, however, is sometimes referred to as "the veal of the sea".

1½ lb (750 g) monkfish fillets

½ cup (2½ oz/75 g) all-purpose (plain) flour

Salt and freshly ground pepper to taste

3 tablespoons unsalted butter

2 tablespoons olive oil

½ cup (4 fl oz/125 ml) dry white wine

3 tablespoons fresh lemon juice

2 tablespoons capers, chopped

2 tablespoons chopped fresh flat-leaf (Italian) parsley

Lemon slices

Serves 4

1 Cut the fish fillets on an angle into slices ½ inch (12 mm) thick (or have the fishmonger do this for you). Rinse the fish and pat dry. Working with 1 slice at a time, place between 2 sheets of plastic wrap and pound gently with a meat pounder to ¼ inch (6 mm) thick.

2 Spread the flour on a plate and season with salt and pepper. Lightly dust the fish slices with the flour, shaking to remove the excess.

3 In a large frying pan over medium heat, melt the butter with the olive oil. Add the fish in batches and cook, turning once, until browned on both sides, about 4 minutes total. Transfer to a warmed platter and keep warm.

4 When all the fish is cooked, pour the wine and lemon juice into the pan and add the capers. Raise the heat and cook until the liquid is reduced and slightly thickened, about 1 minute. Stir in the parsley. Pour the sauce over the fish and garnish with the lemon slices. Serve at once.

Stuffed Mussels

Cozze Ripiene • Tuscany • Italy

For this dish, be sure to look for the common blue mussel, with its deep blue-black shell, rather than the much larger green-lipped mussel.

About 2 cups (16 fl oz/500 ml) dry white wine

5 lb (2.5 kg) large mussels (see note), scrubbed and debearded

¼ cup (2 fl oz/60 ml) extra-virgin olive oil

2 tablespoons finely chopped shallots

2 cloves garlic, minced

3 tablespoons coarse dried bread crumbs

3 tablespoons finely chopped fresh flat-leaf (Italian) parsley

Salt and freshly ground pepper to taste

Lemon wedges

Serves 6

1 Pour the wine into a large pot to a depth of about ½ inch (12 mm). Add the mussels, discarding any that fail to close to the touch, cover, and place over high heat. Cook, shaking the pot occasionally, until the shells open, 5–6 minutes. Transfer the mussels to a large roasting pan. Discard any mussels that failed to open. Reserve the cooking liquid.

2 Preheat a broiler (grill).

3 In a heavy frying pan over medium-high heat, warm the olive oil. Add the shallots and garlic and sauté for 1 minute. Add 1 tablespoon of the cooking liquid and cook for 1 minute. Remove from the heat and stir in the bread crumbs, parsley, salt, and pepper.

4 Remove the top shell of each mussel and discard. Using a sharp knife, sever the muscle connecting each mussel to its bottom shell, leaving each mussel on its half shell. Top with about 1 teaspoon of the bread crumb mixture. Place on a baking sheet and slip under the broiler until the mussels begin to sizzle and brown, 1–2 minutes. Transfer the mussels from the sheet to a warmed platter. Garnish with lemon wedges and serve.

Hot Anchovy and Garlic Dip

Bagna Cauda • Piedmont • Italy

In Piedmont, eating *bagna cauda* is a fall and winter ritual. The name means "hot bath," and the dish is so called because the mixture of garlic and anchovies is traditionally kept warm in a chafing dish or fondue pot. *Bagna cauda* is served with assorted vegetables for dipping and crusty bread to catch the drips. Among the possible vegetables are raw Jerusalem artichokes, cardoons, bell peppers (capsicums), carrots, spinach, green onions, or celery; cooked potatoes; roasted onions or beets; and blanched cauliflower or broccoli.

¾ cup (6 fl oz/180 ml) olive oil

8–10 cloves garlic, very finely chopped

12 anchovy fillets

¼ cup (2 oz/60 g) unsalted butter

About 8 cups (2½ lb/1.25 kg) trimmed, cut-up vegetables (see note)

Slices of coarse country bread

Serves 6–8

1 In a small saucepan over low heat, combine the olive oil, garlic, and anchovies. Cook, mashing the anchovies with the back of a wooden spoon, until smooth, about 5 minutes. Remove from the heat and stir in the butter.

2 Pour the mixture into a warmed chafing dish or fondue pot set over a warming candle or spirit lamp. Serve at once with vegetables for dipping. Pass the bread slices at the table.

PORCINI MUSHROOMS

Porcini mushrooms, with their smooth, pale brown heads and thick, bulbous stems can cost a small fortune at the market, so it's no surprise that the hunting of porcini (and of truffles even more so) is generally a secretive and solitary affair.

Porcini are most popular in central and northern Italy, and the largest body of recipes using the mushrooms comes from the north, but Tuscans do love their porcini and eat them whenever they can. Italian chefs won't waste any part of these treasured fungi. If the caps are spiked with slivers of garlic and mint-scented nepitella, then sprinkled with salt and pepper and grilled like steaks, then the stems will be used as well, perhaps sliced thinly, sautéed in garlic, parsley, and white wine, and tossed with fresh *tagliolini*. These woodland mushrooms grow in the spring and fall, when the weather is warm and damp, and are often found in the vicinity of chestnut trees. They are also perhaps the world's best drying

mushrooms. Whole porcini are cut into slices, dried, and sold in small (not inexpensive) cellophane packages. Their musky earthiness is a wonderful addition to pasta sauces and risottos or they can deliver a welcome boost of flavor to the more subtle flavors of most cultivated mushrooms.

Fresh mushrooms should be kept in a paper bag to absorb excess moisture and refrigerated for no more than 3–4 days. While some cooks insist that you you should not wash mushrooms at all, a quick rinse and thorough drying before cooking them won't harm them. If you have time or are planning to cook only a few mushrooms, wipe them clean with a damp cloth or soft brush. Special mushroom brushes are available for the gentle removal of dirt, but a toothbrush with soft bristles will work as well. Trim the dried end of tender stems. If the stems are tough, remove them completely; these can be stored for later use, such as a soup or stock.

Fillet of Sole with Mushrooms

Sogliola alla Boscaiola · Tuscany · Italy

Boscaiolo means "woodsman," and anything cooked *alla boscaiola* typically includes mushrooms. Substitute 1½ pounds (750 g) sole fillets if small sole are not available.

3 tablespoons unsalted butter

3 tablespoons extra-virgin olive oil

1 small yellow onion, thinly sliced

Salt and freshly ground pepper to taste

4 small sole, cleaned, skinned, and head and tail removed

1 lb (500 g) mixed fresh mushrooms such as portobello, porcino, and/or cultivated white, brushed clean and thinly sliced

½ cup (4 fl oz/125 ml) dry white wine

Serves 8–10

1 Preheat the oven to 375°F (190°C).

2 In a frying pan over low heat, melt 1 tablespoon of the butter with 2 tablespoons of the olive oil. Add the onion and sauté, stirring frequently, until translucent, about 6 minutes. Remove from the heat. Spread half of the onion slices evenly over the bottom of a baking dish large enough to accommodate the fish in a single layer. Drizzle with the remaining 1 tablespoon olive oil and season with salt and pepper. Lay the fish over the onions. Cut the remaining 2 tablespoons butter into small pieces and use to dot the fish. Bake for 10 minutes.

3 While the fish is baking, add the mushrooms to the pan holding the remaining onions, season with salt and pepper, and sauté over medium-high heat until the mushrooms soften and expel their liquid, about 10 minutes.

4 Remove the fish from the oven, spoon the mushroom mixture evenly over them, pour the wine evenly over the surface, and return the dish to the oven. Bake until the fish is opaque throughout and the wine has evaporated, about 5 minutes longer. Transfer to a warmed platter and serve.

Stuffed Clams

Vongole Ripiene • Campania • Italy

On the tiny island of Procida, off the coast of Naples, fisherman deliver basketfuls of just-caught fish and shellfish to little port-side restaurants. The chefs at each establishment turn that bounty into simple but satisfying dishes like this heaping platter of fresh clams dusted with a crunchy crumb topping.

36 hard-shell clams, well scrubbed

⅓ cup (1½ oz/45 g) fine dried bread crumbs, preferably homemade from coarse country bread

3 tablespoons grated Parmigiano-Reggiano or pecorino romano cheese

3 tablespoons chopped fresh flat-leaf (Italian) parsley

1 clove garlic, minced

6 tablespoons (3 fl oz/90 ml) olive oil

Salt and freshly ground pepper to taste

Lemon wedges

Serves 8

1 Working with one clam at a time, and protecting your hand with a heavy towel, hold the clam in one hand with the hinge facing you. Push a round-tipped knife gently into the crack between the halves of the shell. Once the shell opens slightly, slide the knife around from side to side to separate the halves. Holding the clam over a bowl to catch the juices, scrape the flesh from one shell into the other. Discard the empty shell. Arrange the clams in a shallow baking pan. Strain the juices and pour some over each clam.

2 Preheat a broiler (grill). In a small bowl, combine the bread crumbs, cheese, parsley, garlic, 3 tablespoons of the olive oil, salt, and pepper. Spoon the crumb mixture onto the clams. Do not pack the crumbs down or they will become soggy. Drizzle evenly with the remaining 3 tablespoons oil.

3 Broil (grill) until the crumbs are lightly browned, about 4 minutes. Remove from the broiler and arrange on warmed individual plates. Serve at once with the lemon wedges.

Mussels with Black Pepper

Impepata di Cozze • Campania • Italy

Ancient Romans loved to eat mussels and other bivalves and farmed them in the Mediterranean as early as the first century AD. Here, glistening black mussels steamed in a spicy wine and black pepper broth call for spoons at each table setting and lots of crusty bread. Tiberio, a fresh white wine from the island of Capri, is a great accompaniment.

⅓ cup (3 fl oz/80 ml) olive oil

4 cloves garlic, finely chopped

⅓ cup (½ oz/15 g) chopped fresh flat-leaf (Italian) parsley

About 1 tablespoon coarsely ground pepper

½ cup (4 fl oz/125 ml) dry white wine

4 lb (2 kg) mussels, well scrubbed and debearded

Lemon wedges

Serves 8–10

1 In a large, heavy pot over medium heat, combine the olive oil, garlic, parsley, and pepper. Heat until the garlic is fragrant, about 1 minute.

2 Add the wine and the mussels, discarding any that do not close to the touch. Cover and cook, shaking the pan occasionally, until the mussels open, about 5 minutes.

3 Using a slotted spoon, transfer the opened mussels to a serving bowl. If some have failed to open, cook them for a minute or two longer; add the opened ones to the bowl, and discard the others.

4 Pour the pan juices over the mussels and serve with lemon wedges.

Smoked Swordfish Toasts

Crostini di Pesce Spada · Tuscany · Italy

Tuscan kitchens are notoriously gadget free. Vegetables are chopped by hand, using one of the few tools of the kitchen, the *mezzaluna*, or "half moon," a curved knife with a handle at each end. Tuscan cooks will almost always use this implement for a recipe such as this one, rolling the blade back and forth over the ingredients until everything is chopped to the perfect consistency. If you cannot find smoked swordfish, smoked trout can be used.

1 green (spring) onion, white part only, finely chopped

1 carrot, peeled and finely chopped

1 tender inner celery stalk, finely chopped

2 tablespoons finely chopped fresh flat-leaf (Italian) parsley

¼ lb (125 g) smoked swordfish fillet, thinly sliced

¼ cup (2 fl oz/60 ml) extra-virgin olive oil

Juice from ½ lemon

Freshly ground pepper to taste

1 loaf ciabatta or 1 baguette

Snipped fresh chives

Serves 6

1 Combine the green onion, carrot, celery, and parsley on a cutting board. Add the smoked fish and finely chop the ingredients.

2 Transfer the fish mixture to a glass bowl. Pour in the olive oil and lemon juice, combine to mix well, and season with pepper. Cover and refrigerate for at least 4 hours or for up to 24 hours.

3 Just before serving, cut the bread into slices ¼ inch (6 mm) thick and toast lightly.

4 Spread the fish mixture on the slices of toast, dividing evenly. Garnish with the chives and serve the toasts at once.

Roasted Fish with Pine Nuts and Raisins

Pesce al Forno con Pinoli e Uva Passa • Tuscany • Italy

Tuscans are known for their simple techniques for cooking meats, often marinating them first with fresh rosemary. But along the region's Mediterranean coastline, fish is also flavored with the highly aromatic herb. In this recipe, it permeates the flesh, while the vinegar balances out the sweetness of the raisins. Any leftovers are good served cold. A red wine from the Chianti region makes a surprisingly good partner.

2 tablespoons olive oil

2 small red snappers or sea bass, 1¼–1½ lb (625–750 g) each, cleaned with heads and tails intact

2 tablespoons chopped fresh rosemary, plus sprigs for garnish

Salt and freshly ground pepper to taste

⅔ cup (4 oz/125 g) raisins

¼ cup (1¼ oz/37 g) pine nuts

¼ cup (2 fl oz/60 ml) balsamic vinegar

¼ cup (2 fl oz/60 ml) water

Serves 4

1 Preheat the oven to 400°F (200°C). Oil a large roasting pan with a little of the olive oil.

2 Rinse the fish, pat dry, and place in the prepared pan. Drizzle the inside of each fish with the remaining oil and sprinkle the insides with the rosemary and the salt and pepper. Scatter the raisins inside the fish, then sprinkle the pine nuts over the tops. In a small bowl, stir together the vinegar and water and pour evenly over the fish.

3 Roast until the flesh is opaque when cut near the bone, 25–30 minutes.

4 Transfer the fish to a large warmed platter. Spoon the pine nuts, pan juices, and any raisins that tumbled from the cavities over the fish. Garnish with rosemary sprigs and serve at once.

LA GASTRONOMIE

Gastronomie, the fancy food stores of Italy, are easy to spot, whether they anchor a piazza or are tucked away on a narrow *vicolo*. Golden loaves of bread are invariably piled against the windows, and wheels of Parmigiano-Reggiano are stacked next to the doorway, twin invitations difficult to turn down. Inside, refrigerator cases are filled with all kinds of cheeses: balls of fresh mozzarella swimming in milky liquid, swirled mounds of buttery mascarpone, ricotta molded in little basket shapes. Trays of freshly-made pasta, in various shapes and sizes, curled into loose skeins or stuffed and arranged in neat rows, are lined up below a canopy of *salumi*, cured meats hung from the rafters, their mouthwatering aromas perfuming the air.

Many *gastronomie* sell delicious prepared foods, too, such as salads, stuffed vegetables, and roasted chickens and other meats, perfect fare for a picnic or a quick supper. At the more elegant shops, such as Milan's Gastronomia Peck, you will find plump stuffed squabs, rosemary-scented *porchetta*, chestnut brown spit-roasted rabbits, vegetable flans made of greens or asparagus, sautéed porcini, and much more.

Squid with Spinach

Calamari in Zimino • Tuscany • Italy

In zimino refers to a particular sauce—a combination of spinach, tomatoes, and aromatic vegetables cooked with wine.

2 lb (1 kg) squid

2 lb (1 kg) spinach, stems removed

1 cup (8 fl oz/250 ml) water

Salt to taste

⅓ cup (3 fl oz/80 ml) extra-virgin olive oil

1 yellow onion, chopped

1 small carrot, peeled and chopped

1 small celery stalk, chopped

2 cloves garlic, minced

1 tablespoon chopped fresh flat-leaf (Italian) parsley

1 or 2 small dried hot chiles, crumbled

½ cup (4 fl oz/125 ml) dry white wine

¾ lb (375 g) tomatoes, peeled, seeded, and coarsely chopped

Serves 4–6

1 First, clean the squid: Working with 1 squid at a time, pull the head from the body. Cut off and reserve the tentacles; discard the head. Squeeze out and discard the small, hard "beak" at the base of the tentacles; leave the tentacles whole. Using your fingers, pull out any internal matter from the body, including the quill-like cartilage, and discard. Peel off the mottled skin that covers the body. Rinse the body well. Cut the bodies crosswise into rings ¼ inch (6 mm) wide, and cut the tentacles into pieces 2 inches (5 cm) long.

2 Stack 10 spinach leaves, roll up, and coarsely slice crosswise. Pour the water into a saucepan, place over medium heat, salt lightly, and add the spinach. Cover and cook until wilted, about 3 minutes. Drain well in a colander, pressing against the spinach with a wooden spoon to extract as much water as possible.

3 In a frying pan over medium heat, warm the olive oil. Add the onion and sauté until soft, 2–3 minutes. Add the carrot, celery, garlic, parsley, and chiles. Sauté, stirring often, until the garlic begins to color, 3–4 minutes. Season with salt. Add the squid to the pan with the vegetables, douse with the wine, and cook until the squid is opaque, 4–5 minutes. Add the spinach and stir to coat it with the pan juices. Sauté until the flavors are blended, about 5 minutes. Stir in the tomatoes, season with salt, and reduce the heat to low. Cover and simmer until the stew is dark, about 30 minutes. Transfer to warmed bowls and serve.

Red Mullet in White Wine, Garlic, and Parsley

Triglie dell'Argentario • Tuscany • Italy

Triglie are beautiful fish whose silvery pink skins are speckled with red. Known in English as red mullets, they are a bit of work to eat (because of their many bones), but the extra effort is a small price to pay for the full flavor and strong, lean meat.

3 cloves garlic

8 red mullets, ½ lb (250 g) each, cleaned, with head and tail intact

Salt to taste

3 tablespoons chopped fresh flat-leaf (Italian) parsley

½ cup (4 fl oz/125 ml) extra-virgin olive oil

½ cup (4 fl oz/125 ml) dry white wine

Juice of ½ lemon

2 lemons, cut into wedges

Serves 4–6

1 Crush 1 garlic clove. Thinly slice the remaining 2 cloves. Rinse the fish and pat dry. Sprinkle the cavity of each fish with salt and divide the garlic slices and the parsley evenly among them.

2 In a large frying pan over medium heat, warm the olive oil. Add the crushed garlic to the pan and sauté until it begins to color, about 2 minutes. Remove and discard the garlic.

3 Lay the fish in the pan, pour in the wine, and let the alcohol bubble away for a couple of minutes. Turn the fish, reduce the heat to low, cover, and cook, shaking the pan from time to time, until opaque throughout, about 15 minutes longer.

4 When the fish are ready, uncover, pour the lemon juice evenly over them, and then carefully transfer to a warmed platter. Garnish with the lemon wedges and serve at once.

Red Mullet in Tomato Sauce

Triglie in Salsa Rossa • Liguria • Italy

A quiet trattoria in Rapallo, a town along the Ligurian coast, serves fat shrimp grilled in their shells, followed by red mullet seasoned with thyme and cloaked in a light tomato sauce.

1 yellow onion, finely chopped

2 cloves garlic, lightly crushed

¼ cup (2 fl oz/60 ml) olive oil

4 tomatoes, peeled, seeded, and chopped

Pinch of red pepper flakes

Salt and freshly ground pepper to taste

½ cup (4 fl oz/120 ml) dry white wine

4 small red mullets or porgies, about ¾ lb (375 g) each, cleaned with heads and tails intact

4 fresh thyme sprigs

Serves 4

1 Preheat the oven to 425°F (220°C). Oil a baking dish large enough to hold the fish in a single layer.

2 In a saucepan over medium heat, sauté the onion and garlic in the olive oil until tender, about 5 minutes. Add the tomatoes, red pepper flakes, salt, and pepper. Bring to a simmer, add the wine, and cook until most of the juices have evaporated, about 10 minutes. Discard the garlic.

3 Rinse the fish and pat dry. Tuck a thyme sprig inside each fish and sprinkle inside and out with salt and pepper. Arrange the fish in the prepared baking dish and pour the sauce over the fish.

4 Bake until the fish are opaque when cut near the bone, about 20 minutes.

5 Divide the fish among warmed individual plates and serve at once.

Tuna with Garlic, Basil, and Tomato

Tonno alla Livornese • Tuscany • Italy

This sauce marries the best flavors of the Mediterranean: tomatoes, olives and olive oil, capers, garlic, and basil. It is a particular treat over fresh tuna.

6 tablespoons (3 fl oz/90 ml) extra-virgin olive oil

1 large yellow onion, chopped

3 cloves garlic, 2 minced and 1 crushed

1 lb (500 g) tomatoes, peeled, seeded, and chopped

8 fresh basil leaves

2 tablespoons chopped fresh flat-leaf (Italian) parsley, plus chopped parsley for garnish

4 tuna steaks, each about ½ lb (250 g)

Salt and freshly ground pepper to taste

1 cup (5 oz/155 g) pitted brine-cured black olives

4 teaspoons capers, rinsed

Serves 4

1 In a frying pan over medium heat, warm 3 tablespoons of the olive oil. Add the onion and sauté gently until it begins to soften, about 3 minutes. Add the minced garlic and sauté until golden, about 2 minutes longer. Stir in the tomatoes, basil, and 2 tablespoons parsley and cook uncovered, stirring occasionally, until thickened, about 15 minutes. Remove from the heat and pass through a food mill fitted with the medium disk. Set aside.

2 In a frying pan large enough to hold the fish in a single layer, warm the remaining 3 tablespoons oil over medium heat. Add the crushed garlic and sauté until golden, about 2 minutes. Remove and discard the garlic clove. Lightly season the tuna steaks with salt and pepper and place in the pan. Raise the heat to medium-high and cook, turning once, until lightly browned on both sides, about 2 minutes. Pour the reserved sauce directly over the fish, reduce the heat to low, add the olives and capers, and cook until the sauce thickens, about 5 minutes.

3 Transfer to warmed individual plates, sprinkle with parsley, and serve at once.

Sea Bass with Potatoes and Olives

Spigola al Forno • Liguria • Italy

More than any other herb, marjoram is associated with Ligurian cooking. Similar to oregano, although more delicate and with a hint of citrus, fresh marjoram is used in stuffings, sauces, and marinades for both fish and meat. It is a perennial with small green to golden leaves and tiny white or pale pink flowers in summer. Striped bass and red snapper are also good prepared this way.

2 sea bass, 1½–2 lb (750 g–1 kg) each, cleaned with heads and tails intact

2 tablespoons chopped fresh flat-leaf (Italian) parsley

1 tablespoon chopped fresh marjoram

6 tablespoons (3 fl oz/90 ml) olive oil

2 tablespoons fresh lemon juice

Salt and freshly ground pepper to taste

4 lemon slices

2 lb (1 kg) waxy boiling potatoes, peeled and sliced

½ cup (2½ oz/75 g) Gaeta or other Mediterranean-style black olives

Serves 4

1 Preheat the oven to 450°F (230°C).

2 Rinse the fish and pat dry. Using a sharp, heavy knife, make slashes on both sides of each fish, cutting down to the bone. In a small bowl, stir together the parsley, marjoram, 4 tablespoons (2 fl oz/60 ml) of the olive oil, and the lemon juice, salt, and pepper. Rub the mixture inside the cavities and over the outside of each fish. Tuck the lemon slices inside. Cover and let stand while you prepare the potatoes.

3 Rinse the potato slices under cold running water and pat dry. Place in a bowl and add the remaining 2 tablespoons oil, the salt, and pepper. Toss well, then spread them in a roasting pan large enough to hold them in a shallow layer.

4 Bake until the potatoes begin to brown, 25–30 minutes. Turn the potatoes, stir in the olives, and place the fish on top. Continue to bake until the flesh is opaque when cut near the bone and the potatoes are tender, 20–30 minutes longer.

5 Transfer the fish to a warmed platter. Surround with the potatoes and olives. Serve at once.

Oven-Roasted Trout with Potatoes

Trota al Forno con Patate • Tuscany • Italy

Trout is the most common freshwater fish found in Tuscan fish markets. The clear, cold streams that course through the mountains in the Casentino above Arezzo have given Tuscany the lion's share of recipes for trout. To the north lies the town of Pontassieve, known for its soft, pleasing Chardonnays, ideal for pairing with this delicate dish.

2 fresh rosemary sprigs

2 cloves garlic, minced

Salt and white pepper to taste

1½ lb (750 g) new potatoes, peeled and thinly sliced

4 tablespoons (2 fl oz/60 ml) extra-virgin olive oil

2 tablespoons unsalted butter, cut into small pieces

4 small trout, ¾ lb (375 g) each, cleaned and filleted

Serves 4

1 Preheat the oven to 375°F (190°C). Set aside 1 rosemary sprig and finely chop the leaves of the other. In a cup, combine the chopped rosemary and garlic. Season generously with salt and pepper.

2 Oil a large baking pan. Arrange half of the potato slices in rows on the bottom, slightly overlapping the slices and the rows. Sprinkle evenly with one-third of the garlic mixture, drizzle with 1½ tablespoons of the olive oil, and dot with 1 tablespoon of the butter. Layer with the remaining potato slices, then top with another third of the garlic mixture and 1½ tablespoons of the oil and the remaining 1 tablespoon butter. Cover the dish and bake for 20 minutes. Uncover and continue to bake until the potatoes are almost tender, about 20 minutes longer.

3 Remove from the oven and arrange the fish in a single layer on top of the potatoes. Drizzle with the remaining 1 tablespoon olive oil and sprinkle with the remaining garlic mixture. Lay the whole rosemary sprig on top. Return to the oven and bake until the fillets are opaque throughout, about 10 minutes. Remove from the oven and let rest for 10 minutes before serving directly from the baking pan.

Clams with White Wine, Garlic, and Tomatoes

Zuppa di Arselle • Tuscany • Italy

Arsella is another word for *vongola*, or "clam." When used in Versilia, it generally refers to the smallest, most tender clam with the sweetest meat of any clam you'll ever eat.

2 lb (1 kg) small hard-shelled clams such as manila or littleneck

6 tablespoons (3 fl oz/90 ml) extra-virgin olive oil

2 cloves garlic, thinly sliced, plus 1 clove, halved lengthwise

1 tablespoon finely chopped fresh flat-leaf (Italian) parsley, plus 2 teaspoons for garnish

½ cup (4 fl oz/125 ml) dry white wine

1 lb (500 g) tomatoes, peeled, seeded, and chopped

¼ teaspoon red pepper flakes

Salt to taste

4 slices coarse country bread, toasted

Serves 8–10

1 Scrub the clams. Place in a bowl with lightly salted water and let soak for 2 hours. Drain and rinse well, discarding any that fail to close to the touch.

2 In a large, wide pot over medium heat, warm the olive oil. Add the sliced garlic and 1 tablespoon parsley and sauté for about 2 minutes. Pour in the wine and let the alcohol evaporate, about 2 minutes. Stir in the tomatoes and the red pepper flakes, season with salt, cover, and cook, stirring occasionally, until the liquid has reduced, about 10 minutes. Add the clams, cover, and cook until the shells open, about 5 minutes. Discard any that have not opened.

3 Rub the toasted bread with the cut sides of the garlic clove and set a slice in each warmed bowl. Ladle the clams and their juices into the bowls, dividing evenly. Sprinkle the *zuppa* with the 2 teaspoons parsley and serve.

Whipped Salt Cod

Baccalà Mantecato • Veneto • Italy

This dish can be made with either *baccalà*, salt cod, or with *stoccafisso* (also known as *pesce stocco*), or stockfish, which is air-dried. However, the stockfish may take up to 3 days to soak.

1 lb (500 g) salt cod or stockfish, soaked (page 225)

8 cups (64 fl oz/2 l) water

4 potatoes, unpeeled

1 clove garlic

Salt to taste

½ cup (4 fl oz/125 ml) extra-virgin olive oil

3–4 tablespoons fresh lemon juice

¼ cup (⅓ oz/10 g) chopped fresh flat-leaf (Italian) parsley

Freshly ground pepper to taste

12 slices coarse country bread, toasted

½ cup (2½ oz/75 g) chopped Gaeta or other Mediterranean-style black olives

Serves 6

1 In a saucepan, bring the 8 cups (64 fl oz/2 l) water to a boil. Add the fish and cook until tender, 15–20 minutes.

2 Place the potatoes in another saucepan and add water to cover and the garlic and salt. Cover, and bring to a simmer over medium heat. Reduce the heat to low and cook until tender, about 20 minutes.

3 When the fish is ready, drain and let cool. Using your fingers, break into very fine pieces, discarding any skin and bones, and place in a bowl. Gradually beat in the olive oil until light and fluffy.

4 Drain the potatoes and garlic and transfer to a bowl. Mash with a fork until smooth, then stir into the fish. Add the lemon juice, parsley, salt, and pepper. Mix well.

5 Mound in the center of a platter, arrange the toast around it, sprinkle with the olives, and serve.

STOCKFISH AND SALT COD

Due to the regional nature of Italian ingredients, few foods are used throughout the country. One exception is preserved cod, in the forms of stockfish, or *pesce stocco*, and salt cod, or *baccalà*, both of which originated in and are still imported from Scandinavia.

The former is made by hanging cod fillets on wooden A-frames and leaving them to desiccate in the cold, dry wind. Having lost much of its natural moisture, the fish is light in weight and resistant to spoilage, yet high in protein. Viking sailors packed it as a staple on their long sea voyages, and introduced the fish to Italy, where it caught on quickly in port cities like Venice, Genoa, and Livorno.

Stockfish, from the Norwegian *stokfisk*, which originally meant "stick fish" because it resembles a wooden plank, was Italianized to *pesce stocco* or *stoccafisso*. It was popular in Italy and other Catholic countries for fast days because fresh fish was expensive and difficult to transport. *Baccalà* is made from the same type of fish, but the fillets are salted before drying. The names *pesce stocco* and *baccalà* are used interchangeably in Italy, and recipes that call for one can be made with the other. In Rome, *baccalà* fried in a crispy batter is so popular that there is even a trattoria named Filetti di Baccalà. In Liguria, the fish is made into fritters or stewed with wine, olives, and potatoes, while Neapolitans serve it in a salad with roasted peppers, olive oil, and lemon juice. Cooks in Florence dust squares of salt cod with flour, fry it with a shower of garlic, and then spoon a robust tomato sauce over it, while those in Bologna prepare it with lemon, garlic, and parsley. Romans, in contrast, marry it with tomatoes, pine nuts, and raisins or with sweet peppers (capsicums).

The most significant difference between the two types of preserved fish is how to prepare them for cooking. Stockfish must be rehydrated by long soaking in frequent changes of cold water. As it soaks, the fish softens, puffs up, and lightens in color. Depending on the quality, it may take as much as a week to rehydrate fully, and during that time it gives off a powerful aroma. *Baccalà*, on the other hand, needs only a day or two of soaking to eliminate some of the salt. Both the aroma and flavor of *baccalà* are much milder than those of stockfish. In Italy, many vendors sell the fish already soaked. Indeed, a common sight in markets in big cities and small towns alike is a basin of salt cod beneath a steady light shower of water.

Sea Bass in Parchment with Caper Sauce

Spigola al Cartoccio con Salsa di Capperi • Tuscany • Italy

The method of cooking in parchment paper is an old one, used mostly for cooking fish. The parchment holds in both the flavor and the juices of the fish, and the presentation is both elegant and intriguing, but simple to execute. Before even picking up your fork, peer inside the open package and inhale a whiff of the rising steam for the full dramatic effect.

1 tablespoon unsalted butter

1 tablespoon extra-virgin olive oil

2 cloves garlic, minced

2 tablespoons capers, rinsed

Juice of ½ lemon

Freshly ground pepper to taste

4 sea bass fillets, each about ½ lb (250 g) and 1 inch (2.5 cm) thick

Salt to taste

Handful of fresh basil leaves

Serves 4

1 Preheat the oven to 425°F (220°C).

2 In a small frying pan over medium heat, melt the butter with the olive oil. Add the garlic and sauté until fragrant, about 1 minute. Add the capers and cook for 1 minute longer. Remove from the heat, stir in the lemon juice, and season lightly with pepper.

3 Cut 4 large rectangles of parchment (baking) paper or aluminum foil. Lay a fish fillet on each rectangle and sprinkle lightly with salt. Distribute the garlic-caper mixture over the fillets, then scatter a few basil leaves on top. Wrap each fillet in the paper or foil, bringing together the long edges and folding them over to seal well, then folding in the sides and sealing them. Transfer the parcels to a baking dish.

4 Bake until the fish is opaque throughout, 10–15 minutes. To check for doneness, unwrap a parcel and pierce the fillet with a knife. Serve the fish fillets, still in their wrappers, on warmed individual plates.

Roast Eel Kabobs

Spiedini di Anguilla Arrosta • Tuscany • Italy

Old Tuscan cookbooks are filled with a variety of recipes for preparing eel, although eel is rarely found at fishmongers' stands or on restaurant menus. Eel fishing, raising, and cooking are all still very much alive in Orbetello, which is in the southern Maremma. The lagoons there are reputed to have the finest quality eel available in all of central Italy.

2 lb (1 kg) baby eels

2 tablespoons extra-virgin olive oil

2 cloves garlic, minced

2 tablespoons chopped fresh flat-leaf (Italian) parsley

Juice of 1 lemon

Salt and freshly ground pepper to taste

1 baguette, cut into ½-inch (12-mm) slices

16 bay leaves

1 cup (8 fl oz/250 ml) dry red wine

Serves 4

1 Wearing rubber gloves and using a sharp knife, slit the skin around each eel's head. Holding the head, grasp the skin with a coarse cloth, pull it toward the tail to remove it, and discard. Make a slit up the length of the eel and remove the viscera. Cut off the head. Wash the body thoroughly. Cut the eels crosswise into sixteen 2-inch (5-cm) pieces.

2 In a bowl, combine the oil, garlic, parsley, and lemon juice. Season with salt and pepper and mix well. Add the eel pieces and turn to coat well with the marinade. Cover and refrigerate for 2 hours.

3 Preheat the oven to 375°F (190°C). Drain the eel. Thread a bread slice onto a metal skewer, followed by a piece of eel, and then a bay leaf. Repeat until there are 4 pieces of eel on each skewer, then slip a piece of bread the end of each skewer. Lay the skewers in the baking dish. Bake the eel, basting occasionally with the wine, until crisp, about 20 minutes. Turn off the heat and let the eel rest in the oven with the door closed for 15 minutes before serving. Transfer the skewers to a platter or individual plates and serve.

Fried Soft-Shell Crabs

Moleche Fritte • Veneto • Italy

A visit to a Venetian seafood market is an education, for you will see varieties there not available anywhere else in Italy. One of the delights of springtime in Venice is *moleche*, small crabs that are caught and cooked just after they have molted their hard outer shells. The crabs stay soft for only a short time, so they must be taken from the water immediately after the shedding takes place. They are sold live and, for the crispest texture, should be served steaming hot, directly from the pan.

8–12 live soft-shell crabs

1½ cups (7½ oz/235 g) all-purpose (plain) flour

Salt and freshly ground pepper to taste

Vegetable oil for frying

Lemon wedges

Serves 4

1 To clean each soft-shell crab, using kitchen shears, cut off the eyes and mouth, then cut out the spongy, grayish gills. On larger crabs, you can also remove the apron, the hard flap that covers the belly.

2 Spread the flour on a plate and season with salt and pepper. Dust the crabs with the flour, then shake off the excess.

3 In a deep, heavy saucepan, pour in vegetable oil to a depth of 3 inches (7.5 cm) and heat to 375°F (190°C) on a deep-frying thermometer. Using tongs, slip the crabs into the pot, frying only as many at one time as will fit comfortably. The crabs tend to splatter, so stand back. Cook until golden and crisp, about 4 minutes. Using tongs, transfer to paper towels to drain. Sprinkle with salt; keep warm. Repeat with the remaining crabs.

4 Serve at once with lemon wedges.

Salt Cod with Leeks

Baccalà coi Porri • Tuscany • Italy

That Florence has few fish dishes it can call its own is not surprising, given its distance from the sea, but dried salt cod has long provided a practical and economical solution for *il venerdì di magro*, the meatless Friday meal of Catholic tradition.

2 lb (1 kg) salt cod, soaked (page 225)

Vegetable oil for frying

1 cup (5 oz/155 g) all-purpose (plain) flour

Salt and freshly ground pepper to taste

3 tablespoons extra-virgin olive oil

2 cloves garlic, crushed

6 leeks, white part and 1 inch (2.5 cm) of the green, thinly sliced

1 cup (6 oz/185 g) crushed canned plum (Roma) tomatoes with juice

1 lemon, cut into wedges

Serves 6

1 Drain the salt cod and carefully remove the bones. Cut into large pieces and pat dry with paper towels.

2 Pour the vegetable oil into a large frying pan to a depth of ½ inch (12 mm) and place over medium-high heat until hot but not smoking. Meanwhile, pour the flour onto a plate and season with salt and pepper. Coat the fish pieces in the flour, tapping off the excess.

3 When the oil is ready, working in batches, slip the fish pieces into the pan and fry, turning once, until opaque on both sides, about 6 minutes total. Do not worry if the fish sticks; it will be broken up in the sauce. Using a slotted utensil, transfer to a plate.

4 In a pan large enough to hold the fish pieces in a single layer, warm the olive oil over medium-low heat. Add the garlic and sauté until golden and fragrant, about 2 minutes. Remove and discard the garlic. Add the leeks to the pan and season with salt. Sauté gently until the leeks have softened but not browned, about 10 minutes. Add a little water as necessary to prevent the leeks from sticking. Add the tomatoes and cook for 5 minutes. Raise the heat to medium, arrange the fried salt cod and any accumulated juices on top of the leeks and tomatoes, and cook, turning the cod pieces occasionally, until the cod is well flavored with the sauce, about 15 minutes.

5 Transfer the salt cod and leeks to warmed individual plates, garnish with the lemon wedges, and serve at once.

Seafood Stew

Cacciucco • Tuscany • Italy

It has been said that the residents of Livorno are like their well-known seafood stew: a harmonious mixture, a melting pot. Livorno is historically the most heterogeneous city in Tuscany. In the fifteenth century, Florence's Medici family built a new port, fortified the town, and opened it for trade, attracting Greeks and Armenians from the east and south, English and Dutch from the north, and a large population of Jews escaping Spanish persecution. *Cacciucco* is often considered to be Livorno's most famous dish.

4 lb (2 kg) assorted fish and shellfish such as clams, mussels, mullet, smelt, snapper, cod, haddock, striped bass, squid, shrimp (prawns) in the shell, and crabs, in any combination

3 cloves garlic

¼ cup (2 fl oz/60 ml) extra-virgin olive oil

1 large yellow onion, chopped

3 tablespoons chopped fresh flat-leaf (Italian) parsley

1 teaspoon red pepper flakes

1 cup (8 fl oz/250 ml) dry white wine

3 cups (24 fl oz/750 ml) tomato purée

Salt and freshly ground black pepper to taste

6 thick slices coarse country bread

Serves 6

1 If using clams, soak them in lightly salted water to cover for 2 hours, then drain and scrub well, discarding any that fail to close to the touch. If using mussels, scrub well, debeard, and discard any that fail to close to the touch. Clean any whole fish, remove and discard their heads and tails, remove their skin, and cut crosswise into thick slices on the bone. If using squid, working with 1 squid at a time, pull the head from the body. Cut off and reserve the tentacles; discard the head. Squeeze out and discard the small, hard "beak" at the base of the tentacles; leave the tentacles whole. Using your fingers, pull out any internal matter from the body, including the quill-like cartilage, and discard. Peel off the mottled skin that covers the body. Rinse the body well. Cut the bodies into rings and the tentacles into medium-sized pieces. Place all the seafood in a bowl of salted cold water and set aside.

2 Mince 2 of the garlic cloves and cut the third clove in half lengthwise. Set aside.

3 In a large saucepan over medium heat, warm the olive oil. Add the onion and sauté until soft and fragrant, about 3 minutes. Add the minced garlic and 2 tablespoons of the parsley and cook, stirring frequently, until the garlic is fragrant, about 2 minutes.

4 Raise the heat to high, add the red pepper flakes, and pour in the wine. Let the alcohol bubble away for a couple of minutes, then reduce the heat to medium, pour in the tomato purée, and simmer uncovered, stirring occasionally, until the flavors are blended, about 5 minutes.

5 Begin adding the seafood to the soup, starting with the squid, adding the full-fleshed fish pieces after 10 minutes, and ending with the shellfish. After all the seafood is added, reduce the heat to low and cook, uncovered, at a slow simmer for 15 minutes. Season to taste with salt and black pepper.

6 Meanwhile, toast the bread and rub the surface with the cut sides of the halved garlic. Place 1 bread slice in each individual soup bowl.

7 Transfer the stew to a warmed tureen. Sprinkle with the remaining 1 tablespoon parsley.

8 Bring the tureen to the table and serve at once, ladling a mix of fish and shellfish onto the toast in each bowl and covering with broth.

SPAIN AND PORTUGAL

Preceding pages: Portugal's west coast offers dramatic cliffs, bracing Atlantic waves, and fine, deep-colored sand. **Top:** The Alfama, Lisbon's oldest quarter, gives visitors a striking—and romantic—view of the Tagus River. **Above:** Near Barcelona's Port Vell, the Monument a Colom honors Christopher Colombus for his successful return from the New World. **Right:** Succulent snails and myriad ocean delicacies are plucked from Portugal's west coast waters.

A wide array of fish and shellfish comes from the Iberian coastline of the Mediterranean and the Atlantic. Spain holds second place in the world in terms of both the consumption of fish and the size of the fishing fleet, right after Japan. Some of the best seafood comes from the cold Atlantic waters of the Basque provinces, where fishermen catch quisquillas *(tiny shrimp/ prawns),* camarones *(small shrimp),* langostas *(spiny lobsters), and* centollos *(spider crabs).*

Squid cooked in their ink are a specialty of the region, as are eels prepared with garlic, chile, and saffron and small, flavorful sardines, called *bokartas*, either batter-fried or doused with cider. Of course, not only northerners love fish. Tuna is enjoyed all over Spain, and in Andalusia, sardines, sole, mullets, squid, anchovies, shark, and hake are dusted with flour and dropped into hot oil to make the region's popular *fritura de pescados*. In Catalonia, fishermen set sail from the region's many ports in search of shrimp and the lobsterlike crustaceans known as *langoustines* in every color and size. Once back in port, their catches are then transformed into *zarzuela de mariscos*, a festive shellfish mix of prawns, scallops, mussels, clams, and lobsters, served cooked in their shells with a broth of tomato, wine, vegetables, and a touch of saffron. It takes its

name from the Spanish word for operetta, and it is indeed a musical for the senses. Besides tomatoes, the sweet and bitter oranges and lemons that grow throughout southern Spain are used to add freshness and tang to seafood dishes. Wine, olives, herbs, and pine nuts also turn up in many Iberian recipes for fish and shellfish.

As befitting a country that is equally balanced between rich coastlines and rural inland regions, many dishes that originated in Spain and Portugal mix meat and seafood together, especially when it comes to pork and shellfish. Clams are often cooked with spicy pork chorizo, linguiça sausage, or smoked ham, as in the Algarve dish called *ameijoas na cataplana*, in which clams are steamed open inside a hinged, clam-shaped cooking pan that traps the flavors inside as the clams and sausage cook together.

Historically, Spanish cooking styles have been divided into three geographical zones. Central Spain tends to favor roasting, while the south will usually prefer to fry food, and the colder north is known for braising. Over time, of course, these methods migrated, spilling easily over their culinary borders. Two additional signature methods for meats and fish are known as *a la plancha* and *a la parrilla*, cooking on a heavy metal griddle and grilling on a grid over a charcoal fire, respectively. The same cooking techniques prevail in neighboring Portugal, where fried and grilled seafoods are traditionally found along the warm southern coast.

Fish and shellfish are abundant in Portugal, accounting for approximately 40 percent of the population's protein consumption. Sesimbra, a lovely fishing village on the Arrábida Peninsula, is known for its fine swordfish, and Setúbal and the Algarve's small Quartiera ports are recognized for mullet. Tuna, sea bass, skate, sole, whiting, and squid are also served throughout the country, as are clams from Faro and Portimão, shrimp from the resort town of Monte Gordo, eel from lagoon-locked Aveiro, and lobster from Sagres, the promontory-sited village from which Henry the Navigator charted the seas. Fried or grilled sardines are staples on nearly every restaurant's menu.

With this bounty of fresh seafood, it may seem at first surprising to discover that the Portuguese have a passion for salted fish. But Portugal has long been a great seafaring nation. By the sixteenth century, Portuguese sailors fishing the Grand Banks southeast of Newfoundland had perfected the salting of cod caught at sea to preserve it for the long voyage home, where it was dried under the hot coastal sun. Today, the most popular of all the country's fish dishes still revolve around *bacalhau*, or salt cod, an ingredient that the Portuguese fondly call *o fiel amigo*— "the faithful friend"—and for which they claim a repertoire so extensive that a different recipe can be prepared for every day of the year.

The Spaniards, particularly the Basques, began cooking salt cod (*bacalao*) just over a century later, creating such memorable dishes as *bacalao a la vizcaína* (with peppers and pork) and *bacalao al pil pil* (simmered in olive oil and garlic). Although the Spanish enthusiasm for the preserved fish never matched that of the Portuguese, it did become a very important part of the traditional Catholic dietary regimen, as it became incorporated into countless Lenten meals and Friday suppers when eating meat is not allowed by the church. Today, the Grand Banks are nearly fished out and most of the salt cod sold in markets in Portugal and Spain comes from processors in Norway. It seems that this integral part of the Iberian diet that once fed the rich and poor alike has now become a pricey import.

Left: Both the tables and cultures of Spain and Portugal have been influenced for centuries by the abundant seafood from the surrounding waters. **Above, left:** Barcelona's history as a cosmopolitan seaport is evident everywhere you turn. **Above, right:** Vessels of every shape and size can be found in the waterways of Spain and Portugal, which is both ideal for and indicative of any community that depends on seafood for personal and commercial use.

Monkfish with Greens

Rape con Grelos • Galicia • Spain

Plump, meaty monkfish is popular in Spanish fish cookery, especially with cooks who live along the Galician coastline, the most important fishing region in the country.

About ¼ cup (2 fl oz/60 ml) olive oil

2 yellow onions, chopped

3 cloves garlic, finely minced

½ teaspoon red pepper flakes (optional)

1 bay leaf

4 cups (32 fl oz/1 l) fish or chicken stock

Salt and freshly ground pepper to taste

2 tablespoons fresh lemon juice (optional)

2 lb (1 kg) monkfish, rock fish, or sea bass fillet, cut into pieces about 2 by 3 inches (5 by 7.5 cm)

1½ lb (750 g) small clams such as Manila, well scrubbed (optional)

1 lb (500 g) Swiss chard, tough stems removed, cut into fine strips

6 slices coarse country bread, ½ inch (12 mm) thick, grilled or toasted

Serves 6

1 In a saucepan over medium heat, warm enough olive oil to form a film on the pan bottom. Add the onions and garlic and sauté until softened, 3–4 minutes. Add the red pepper flakes, if using, and the bay leaf and sauté until the onions are translucent and tender, 8–10 minutes. Do not allow the garlic to brown. Add the stock and simmer, uncovered, for 15 minutes. Season with salt, pepper, and the lemon juice, if using.

2 Transfer the onion sauce to a wide saucepan. Add the fish, the clams, if using (discard any clams that are open or broken), and the Swiss chard. Place over medium-high heat, cover, and simmer until the clams have opened and the fish is cooked, about 5 minutes. (Discard any clams that failed to open.)

3 Transfer the fish, clams (if used), and sauce to warmed individual bowls. Accompany each serving with a piece of the bread cut into thirds.

Scallops Baked in White Wine

Vieiras a la Gallega • Galicia • Spain

The scallop shell has come to symbolize the journey of pilgrims to the Galician town of Santiago del la Compostela, and scallop dishes are popular on many local menus.

16 large scallops

1 lemon, halved

6 tablespoons (3 fl oz/90 ml) olive oil

1 large yellow onion, finely chopped

1 cup (8 fl oz/250 ml) dry white wine

2 teaspoons sweet paprika

Pinch of cayenne pepper

Salt and freshly ground pepper to taste

¼ cup (⅓ oz/10 g) *each* chopped fresh flat-leaf (Italian) parsley and dried bread crumbs

Serves 2

1 Preheat the oven to 400°F (200°C).

2 Oil a baking dish or 2 individual ramekins. Place the scallops in the prepared dish(es) and squeeze a bit of lemon juice over them. Cover and refrigerate until the sauce is ready.

3 In a frying pan over medium heat, warm the olive oil. Add the onion and sauté until the onion is very soft, about 15 minutes. Add the wine and deglaze the pan, scraping up any browned bits on the pan bottom, then cook until reduced by half, 5–8 minutes. Stir in the paprika, cayenne, salt, pepper, and parsley, and spoon over the scallops. Top evenly with the bread crumbs. Bake until golden and bubbling, about 15 minutes. Remove from the oven and serve at once.

OLIVE OIL

The ancient Romans, responding to the felicitous climate, introduced the olive tree and the olive press to the Iberian Peninsula. The then-named *Hispania* (Spain) quickly became the principal supplier of olive oil (*aceite de oliva*, Spanish; *azeite de oliva* or simply *azeite*, Portuguese) to the empire. The Spanish oil, which traveled in earthenware amphorae, was even stocked in the pantries of the capital's senators: an 1872 archaeological dig centered on Mount Testaccio, a modest hill that rises alongside the Tiber, unearthed the shards of millions of discarded Spanish oil containers.

Today in Spain, about four thousand square miles (10,360 sq km) are given over to olive cultivation, primarily in the Andalusian provinces of Jaén and Córdoba and in Catalonia. Despite little or no rainfall for months at a time, Andalusia alone produces one-fifth of the world's olive oil, much of it sold to Italy, where it is blended and bottled. Olive trees blanket stretches of Portugal as well, their silvery gray-green profiles standing alongside orchards of figs, almonds, and oranges in Algarve and with groves of cork-oaks and fields of wheat in Alentejo.

Spain's Ministry of Agriculture has established production zones for the country's best oils. In Catalonia, where the small, green Arbequina olive is crushed, Borjas Blancas and Siurana are protected by *denominaciones de origen*. In Andalusia, where the Picual, Picuda, and Hojiblanca are the most common oil olives, the zones are Baena, in the province of Córdoba, and Sierra de Segura, in the province of Seville. Notable extra-virgin oils are bottled in these areas, with Nuñez de Prado from Baena and Estornel and Siurana from Catalonia among the finest.

In general, Catalan oil is lighter and less sweet than its Andalusian counterpart. By contrast, Andalusian oil has fruity shadows, a richer color, and a more pronounced olive taste. Portuguese oil, although intensely colored and highly aromatic, is less distinguished. It is not, however, without its vocal partisans.

Sizzling Shrimp with Garlic

Gambas al Pil Pil • Basque Country • Spain

This Basque tapa is traditionally served at the table sizzling—*pil pileando*—in a little metal pan. Sherry or lemon juice adds a nice contrast to the richness of the oil and garlic.

4–5 tablespoons (2–2½ fl oz/60–75 ml) olive oil

4 cloves garlic, finely minced

1 teaspoon red pepper flakes

1 teaspoon sweet paprika

1 lb (500 g) medium shrimp (prawns), peeled and deveined

1–2 tablespoons fresh lemon juice

1–2 tablespoons dry sherry

Salt and freshly ground black pepper to taste

2 tablespoons chopped fresh flat-leaf (Italian) parsley

Serves 4

1 In a sauté pan over medium heat, warm the olive oil. Add the garlic, red pepper flakes, and paprika and sauté for 1 minute until fragrant.

2 Raise the heat to high, add the shrimp, lemon juice, and sherry, stir well, and sauté until the shrimp turn pink and are opaque throughout, about 3 minutes. Season with salt and pepper, sprinkle with parsley, and serve.

Monkfish with Pine Nut Sauce

Rape en Salsa de Piñones • Catalonia • Spain

Many Spanish fish dishes include sauces made with nuts. Here, a pine nut sauce cloaks monkfish pulled from the coastal waters of Catalonia. Add parboiled English peas if you like.

4 tablespoons olive oil

1 large yellow onion, finely chopped

¼ cup (1 oz/30 g) pine nuts, toasted and ground

¼ cup (½ oz/15 g) fresh bread crumbs

1 tablespoon finely minced garlic

1 teaspoon sweet paprika

1½ cups (9 oz/280 g) peeled, seeded, and chopped tomatoes

1 cup (8 fl oz/250 ml) dry white wine

Salt and freshly ground pepper to taste

1½ lb (750 g) monkfish fillets

¼ cup (1 oz/30 g) pine nuts, toasted

¼ cup (⅓ oz/10 g) chopped fresh mint

Serves 4

1 In a frying pan over medium heat, warm 2 tablespoons of the oil. Add the onion and sauté until tender, 8–10 minutes. Add the ground pine nuts, bread crumbs, garlic, and paprika; cook for 3 minutes. Add the tomatoes and wine and cook until thickened, 5–8 minutes. Season with salt and pepper.

2 Cut the monkfish into slices 1 inch (2.5 cm) thick. Sprinkle the fish with salt and pepper. In a large frying pan over medium heat, warm the remaining 2 tablespoons of olive oil. Add the fish and sauté, turning once, for about 3 minutes on each side. Pour the sauce over the fish and simmer until the fish is opaque throughout, 4–5 minutes longer.

3 Transfer the fish and sauce to a platter, garnish with the pine nuts and mint, and serve.

Trout in the Style of Bragança

Truta à Moda de Bragança • Trás-os-Montes • Portugal

Trout in great numbers swim in the many freshwater streams of Trás-os-Montes. In Bragança, the main town of the province, local cooks prepare the fish in this manner

4 whole freshwater trout, cleaned with heads intact, about ¾ lb (375 g) each

Salt and freshly ground pepper to taste

8 thin slices *presunto* or prosciutto

About ¾ cup (4 oz/125 g) all-purpose (plain) flour

⅓ cup (3 fl oz/80 ml) olive oil

½ cup (4 fl oz/125 ml) dry white wine (optional)

Lemon wedges

Serves 4

1 Sprinkle the trout inside and out with salt and pepper. Stuff 1 ham slice inside each trout, and then wrap 1 ham slice around each fish, leaving the head and the tail exposed. Skewer closed with toothpicks or tie with kitchen string.

2 Spread the flour on a large plate. One at a time, dip each trout in the flour, tapping off the excess.

3 In a large frying pan over medium heat, warm the olive oil. Add the trout and fry, turning once, until golden on both sides, about 4 minutes on each side. Transfer the fish to a warmed platter. Discard the toothpicks or string.

4 If desired, pour the wine into the pan, raise the heat to high, and deglaze the pan, stirring to scrape up any browned bits from the pan bottom. Remove from the heat and pour over the fish.

5 Serve at once with the lemon wedges.

Salt Cod, Bay of Biscay Style

Bacalao a la Vizcaína • Basque Country • Spain

The color of this famous Basque dish of salt cod with onions and peppers comes from *choricero* peppers, dried sweet red peppers that impart a smoky quality to the sauce. Dried ancho chiles and *pimentón de La Vera*, the preferred sweet paprika, produce a similar effect. During Lent, the lard is omitted.

1 Drain the cod, reserving a little of the soaking water, and place the cod in a saucepan with water to cover. Bring to a gentle simmer over medium heat and cook until tender, 10–15 minutes. Drain well. Cut into 4 equal pieces, removing any bits of skin and any small bones.

2 Preheat the oven to 400°F (200°C).

3 Bring a saucepan three-fourths full of water to a boil. Add the bell pepper and blanch for 3–4 minutes. Drain and, when cool enough to handle, peel away the skin. Remove the stem and seeds and chop finely; set aside. Place the ancho chiles in a small saucepan, add water to cover, and bring to a boil. Drain immediately, re-cover with fresh water, and bring to a boil again. Drain and repeat one more time. Then drain the chiles, cut them open, and remove the seeds. Scrape the pulp from the skins and reserve. You should have about ¼ cup (2 oz/60 g).

4 In a large frying pan over medium heat, warm the olive oil. Add the onions, garlic, and parsley and sauté until the onions are tender, about 10 minutes. Stir in the sweet paprika and the hot paprika, if using, and cook for a minute or two. Add the bell pepper and the ancho pulp and sauté until soft, about 15 minutes. Remove from the heat.

5 Meanwhile, in a mortar, pound the bread crumbs or crackers with some of the cod soaking liquid until a paste forms. Add the hard-boiled egg yolks, mixing well. Add this mixture to the onion mixture and transfer to a blender. Purée until smooth, then pass through a sieve to strain out any lumps. Season to taste with salt and pepper. Pour 2 tablespoons of the melted lard into a *cazuela* or baking dish in which the fish will fit in a single layer. Tip the dish to coat evenly. Add a few ladlefuls of the sauce. Place the fish on top, then ladle the remaining sauce on top. Drizzle with the remaining 2 tablespoons lard.

6 Bake until the cod is heated through, about 15 minutes. Serve hot directly from the dish.

1½ lb (750 g) salt cod, preferably a single thick, solid piece or 2 thick pieces, soaked (page 225)

1 large red bell pepper (capsicum)

4 ancho chiles

1 cup (8 fl oz/250 ml) olive oil

4 yellow onions, chopped

4 cloves garlic, minced

¼ cup (⅓ oz/10 g) chopped fresh flat-leaf (Italian) parsley

1 tablespoon sweet paprika

½ teaspoon hot paprika (optional)

1 cup (4 oz/125 g) dried bread crumbs or crushed soda crackers

2 hard-boiled egg yolks

Salt and freshly ground pepper to taste

4 tablespoons (2 oz/60 g) lard, melted

Serves 4

Shrimp with Curry

Gambas com Caril · Estremadura · Portugal

In the fifteenth century, Vasco da Gama rounded the Cape of Good Hope and later returned with exotic spices, including cinnamon, cloves, nutmeg, pepper, and curry powder. This recipe is based on one from Goa, a Portuguese colony until it was seized by India in 1961. Serve with rice and *piri-piri* sauce (page 201).

1 lb (500 g) medium or large shrimp (prawns), peeled and deveined

Salt to taste

1 tablespoon curry powder

½ teaspoon ground ginger (optional)

1 tablespoon fresh lemon juice

3 tablespoons unsalted butter

1 yellow onion, chopped

2 cloves garlic, minced

1 red bell pepper (capsicum), seeded and chopped

1 tablespoon all-purpose (plain) flour

½ cup (4 fl oz/125 ml) fish or chicken stock

½ cup (4 fl oz/125 ml) half-and-half (half cream)

Freshly ground pepper to taste

¼ cup (⅓ oz/10 g) chopped fresh flat-leaf (Italian) parsley or fresh cilantro (fresh coriander)

Serves 4

1 Sprinkle the shrimp with salt. In a small bowl, dissolve the curry powder and the ginger, if using, in the lemon juice. (Use the ginger if the curry powder lacks ginger or includes only a small amount.)

2 In a large frying pan over medium heat, melt the butter. Add the onion, garlic, and bell pepper and sauté until tender, about 10 minutes. Add the dissolved spices and the flour and stir well. Add the stock and cream and cook, stirring constantly, until thickened, about 8 minutes. Season with salt and pepper. Add the shrimp and cook until they turn pink, 2–4 minutes.

3 Transfer to a warmed serving dish and sprinkle with parsley or cilantro. Serve at once.

Clams in White Wine

Amêijoas à Bulhão Pato • Estremadura • Portugal

This Portuguese dish is named after the nineteenth-century Lisbon poet Bulhão Pato, a well-known gourmand, and today it is a popular first course in the capital's many *tascas* and *restaurantes típicos*. If you have sandy clams, place them in a large basin of salted water to cover and leave for about 2 hours, stirring occasionally, so they will expel their sand. Drain and discard any open or broken clams before cooking. Serve with warm crusty bread to soak up the delicious juices.

⅓ cup (3 fl oz/90 ml) olive oil

5 cloves garlic, finely minced

Pinch of red pepper flakes (optional)

1 tablespoon fine dried bread crumbs, toasted

3 lb (1.5 kg) small clams, preferably Manila, well scrubbed

½ cup (4 fl oz/125 ml) dry white wine

1 cup (8 fl oz/250 ml) water

¼ cup (⅓ oz/10 g) chopped fresh flat-leaf (Italian) parsley

¼ cup (⅓ oz/10 g) chopped fresh cilantro (fresh coriander)

Serves 4–6

1 In a large sauté pan over medium heat, warm the olive oil. Add the garlic, the red pepper flakes, if using, and the bread crumbs and sauté until softened and pale gold, about 5 minutes. Add the clams, wine, and water, cover tightly, and cook until the clams open, 5–8 minutes, depending upon the size of the clams. Discard any clams that failed to open.

2 Transfer the clams and pan juices to warmed soup bowls, dividing evenly. Sprinkle with the parsley and cilantro and serve.

Shrimp with Hot Sauce

Camarão com Piri-Piri • Estremadura • Portugal

This traditional Portuguese fiery sauce known as *molho de piri-piri* is made all over Portugal and used in many different dishes. It takes its name from the very hot *piri-piri* chile.

PIRI-PIRI SAUCE

½ cup (2 oz/60 g) coarsely chopped fresh hot red chiles

4 cloves garlic, finely minced

1 teaspoon salt

1 cup (8 fl oz/250 ml) olive oil

¼ cup (2 fl oz/60 ml) white wine vinegar

2 cloves garlic, finely minced

2 small fresh red chiles, finely chopped, or 1 teaspoon cayenne pepper

½ cup (4 fl oz/125 ml) olive oil

2 lb (1 kg) jumbo shrimp (prawns), peeled and deveined

Salt to taste

Lemon wedges and coarse country bread

Serves 4–6

1 To make the sauce, in a jar with a tight-fitting lid, combine the chiles, garlic, salt, olive oil, and vinegar. Cover, shake well, and let rest in the refrigerator for about 1 week before using. You should have about 1½ cups (12 fl oz/375 ml). (You will not use it all; store the remainder for up to 2 months.) Shake well before using.

2 In a mortar, grind together the garlic and chiles or cayenne pepper to make a paste. Stir in the olive oil. Rub this mixture over the shrimp, place them in a bowl, cover, and refrigerate for 4 hours.

3 Preheat a broiler (grill), or prepare a fire in a grill. Remove the shrimp from the marinade, reserving the marinade. Thread the shrimp onto skewers, piercing the shrimp twice, once near the tail and again near the head. Sprinkle with salt. Broil or grill, turning once and basting with the marinade, until opaque throughout, 5–6 minutes total.

4 Arrange the skewers on a serving platter and garnish with the lemon wedges. Serve the bread and *piri-piri* sauce for dipping on the side.

EELS

One of the Basque region's most celebrated delicacies is *angulas*, or baby eels. These tiny freshwater denizens, each the size of a tailor's needle, are cooked in small earthenware vessels, or *cazuelitas*, and are usually prepared *al pil pil*— that is, sizzling in a batch of garlic, chile, and olive oil. But their simple appearance belies the arduous journey their ancestors survived.

Eels spawned in the distant Sargasso Sea travel thousands of miles across the Atlantic in a three-year journey to Spain's northern waters. In the past, these tiny eels, or elvers, were so abundant that Basque farmers reportedly fed them to their hogs along with the usual ration of grain. But once their popularity in the Spanish kitchen was established, fishermen began netting them in numbers that threatened the eels with extinction.

Today, both wild and farmed elvers are served in the tapas bars of San Sebastián, Bilbao, and other Basque towns. Crusty bread and a glass of *txakolí*, the local wine, are the perfect accompaniments.

Tuna with Peppers and Potatoes

Marmitako · Basque Country · Spain

Marmitako, a rich blend of potatoes and fish bound with a sauce of peppers, has as many interpretations as there are Basque cooks. Serve with grilled coarse country bread.

1½ lb (750 g) albacore tuna fillet, cut into 2-inch (5-cm) pieces

Salt to taste

3 tablespoons olive oil

1 yellow onion, chopped

2 cloves garlic, minced

2 red or green bell peppers (capsicums), seeded and finely chopped

2 lb (1 kg) boiling potatoes, peeled and cut into 2-inch (5-cm) chunks

½ cup (4 fl oz/125 ml) tomato sauce

¼ teaspoon hot paprika, or to taste (optional)

Freshly ground pepper to taste

Serves 4

1 Sprinkle the fish lightly with salt and refrigerate until ready to cook. In a large frying pan over medium heat, warm the olive oil. Add the onion and sauté until tender, about 8 minutes. Add the garlic and peppers and sauté for a few minutes longer until the peppers begin to soften. Add the potatoes and enough water just to cover. Simmer, uncovered, until the potatoes are tender, about 20 minutes.

2 Add the tuna, the tomato sauce, and the paprika, if using, and mix well. Cover and simmer until the fish is opaque throughout, about 10 minutes longer. Season with salt, pepper, and paprika (if using). Transfer to a warmed platter and serve at once.

Swordfish with Tomatoes and Anchovies

Espadarte à Lisboeta · Estremadura · Portugal

If you cannot find fresh swordfish, thick fillets of cod or sea bass are good substitutes. And if fresh tomatoes are not in season, you may use canned tomatoes for this dish.

6 swordfish steaks, about 7 oz (220 g) each

Salt and freshly ground pepper to taste

5 tablespoons (3 fl oz/80 ml) olive oil

1 yellow onion, chopped

2 cups (12 oz/375 g) peeled, seeded, and chopped plum (Roma) tomato

1 tablespoon finely minced anchovy

2 tablespoons tomato paste dissolved in ¼ cup (2 fl oz/60 ml) dry white wine

20 black olives, pitted and coarsely chopped

¼ cup (⅓ oz/10 g) chopped fresh flat-leaf (Italian) parsley, plus extra parsley for garnish

Lemon wedges

Serves 6

1 Preheat the oven to 400°F (200°C). Oil a baking dish in which the fish steaks will fit in a single layer.

2 Sprinkle the fish with salt and pepper and refrigerate until ready to cook. In a large frying pan over medium heat, warm the olive oil. Add the onion and sauté until tender, about 8 minutes. Add the tomato, anchovy, tomato paste dissolved in white wine, olives, and ¼ cup chopped parsley and simmer until thickened, about 5 minutes.

3 Place the fish steaks in the prepared baking dish. Spoon the tomato sauce over the fish. Bake until the fish is opaque throughout, about 15 minutes.

4 Remove from the oven and sprinkle with additional parsley. Serve at once directly from the dish. Accompany with lemon wedges.

Peppers Stuffed with Salt Cod

Pimientos Rellenos de Bacalao • Basque Country • Spain

Many different kinds of sweet peppers are grown in Spain, but the *piquillo* is the most highly regarded. It is sold fresh and is also roasted and peeled and packed in cans and jars. In California and elsewhere, one can find a similar pepper called the gypsy pepper, but don't hesitate to use jarred or canned Spanish imports for this dish. Large fresh pimientos are also a good choice. If you use fresh red bell peppers, select the smallest ones possible and cut away the thick inner ribs. Poached fresh cod can be used in place of the salt cod.

1½ lb (750 g) boneless salt cod, soaked (page 225)

6 tablespoons extra-virgin olive oil

2 large yellow onions, finely chopped

¼ cup (2 fl oz/60 ml) tomato sauce

1 tablespoon sweet paprika

4 tablespoons (⅓ oz/10 g) chopped fresh flat-leaf (Italian) parsley

2 tablespoons all-purpose (plain) flour, plus extra for dusting

½ cup (4 fl oz/125 ml) dry white wine

½ cup (4 fl oz/125 ml) fish or vegetable stock

3 cloves garlic, minced

1 cup (2 oz/60 g) fresh bread crumbs, soaked in milk to cover and squeezed dry

Salt and freshly ground pepper to taste

2 egg yolks, lightly beaten, plus 1 whole egg

8 canned or jarred roasted whole *piquillo* peppers or 8 large fresh pimiento peppers (capsicums), roasted and peeled

Olive oil for deep-frying

Serves 8

1 Drain the cod and place in a saucepan with water to cover. Bring to a simmer very slowly over low heat. When it comes to a boil, remove from the heat and let cool completely in the water. Drain well and break up the cod into small pieces with your fingers, removing any bits of skin and any small bones. Set the cod aside.

2 In a sauté pan over medium heat, warm 3 tablespoons of the olive oil. Add half of the chopped onions and sauté until soft and pale gold, 10–12 minutes. Add the tomato sauce, paprika, 2 tablespoons of the parsley, and the 2 tablespoons flour. Stir well and pour in the white wine and stock. Bring to a boil, reduce the heat to low, and simmer until thickened, 5–8 minutes. Remove from the heat and set aside.

3 In another sauté pan over medium heat, warm the remaining 3 tablespoons oil. Add the remaining onion and the garlic and sauté until translucent, about 8 minutes. Add the cod and the bread crumbs, season with salt and pepper, and cook gently, stirring from time to time, until well mixed and softened, 8–10 minutes. Add the egg yolks and the remaining 2 tablespoons parsley and remove from the heat. Let cool completely.

4 Cut a slit down one side of each pepper and carefully remove the seeds. Stuff the peppers with the cooled cod mixture. If you like, secure the stuffing with toothpicks.

5 Pour olive oil to a depth of 1½ inches (4 cm) into a deep frying pan and heat to 375°F (190°C) on a deep-frying thermometer. Meanwhile, in a shallow bowl, beat the whole egg until blended. Put some flour for dusting in a separate bowl.

6 When the oil is ready, dip the peppers, one at a time, into the beaten egg and coat with the flour. Slip the peppers into the oil in small batches and fry, turning as necessary, until golden, 4–5 minutes. Using a slotted spoon, transfer the peppers to paper towels to drain.

7 When all the peppers are fried, transfer the tomato sauce mixture to a large frying pan and place over low heat. Add the stuffed peppers and simmer, uncovered, for 10 minutes to blend the flavors.

8 Transfer to a serving dish and serve hot or at room temperature.

Stuffed Squid

Lulas Recheadas • Alentejo • Portugal

Squid are greatly enjoyed in Portugal. At their simplest, they are grilled and dressed with olive oil and lemon. Other times they are braised in a sauce of stock and wine.

12 medium or 16 small squid

¼ cup (2 fl oz/60 ml) olive oil, plus ⅓ cup (3 fl oz/80 ml), plus olive oil for brushing

1½ cups (7½ oz/235 g) chopped yellow onion

4 cloves garlic, minced

½ cup (3 oz/90 g) chopped *presunto* or prosciutto

1½ cups (3 oz/90 g) fresh bread crumbs

¼ cup (2 fl oz/60 ml) fresh lemon juice, plus 3–4 tablespoons

6 tablespoons (½ oz/15 g) chopped fresh flat-leaf (Italian) parsley

Salt and freshly ground pepper to taste

1 egg, lightly beaten

2 tablespoons dried oregano

Serves 4

1 First, clean the squid: Working with 1 squid at a time, pull the head from the body. Cut off and reserve the tentacles; discard the head. Squeeze out and discard the small, hard "beak" at the base of the tentacles; leave the tentacles whole. Using your fingers, pull out any internal matter from the body, including the quill-like cartilage, and discard. Peel off the mottled skin that covers the body. Rinse the body well, leave the squid bodies whole, and chop the tentacles. Set aside. In a frying pan over medium heat, warm the ¼ cup (2 fl oz/60 ml) olive oil. Add the onion and sauté until tender, 8–10 minutes. Add the garlic, ham, tentacles, and bread crumbs and sauté, stirring often, until blended, about 2 minutes. Add the ¼ cup (2 fl oz/60 ml) lemon juice, and the parsley, salt, and pepper. Stir in the egg, remove from the heat, and let cool.

2 Prepare a fire in a grill. Stuff the squid bodies with the cooled filling and skewer closed with toothpicks. Thread the squid onto metal skewers, placing 3 on each. Brush with olive oil and sprinkle with salt and pepper. Grill, turning once, until they are firm and light grill marks appear, about 3 minutes on each side.

3 Meanwhile, in a bowl, stir together the ⅓ cup (3 fl oz/80 ml) olive oil, 3–4 tablespoons lemon juice, and the oregano. When the squid are ready, place them on a warmed platter and spoon the olive oil mixture over them. Serve at once.

Salt Cod and Potato Gratin

Bacalhau à Gomes de Sá • Douro • Spain

Gomes de Sá, a well-regarded nineteenth-century Oporto restaurateur, created this hearty gratin, which is now a considered a traditional national dish.

1 lb (500 g) boneless salt cod

Milk to cover, if needed

1½ lb (750 g) boiling potatoes, peeled

6 tablespoons (3 fl oz/90 ml) olive oil

2 yellow onions, thinly sliced

2 cloves garlic, minced

½ cup (¾ oz/20 g) chopped fresh flat-leaf (Italian) parsley

1 teaspoon freshly ground pepper

20 oil-cured black olives

2 hard-boiled eggs, peeled and sliced

Serves 4

1 Soak the salt cod (page 225). Drain well and break up the cod into small pieces with your fingers, removing any bits of skin and any small bones. Taste the cod. If too salty, cover with milk and let rest for 30 minutes, then drain. Combine the potatoes with water to cover, bring to a boil, and boil until just tender, 20–25 minutes. Drain and slice ¼ inch (6 mm) thick. In a frying pan over medium heat, warm 2 tablespoons of the oil. Add the onions and sauté until just tender, 7–8 minutes. Add the garlic and cook for 2 minutes. Transfer to a bowl. In the same pan, warm 3 tablespoons of the oil over medium heat. Add the potatoes and sauté until golden, about 5 minutes.

2 Preheat the oven to 400°F (200°C). Oil a large gratin dish. Layer half of the potatoes in the bottom, top with half of the cod, and then half of the onions. Sprinkle with a little of the parsley and pepper. Repeat the layers, then drizzle the top with the remaining oil. Bake until golden, about 25 minutes. Garnish with the olives and hard-boiled eggs and sprinkle with the remaining parsley. Serve at once.

Mullet with Orange-Wine Sauce

Salmonete Setubalense · Alentejo · Portugal

Orange groves surround the fishing port of Setúbal, which is known for its bitter oranges. The traditional sauce for this fish is a wine- and orange-flavored butter accented by the fish's liver. Rubbing the fish with orange zest, salt, and sugar before cooking heightens the flavor. Red mullet is the star of this dish, but salmon or snapper can also be used.

¼ cup (2 oz/60 g) sugar

2 tablespoons grated orange zest

2 tablespoons kosher salt

1 teaspoon freshly ground pepper

6 small, whole red mullet, salmon trout, or red snapper, about 1 lb (500 g) each, cleaned with heads intact, or 6 salmon fillets, 6–7 oz (185–220 g) each

1 cup (8 fl oz/250 ml) dry white wine

½ cup (4 fl oz/125 ml) fresh orange juice

6 tablespoons (3 oz/90 g) unsalted butter, melted, plus extra butter as needed

2 small oranges, sliced

¼ cup (⅓ oz/10 g) chopped fresh mint or flat-leaf (Italian) parsley

Serves 6

1 In a small bowl, stir together the sugar, orange zest, salt, and pepper. Rub this mixture on the fish, place the fish in a covered container, and refrigerate for about 3 hours.

2 Preheat the oven to 450°F (230°C). Butter a baking dish in which the fish will fit in a single layer.

3 Place the fish in the prepared dish and drizzle evenly with the wine, orange juice, and melted butter. Bake until the fish is opaque throughout when a knife is inserted at the thickest point, 8–10 minutes. Transfer the fish to a warmed platter. Add more butter to the pan juices as needed to thicken it into a sauce, then spoon over the fish.

4 Garnish the fish with the orange slices and sprinkle with the mint or parsley and serve.

SPANISH WINE

Thanks to the Phoenicians and Greeks, the Spanish were drinking wine long before the ancient Romans arrived and replanted existing vines with Italian varieties. Today, thirty carefully drawn areas, called *denominaciones de origen*, fall under the watchful eye of a national institute whose sole job is to maintain the high standards of the country's wines.

Many of the best bottlings come from the Old Castile regions of Rueda, Ribera del Duero, and Rioja. Rueda is famous for its modestly complex whites made from the Verdejo grape. Not far from the bustling, rather homely city of Valladolid, in an area known as Tierra de Vino, Vega Sicilia, one of the rarest and most sought-after Spanish reds, is produced. Its label carries the *Ribera del Duero denominación*, as do a pair of other superb red wines of the area, Tinto Pesquera and Vina Pedrosa. The wines of Rioja have long enjoyed a higher profile than those of their Castilian cousins. Production from these rugged foothills was poured at countless feasts in ancient Rome, and the area's historic monasteries, which lay along the popular pilgrimage route to Santiago de Compostela, made wines for the constant stream of travelers. Today, the same area is home to Spain's most familiar red table wines, at home and abroad, as well as a few light and fruity whites.

Next door, Navarre, a rich stretch of oak forests, snowcapped mountains, clear rivers, and fertile valleys, is the source of some well-regarded reds made from the same varieties used in Rioja. The most celebrated wines of Aragon, to the south, are the big, bold, dark reds from the *Cariñena denominación*. Farther south still, Catalonia, with six designated areas, produces respectable wines of every kind: red, white, sweet dessert, and the country's best *cava*, or sparkling wine.

Fish in a Tart Vinaigrette

Escabeche • Catalonia • Spain

The name *escabeche* comes from the Arabic *sikbaj*, or "vinegar stew." Originally it was made with meat and only rarely with fish, but today it is primarily a dish of pickled fish. Small, oily fish such as sardines or local Portuguese *carapau* (small mackerel) are traditionally used, as they develop a smooth, velvety texture when marinated. You can substitute fillets of a firm white fish, although they will not produce the same extraordinary texture. For maximum flavor, let the fish marinate for a couple of days before serving.

1½ lb (750 g) whole fresh sardines or 1 lb (500 g) tuna or white fish fillets

Kosher salt

½ cup (4 fl oz/120 ml) olive oil

2 white onions, sliced paper-thin

2 carrots, peeled and grated (optional)

2 or 3 cloves garlic, smashed

2 small bay leaves, torn into pieces

⅔ cup (5 fl oz/160 ml) white vinegar

2 teaspoons salt

1 teaspoon sweet paprika (optional)

Freshly ground pepper to taste

1 small lemon, sliced paper-thin

2 tablespoons chopped fresh cilantro (fresh coriander)

Serves 6–8

1 If using fresh sardines, lay the sardines on a plate, sprinkle with kosher salt, cover, and refrigerate overnight. The next day, slit each fish along its belly, gut it, and then remove its backbone and head. Rinse the sardines.

2 Lay the sardines or fish fillets on a plate, sprinkle with kosher salt, and let stand for about 15 minutes.

3 In a large frying pan over medium heat, warm 2 tablespoons of the olive oil. Add half of the fish and sauté, turning once, until golden on both sides and opaque throughout, 2–3 minutes total for the sardines or 4 minutes for the fish fillets. Transfer to a plate. Repeat with the remaining fish and 2 more tablespoons of the oil. Set the fish aside.

4 Add the remaining ¼ cup (2 fl oz/60 ml) oil to the same pan over medium heat, add the onions, and sauté until limp, 8–10 minutes. Add the carrots (if using), garlic, bay leaves, vinegar, salt, paprika (if using), and pepper and let bubble for a minute or two. Remove from the heat and let cool. Toss in the lemon slices and cilantro.

5 Arrange the fish on a deep platter, alternating layers of fish and the onion mixture. Cover, pouring any remaining liquid over the top, and refrigerate for 2 days before serving.

Salt Cod with Chickpeas

Meia Desfeita de Bacalhau · Estremadura · Portugal

The cooks of Estremadura specialize in creative dishes made with chickpeas, combining them here with Portugal's ubiquitous salt cod.

1½ lb (750 g) salt cod, soaked (page 225)

4 hard-boiled eggs, peeled

¾ cup (6 fl oz/180 ml) olive oil

3 yellow onions, chopped

3–5 cloves garlic, minced

1 teaspoon sweet paprika

2 cups (14 oz/440 g) drained, cooked chickpeas (garbanzo beans)

½ cup (4 fl oz/125 ml) white wine vinegar

1 cup (1½ oz/45 g) chopped fresh flat-leaf (Italian) parsley

Few drops of *piri-piri* sauce (page 201)

Salt to taste

18 oil-cured black olives

Olive oil and white wine vinegar for serving

Serves 6

1 Drain the salt cod and place in a saucepan with water to cover. Bring to a gentle simmer over medium heat and cook until tender, 10–15 minutes. Drain well and, when cool enough to handle, flake the cod, removing any bits of skin and any small bones. Set aside. Slice 3 of the hard-boiled eggs, then chop the remaining egg. Set aside separately.

2 In a large frying pan over medium heat, warm the olive oil. Add the onions and sauté until tender, 8–10 minutes. Add the garlic and paprika and sauté until the garlic is translucent, about 2 minutes longer. Add the cod, chickpeas, sliced eggs, vinegar, half of the parsley, and the *piri-piri* sauce and cook, stirring, until heated through, a few minutes. Season with salt.

3 Transfer to a warmed platter and garnish with the chopped egg and olives and the remaining parsley. Pass olive oil and vinegar at the table.

Squid with Peas

Calamares con Guisantes • Catalonia • Spain

Most proprietors of waterfront restaurants in Catalonia put together attractive displays of their offerings, making it easy for diners to survey the bountiful harvest before selecting a place to eat. One of the most popular treatments for seafood on these menus is to combine it with peas in a *salsa verde*, a sauce made from fresh mint or parsley and olive oil.

2 lb (1 kg) squid

4 lb (2 kg) English peas in the pod, shelled

½ cup (4 fl oz/125 ml) olive oil

2 heads garlic, cloves separated and peeled

2 slices coarse country bread, crusts removed

1 tablespoon all-purpose (plain) flour

3 tomatoes, peeled, seeded, and chopped

½ cup (4 fl oz/125 ml) dry white wine, or as needed

¼ cup (⅓ oz/10 g) chopped fresh mint

¼ cup (⅓ oz/10 g) chopped fresh flat-leaf (Italian) parsley

Serves 6

1 First, clean the squid: Working with 1 squid at a time, pull the head from the body. Cut off and reserve the tentacles; discard the head. Squeeze out and discard the small, hard "beak" at the base of the tentacles; leave the tentacles whole. Using your fingers, pull out any internal matter from the body, including the quill-like cartilage, and discard. Peel off the mottled skin that covers the body. Rinse the body well. Cut the squid bodies crosswise into 1-inch (2.5-cm) rings; set aside with the tentacles.

2 Bring a saucepan three-fourths full of salted water to a boil. Add the peas and cook until tender, 3–5 minutes. Drain and immerse in cold water, then drain again and set aside.

3 In a large frying pan over medium heat, warm the olive oil. Add the garlic and sauté until golden, about 5 minutes. Using a slotted spoon, transfer to paper towels to drain. Add the bread to the same oil over medium-high heat and fry, turning once, until crisp and golden, 5–7 minutes. Transfer to paper towels to drain. Break up the bread and place in a blender or food processor along with the garlic. Process until finely ground. Add the flour to the same oil over medium heat and, when it starts to color, add the tomatoes and wine, stirring well. Add the bread-garlic mixture along with half each of the mint and parsley and simmer for 15 minutes. If the sauce is too thick, add a little more wine or water. It needs to be spoonable and have a nice liquid consistency. Remove from the heat, let cool slightly, and pour into a blender or food processor. Process until smooth.

4 Return the sauce to the pan and bring to a boil. Add the squid, stir, and cook for about 2 minutes. Add the peas and heat for 1 minute longer until the peas are heated and the squid is tender. Transfer to a platter, garnish with the remaining mint and parsley, and serve.

Hake with Cider

Merluza a la Sidra • Asturias • Spain

As grapes are hard to cultivate in Galicia and Asturias and apple trees thrive, it's not surprising to find that hard cider, instead of wine, is used in the local cooking, just as it is in the apple orchard–rich French regions of Normandy and Brittany. This dish is usually made with hake or sea bass (*lubina*), but you may use cod, flounder, or another mild white fish. Not all versions call for apples, but they do heighten the flavor of the cider.

1 In a frying pan over medium heat, warm 2 tablespoons of the olive oil. Add the onion and garlic and sauté until the onion is tender, about 8 minutes. Add 1 tablespoon of the flour, the soaked chile, the tomatoes, and the apples. Stir well and pour in the cider. Bring to a boil over medium heat, adjust the heat to maintain a simmer, and simmer until the apples are soft, 8–10 minutes. Remove from the heat and pass the mixture through a food mill or purée in a blender or food processor. Set the sauce aside.

2 Preheat the oven to 450°F (230°C).

3 Bring a pot of water to a boil over high heat. Add the potato slices and boil until about half-cooked, about 5 minutes. Drain and set aside.

4 Spread the remaining flour on a plate. Sprinkle the fish pieces with salt and pepper and then dip them in the flour, tapping off the excess. In a large frying pan over high heat, warm the remaining 6 tablespoons (3 fl oz/90 ml) oil. Add the fish and fry, turning once, to brown lightly on both sides. Transfer to a *cazuela* or other baking dish and set aside.

5 Add the potatoes to the same oil over high heat and fry, turning once, until golden on both sides. Transfer to the *cazuela* and add the clams, discarding any that are open or broken, and the cider sauce.

6 Place in the oven and bake until the clams open and the fish is heated through, about 15 minutes. (If you prefer, you can finish cooking this dish on the stove top, using a deep frying pan and covering it with a lid.)

7 Remove from the oven and discard any clams that failed to open. Sprinkle with the parsley and serve directly from the dish.

8 tablespoons (4 fl oz/125 ml) olive oil

1 yellow onion, finely chopped

2 cloves garlic, minced

About ¾ cup (4 oz/125 g) all-purpose (plain) flour

1 dried chile, soaked in lukewarm water for 30 minutes to soften, drained, and stem removed

2 tomatoes, peeled, seeded, and chopped

2 small apples, peeled, cored, and chopped

1 cup (8 fl oz/250 ml) hard apple cider

2 large boiling potatoes, peeled and sliced ½ inch (12 mm) thick

1½ lb (750 g) hake or other white-fleshed fish fillet, cut into 4 equal pieces (see note)

Salt and freshly ground pepper to taste

16 clams, well scrubbed

3 tablespoons chopped fresh flat-leaf (Italian) parsley

Serves 4

CIDER

While the rest of Spain makes and sips wine, many Asturians and Basques prefer lightly fermented *sidra*, or cider. They have been quaffing the amber-gold beverage since the time of the ancient Greeks, and, not surprisingly, considerable ritual has grown up around the making and the consumption of this favorite spritzy drink.

The cider is made in houses called *sidrerías*. Apples are harvested in the autumn, fed into a press, and crushed to a pulp. The juices from the pulp slowly drip through mesh into vats, where the first fermentation occurs within a few hours and the second shortly after. For the next three months, the fermentation and aging continue and the cider eventually reaches about five percent alcohol. In January, it is tasted to judge its progress, and four months later it is ready to drink.

In days gone by, the cider was left in its natural state in the barrels in which it was aged. Today, however, most of it is very lightly aerated and bottled for sale. Despite this nod to modernization, strict rituals still surround the serving of cider, as one can see on a visit to the sawdust-strewn bar of a cider house or to a *chigre* (tavern) in the ancient Asturian capital of Oviedo.

The bars, no-frills establishments, their air thick with the pungent aroma of cider, are primarily male bastions, places to gather, visit, and drink. The pouring of the cider is startlingly showy and utterly practical: With one fully extended arm, the barman grasps a bottle above his head. In his other hand he holds a large, widemouthed glass as close to the floor as possible. The liquid travels from the bottle in a narrow, continuously flowing stream and strikes the side of the glass, the pressure producing a light, lacy golden foam. This is the source of the faint effervescence that marks every good Spanish cider. It traditionally is poured to a depth of only two fingers, and because the foam lasts only briefly, the nicely tart cider is drunk immediately, usually in a single gulp. The pleasantly musky beverage is used in the local cooking as well, in such dishes as hake with cider (see recipe at left) or clams steamed in cider.

Clams with Sausage and Tomatoes

Amêijoas na Cataplana • Algarve • Portugal

A *cataplana* is a clam-shaped hinged pan typical of the Algarve. It is used on the stove top and can be turned over to ensure even cooking of its contents. You can buy a *cataplana* in a specialty cookware store, or you can make this dish in a deep frying pan with a tight-fitting lid. Serve the clams in shallow bowls, either spooned over wedges of boiled potatoes or accompanied with lots of coarse country bread.

2 tablespoons olive oil

3 yellow onions, thinly sliced

4 cloves garlic, finely minced

1–2 teaspoons red pepper flakes or 2 fresh chiles, finely minced

1 bay leaf, torn into pieces

¼ lb (125 g) *presunto* or prosciutto, diced

¼ lb (125 g) *linguiça* or *chouriço*, casings removed and crumbled

1 cup (8 fl oz/250 ml) dry white wine

2–3 cups (12–18 oz/375–560 g) diced canned tomatoes with juice

3 lb (1.5 kg) small clams such as Manila, well scrubbed

½ cup (¾ oz/20 g) chopped fresh flat-leaf (Italian) parsley

Freshly ground black pepper to taste

Lemon wedges (optional)

Serves 8

1 In a large sauté pan over medium heat, warm the olive oil. Add the onions and sauté until tender, about 8 minutes. Add the garlic and the red pepper flakes, if using, and sauté until softened, about 3 minutes more. Add the bay leaf, ham, sausage, wine, tomatoes, and the fresh chiles, if using. Simmer for 10 minutes. Add the clams, hinge side down, discarding any that are open or broken. Cover and cook until the clams open, 3–5 minutes.

2 Spoon the clams and juices into warmed bowls, discarding any clams that failed to open. Sprinkle with the parsley and a liberal grinding of black pepper. Serve with lemon wedges, if desired.

Tuna with Garlic and Chile

Atum à Portuguesa · Algarve · Portugal

As this marinade is quite intense, rub it on the fish no more than two hours before cooking. This recipe, like the Spanish *atún adobado*, is essentially tuna with garlic and paprika.

3 or 4 fresh hot red chiles, finely minced

1 cup (1½ oz/45 g) finely chopped fresh cilantro (fresh coriander)

2 tablespoons finely minced garlic

1 tablespoon sweet paprika

1 tablespoon freshly ground pepper

½ cup (4 fl oz/125 ml) olive oil

¼ cup (2 fl oz/60 ml) fresh lemon juice

1½ lb (750 g) tuna fillet, cut into 4 equal pieces

Salt to taste

Serves 4

1 In a nonreactive container, stir together the chiles, half of the cilantro, and the garlic, paprika, and pepper. Stir in the olive oil and lemon juice. Add the tuna and rub the mixture into the fish. Cover and refrigerate for 2 hours.

2 Prepare a fire in a charcoal grill, or preheat a broiler (grill).

3 Sprinkle the fish with salt. Place on an oiled grill rack or broiler pan and slip under the broiler. Grill or broil, turning once, for about 3 minutes on each side for medium-rare, or until done to your liking.

4 Transfer to a warmed platter or individual plates. Garnish with the remaining cilantro and serve at once.

Crab in a Cart

Santola no Carro · Minho · Portugal

If you have purchased fresh crabs and picked the crabmeat from them, reserve some of the tomalley and use instead of mayonnaise.

8 tablespoons (4 oz/125 g) unsalted butter

1 large or 2 small yellow onions, minced

3 cups (18 oz/560 g) crabmeat, picked over for shell fragments

1 cup (2 oz/60 g) fresh bread crumbs

2 tablespoons chopped fresh flat-leaf (Italian) parsley

½ cup (2½ oz/75 g) sliced brine-cured black olives

¼ cup (2 fl oz/60 ml) mayonnaise

Piri-piri sauce (page 201) to taste

Salt and freshly ground pepper to taste

Lemon wedges

Serves 4

1 Preheat the oven to 450°F (230°C). Generously butter 4 ramekins or large scallop shells.

2 In a frying pan over medium heat, melt 6 tablespoons (3 oz/90 g) of the butter. Add the onion and sauté until golden, about 15 minutes. Remove from the heat and place in a bowl.

3 Add the crabmeat, bread crumbs, parsley, olives, and mayonnaise and mix well. Season with the *piri-piri* sauce, salt, and pepper. Gently spoon the crab mixture into the prepared ramekins or scallop shells. Cut the remaining 2 tablespoons butter into bits and use to dot the surface.

4 Bake until golden and heated through, 8–10 minutes. Garnish with lemon wedges and serve at once.

GLOSSARY

AJOWAN SEEDS Ajowan seeds (also known as *ajwain*) come from the thymol plant, a close relative of caraway and cumin. The seeds resemble large celery seeds. They have a sharp taste and, when crushed, smell strongly of thyme. Ajowan has been used for centuries in India to flavor vegetable dishes, breads, pickles, and *pappadums*. It helps control digestive problems, so it is often added to starchy dishes and those containing legumes. If unavailable, thyme imparts a similar flavor.

ANCHOVIES These shimmering blue-green fish measure about 6 inches (15 cm). When freshly caught, they may be fried or pickled in vinegar and eaten whole. The bulk of the catch is preserved by layering the fish with salt. Buy salted anchovy fillets in olive oil in small, flat tins or in glass jars.

ARTICHOKES Prickly on the outside but tender within, artichokes are one of nature's more peculiar vegetables. They are actually the flower bud of a large-leaved perennial in the sunflower family. If left on the plant, the buds would gradually open to reveal glorious purple blossoms, but harvesters cut them when they are tightly closed.

To trim artichokes, cut the stem flush with the bottom. Using a serrated knife, cut about 1½ inches (4 cm) off the top of the artichoke. Using scissors, snip off the pointed tips of each leaf. Rub the artichoke with a lemon half to preserve its color while you prepare it.

BAMBOO SHOOTS The edible shoots of certain types of bamboo are known as *qingsun*. Fresh, untreated shoots have tough outer leaves over a golden-colored, horn-shaped, tender shoot of layered construction. Ready-to-use shoots are sold fresh, frozen, or canned in whole pieces, slices, or shreds, and what is not used can be kept fresh in the refrigerator in lightly salted water for up to one week. Winter bamboo shoots (*dongsun*) are small and tender. Salted dried bamboo shoot should be soaked and rinsed before use.

BELL PEPPERS Also called capsicums and sweet peppers, large and meaty green bell peppers turn red and become sweeter when fully ripened. As attractive as they are versatile, red bell peppers add crunch when used raw in appetizers; take on a silky sweetness when cooked slowly in soups, stews, or sauces; and contribute a distinctive smokiness when roasted over an open flame.

BREAD CRUMBS Used to make crisp toppings for oven-baked dishes or to lend body to fillings, bread crumbs should be made from a slightly stale coarse country white loaf.

To make dried bread crumbs, trim the loaf of its crusts and process in a food processor to form crumbs. Dry the crumbs on a baking sheet in a preheated 325°F (165°C) oven for about 15 minutes; let cool, process again until fine, and then bake, stirring once or twice, until pale gold, about 15 minutes longer.

CALVADOS Calvados is an apple brandy that comes from northern France where apples are plentiful but grapes are not grown. A dry brandy aged in oak, Calvados is taken after dinner and even, in Normandy, as a digestive between two courses of a long meal.

CAPERS Growing wild throughout the Mediterranean, the caper bush yields tiny gray-green buds that are preserved in salt or pickled in vinegar to produce a piquant seasoning or garnish.

CASSIA LEAVES The leaves of the cassia tree, also known as Indian bay leaves, have a slightly clovelike aroma and flavor and are available dried from Indian grocers. Despite their alternative name, they are not related to European bay leaves (*Laurus nobilis*). If cassia leaves are unavailable, the same quantity of European bay leaves may be used, although they will give a somewhat different taste.

CHILE PASTE, ROASTED This paste is made from red chiles, garlic, shallots, dried shrimp, dried shrimp paste, tamarind, brown sugar, salt, and vegetable oil. A variety of commercial pastes are available in Asian markets.

CHILES, DRIED Buy dried chiles with skins that are flexible rather than brittle in texture, and store them in airtight containers, away from both light and moisture.

ANCHO A dried form of the poblano, anchos measure 4½ inches (11.5 cm) long, with wide shoulders and wrinkled, deep reddish brown skin, and have a mild bittersweet chocolate flavor and a slight aroma of prunes.

ÁRBOL Smooth-skinned, bright reddish orange chile about 3 inches (7.5 cm) long, narrow in shape and fiery hot.

CHIPOTLE The smoke-dried form of the ripened jalapeño, rich in flavor and very hot. Sold in its dried form, it is typically a leathery tan, although some varieties are a deep burgundy. It is available packed in a vinegar-tomato sauce (*chiles chipotles en adobo*) as well as lightly pickled (*en escabeche*).

PASILLA Skinny, wrinkled, raisin-black pasillas are about 6 inches (15 cm) long, with a sharp, fairly hot flavor.

To seed dried chiles, clean them with a damp cloth, then slit them lengthwise and use a small, sharp knife to remove the seeds.

To toast dried chiles, clean them with a damp cloth, then heat a heavy frying pan over medium heat. Add the whole or seeded chiles, press down firmly with a spatula, turn the chiles, and press down once more before removing. The chiles will change color only slightly and start to give off their aroma.

Caution The oils naturally present in chiles can cause a painful burning sensation when they come in contact with your eyes or other sensitive areas. After handling them, wash your hands thoroughly with warm, soapy water. If you have particularly sensitive skin, wear latex kitchen gloves or slip plastic bags over your hands before working with chiles.

CHILES, FRESH Choose firm, bright fresh chiles. Smaller chiles are usually hotter. Store them in the refrigerator for 1 week.

ANAHEIM This long green mild to moderately spicy chile is found in most markets. It is similar to the New Mexican chile variety.

JALAPEÑO This popular chile, measuring 2–3 inches (5–7.5 cm) in length, has thick flesh and varies in degree of hotness. It is found in green and sweeter ripened red forms.

POBLANO Named for the Mexican state of Puebla, this moderately hot chile is 5 inches (13 cm) long with polished deep green skin.

SERRANO Slender chiles measuring 1–2 inches (2.5–5 cm) long that are very hot, with a brightly acidic flavor. Available in both green and ripened red forms at most markets.

To roast, peel, and seed fresh chiles, using tongs, hold a whole chile over the flame of a gas burner for 10–15 minutes (5–8 minutes for smaller chiles), turning it to char and blister the skin evenly. Place in a bowl, cover, and leave for 10 minutes. The steam will loosen the skin and make it easier to peel. When the chile is cool, peel off the blackened skin, then slit the chile lengthwise and remove the stem, seeds, and membranes. If you have a large number of chiles to roast or if you have an electric range, broil (grill) the chiles, turning as needed, until charred on all sides.

CLAMS Buy the freshest clams you can find from a reputable fish merchant. They are sold live in the shell or freshly shucked and packed in pint and quart containers that contain clam liquor (or liquid), too. Hard-shelled quahog clams should have firm, finely textured gray shells with no yellowing; other hard-shelled clams should have even-colored, firm shells. The clams should not be open—if one gapes a little, prod it gently. If it does not close immediately, do not buy it. An open shell is a sign of a dead clam. Shucked hard-shell clams should be plump and moist with clear liquor and a fresh and briny aroma.

LITTLENECK The smallest of the hard-shelled clams, Atlantic littlenecks measure from 1½–2 inches in diameter. These are sweet and delicious raw or very gently cooked. Pacific littlenecks are not related. Because they are a little tough, they should be steamed.

MAHOGANY These hard-shelled clams from Atlantic waters have a dark, reddish brown shell and pinkish meat. They are also called ocean quahogs because they have a flavor similar to that of large quahogs.

MANILA Also called Japanese clams, these small, sweet clams are farmed off the Pacific coast of the United States, although they are not native. Most of them are harvested when they are 1 inch (2.5 cm) in diameter. They can be served raw or very lightly steamed.

CRAB, FRESH To clean a freshly cooked crab, hold the top shell of the crab in one hand while grasping the legs and claws with the other hand. Gently twist and pull away the shell. Turn the crab's body over and twist off and discard the triangular apron. Pull off and

discard the feathery gills, then cut out the mandibles at the face end. Gently bend each leg and claw backward and twist them free from the body. Spoon out the creamy yellow tomalley and reserve it for another use, if desired. Rinse the body and pat dry with paper towels. Using a cleaver, chop the body into quarters. Crack each leg and claw at the joint with a mallet. At this point, the crab is ready to stir-fry or braise. Or, to extract the crabmeat, pick it out from the body and legs.

COCONUT CREAM AND COCONUT MILK Coconut cream and coconut milk are both derived from an infusion of grated coconut flesh in water or, less commonly, milk. (They are not to be confused with the clear juice inside the whole nut.) The first infusion yields coconut cream, a thick liquid with a high fat content. If the same batch of coconut is steeped again, the resulting liquid is called coconut milk. A third steeping produces thin coconut milk. Freshly grated coconut gives the best results, but commercially packaged, unsweetened coconut can also be used. Good-quality unsweetened canned coconut milk is a welcome shortcut when time is at a premium. Do not shake the can before opening. Once it is open, first scrape off the thick mass on top, which is the cream. The next layer is opaque white coconut milk, and finally there is a clear liquid, which is thin coconut milk.

CRÈME FRAÎCHE Thick enough to spread when chilled, but fluid enough to pour at room temperature, this tangy, slightly acidulated fresh cream is often used as a dessert topping or an enrichment for sauces and soups.

CUTTLEFISH Abundant in the waters of the Mediterranean, the cuttlefish is flatter, thicker, meatier, and more succulent than its close relative, the squid. The solid cuttlebone in the center differentiates the two; the squid has a transparent quill. Cuttlefish are cleaned in the same manner as squid.

FISH SAUCE In many Southeast Asian kitchens, fish sauce assumes the same seasoning role played by soy sauce throughout Chinese and Japanese cuisine. Made by layering anchovies or other tiny fish with salt in barrels or jars and leaving them to ferment, the dark amber liquid adds a pungent, salty flavor. The two

most common types are Thai *nam pla* and Vietnamese *nuoc mam*, with the latter having a milder flavor.

GARAM MASALA This Indian spice blend—sold commercially or made at home—features coriander seeds, cumin, black pepper, cardamom, cloves, cinnamon, nutmeg, and mace. It is typically used to season dishes at the beginning of cooking and is sometimes sprinkled over finished dishes.

GARLIC, PICKLED These popular Thai and Chinese pickles are made by preserving whole peeled heads of garlic in vinegar. Both tart and sweet varieties may be found, ready to eat as a relish or to add a spike of aromatic flavor to meat or noodle dishes or to sauces.

GHEE Used throughout Indian cooking, *ghee* literally means "fat." There are two types: *usli ghee* (clarified butter) and *vanaspati ghee* (vegetable shortening). A recipe that calls simply for ghee is understood to mean *usli ghee*. Indian clarified butter differs from the European equivalent in having been simmered until all the moisture is removed from the milk solids and the fat is amber colored. This gives *usli ghee* its unique nutty taste. Clarification also increases the butter's storage life. *Vanaspati ghee* is a pale yellow, hydrogenated blend of various vegetable oils that is processed to look, smell, and taste very similar to *usli ghee*. Both are readily available in Indian markets; *usli ghee* can also be easily made at home.

To make *usli ghee*, heat ½ lb (250 g) unsalted butter in a pan over medium-low heat, uncovered, until it melts. Increase the heat to medium and simmer the butter, stirring often, until the clear fat separates from the milk solids, about 15 minutes. During this process a layer of foam will rise to the top of the butter and the butter will crackle as its milk solids lose moisture. When the milk solids lose all moisture, the fat as well as the milk residue will turn amber colored. When this occurs, remove the pan from the heat and let the residue settle on the bottom. When cool enough to handle, pour the clear fat, which is the *usli ghee*, into a jar, ensuring that no residue gets in. Alternatively, strain it through two layers of cheesecloth (muslin). Discard the residue. *Usli ghee* may be refrigerated, covered, for up to 6 months or frozen for up to 12 months. Allow to thaw before use. Makes ¾ cup/6 fl oz/180 ml *usli ghee*.

GINGER The edible root or rhizome of ginger is buff colored and smooth when young. When older, root ginger becomes a dull, deep buff color with slightly wrinkled skin; its flavor intensifies and the flesh becomes fibrous. It is peeled and grated, minced, sliced, or chopped for use as a flavoring of unique taste and appealing spiciness. Dried powdered ginger is not a suitable substitute; processed products packed in brine or vinegar may be appropriate, if rinsed first.

To make ginger juice, peel and finely grate fresh root ginger onto a piece of fine cloth, gather up into a ball, and squeeze to extract the juice. The pulp can be discarded or used in a soup or stir-fry. One tablespoon of grated ginger will produce about 1½ teaspoons of ginger juice. Ginger wine is a seasoning and marinade made by combining 1 part ginger juice with 2–3 parts rice wine.

HERBS

BASIL This sweet and spicy fresh herb is especially popular in the cooking of Italy and the south of France. It pairs perfectly with sun-ripened tomatoes.

BASIL, THAI Three types of basil are used in Thailand: *kraprow*, *maenglak*, and *horapa*. *Kraprow* has serrated green leaves with a tint of purple and a hint of anise flavor overlaying the familiar basil scent. *Maenglak*, also known as lemon basil, has smaller leaves and a lemony scent. *Horapa* has purple stems, shiny leaves, and an anise aroma. All three can be used interchangeably, or European sweet basil can be substituted.

CHIVE This thin green shoot of a member of the onion family is used fresh to add a hint of onion flavor to salads and ingredients such as eggs, cheese, and seafood.

CILANTRO This lacy-leafed annual herb, also known as fresh coriander, has a fresh, assertive scent and bright, astringent flavor—an acquired taste for some. Cilantro leaves should be added at the end of the cooking time or used raw, as long cooking destroys their delicate flavor.

DILL This feathery, grassy-tasting herb is often used to season vinegars and pickling brines. It is frequently used to flavor cucumber salads .

KAFFIR LIME LEAVES The kaffir lime contributes its rich, citrusy flavor to curry pastes and other savory and sweet dishes through its dried, fresh, or frozen leaves and its gnarled rind. Its juice, however, is not used. Pesticide-free lemon or lime leaves may be substituted.

MINT More than 600 different types of mint exist, although peppermint and spearmint are the most common. Mint is typically used as an accompaniment to lamb and as a salad-like garnish (often in combination with Thai basil and cilantro) to many Thai and Vietnamese dishes. Fresh mint leaves are also infused in hot water to make an herbal tea.

OREGANO Related to mint and thyme, this strongly scented herb actually gains in flavor from drying, unlike most herbs. It is the signature seasoning of pizza and is added to many sauces and marinades.

OREGANO, MEXICAN Although similar in flavor to the more familiar Mediterranean oregano, Mexican oregano is more pungent and less sweet than its Mediterranean kin, making it a perfect match for the spicy, cumin-laden dishes of the Southwest. Add it at the beginning of cooking to allow time for its flavor to emerge and meld with others.

PARSLEY Southern European in origin, this widely versatile herb adds its bright, fresh flavor to many different kinds of savory foods. The flat-leaf variety, also known as Italian parsley, has a more pronounced flavor than the curly type, which is used predominantly as a garnish.

ROSEMARY Taking its name from the Latin for "rose of the sea," this spiky evergreen shrub thrives in Mediterranean climates. Its highly aromatic, piney flavor goes well with lamb and poultry, as well as with tomatoes and other vegetables.

SAGE Sharply fragrant, with traces of both bitterness and sweetness, this gray-green herb is often used in seasoning pork, veal, game, and sausages.

TARRAGON Native to Siberia, this heady, anise-flavored herb can perfume wine vinegar and Dijon mustards, flavor sauces and dressings, and season seafood, poultry, and eggs.

THYME This low-growing, aromatic herb grows wild throughout the Mediterranean, and often flavors food without the cook's help, as game birds and wild rabbits like to feed upon it. A key element of many slow-cooked savory dishes, it is also considered a digestive aid.

KARI LEAVES These small, shiny, highly aromatic leaves come from the kari tree, native to southern India and Sri Lanka. Although sometimes called curry leaves and used in curries, they bear no relation to curry powder and are not interchangeable with it. Rather, both their flavor and aroma are citrusy, as befits a member of the citrus family. Kari leaves are available in Indian grocery stores. Fresh leaves have the best flavor, but dried are usually more easily found and may be substituted: Use double the quantity of dried leaves as for fresh. If unavailable, substitute 2 teaspoons minced parsley and 1 teaspoon grated lemon zest for every 20 kari leaves.

LEMONGRASS This stiff, reedlike grass has an intensely aromatic, citrusy flavor that is one of the signatures of Southeast Asian cooking. Use only fresh lemongrass, as it lacks good flavor when dried. Lemon zest, often mentioned as a substitute, can play its role but in no way equals its impact.

To prepare lemongrass, if a recipe calls for the tender midsection of a stalk, use only its bottom 4–6 inches (10–15 cm). Peel off any tough outer layers of the stalk to reveal the inner purple ring. To release the aromatic oils, smash or chop the stalk before use.

LOBSTER When buying a live lobster, choose one that proves especially feisty. Hold a lobster up, grasping its sides safely behind its claws, to check that it quickly snaps its tail tightly under its body. Any that are sluggish and apathetic have been in the tank too long. Captured lobsters are not fed, so their meat will shrink away with time. Likewise, when purchasing a whole cooked lobster, make sure that its tail curls, an indication that it was still alive when it was put in the cooking pot.

MASA Kernels of dried field corn are treated with a solution of calcium hydroxide (powdered lime) and water to loosen and remove their tough outer skins and are then ground and mixed with water to make *masa*, literally "dough," used primarily for preparing tortillas and tamales. Fresh-ground *masa* comes in 5- or 10-lb (2.5- or 5-kg) plastic bags.

Use as needed, divide the rest into small amounts, and freeze. Use fresh or frozen *masa* within 1 day of purchase or thawing.

MASA HARINA This flour is ground from dried corn and used to make tortillas and tamales. Two basic types are available, the fine-ground *masa harina* for tortillas and the more coarsely ground *masa harina* for tamales.

MEYER LEMONS Although the exact derivation of the Meyer lemon is disputed, many believe it is a cross between a lemon and a mandarin orange, as hinted at by its rounder shape, yellow-orange color, sweeter flavor, and flowery fragrance. Its peak season is from November to May.

MUSHROOMS, DRIED BLACK Sold fresh or dried in Asian stores, black fungi are also known as wood ear fungi (larger, thicker tree fungi) and cloud ear fungi (smaller, dark, curled fungi). Dried black fungus is sold whole, in pieces of approximately 2 inches (5 cm) square, or shredded. It must be soaked to soften, and any woody root sections should be trimmed off before use. Store in an airtight container for many months. Fresh fungus should be used within 3 to 4 days of purchase.

MUSSELS Buy live mussels from a reputable fishmonger. They should have a fresh sea smell with no trace of ammonia. Tap the mussels, and do not buy them if they stay open, indicating a dead or at least dehydrated mussel. To cut preparation time, look for already-shucked and cooked mussels chilled in the seafood section or freezer case of your supermarket. Already-shucked mussels are also available frozen, and occasionally mussels can be found frozen on the half shell.

NUTS When purchasing nuts, seek out only those that are free of cracks, holes, and discoloration. To make sure the nutmeat is not dried out inside, shake the shells.

CASHEWS Cashew trees measure up to 40 feet (12 m) in height and produce fruits called cashew apples (though actually pear shaped), inside of which the nut develops. When the fruits ripen, the nuts protrude from the end of them. The shells of the nuts contain an acidic, oily substance that can burn and blister the skin but which is neutralized by heating.

PEANUTS Not really a nut at all, but rather a type of legume that grows underground, peanuts are seeds nestled inside waffle-veined pods that become thin and brittle when dried.

WALNUTS The furrowed, double-lobed nutmeat of the walnut has an assertive, rich flavor. The most common type is the English walnut, also known as the Persian walnut, which has a light brown shell that cracks easily. Black walnuts have a stronger flavor and tougher shells but can be hard to find.

To toast nuts, spread them on a baking sheet and toast in a 325°F (165°C) oven until they are fragrant and take on a golden color, 10–20 minutes; the timing depends on the type of nut and the size of the nut or nut pieces. Stir once or twice to ensure even cooking. Remove from the oven and immediately pour onto a plate, as they will continue to darken if left on the hot pan. Toast small amounts of nuts in a frying pan over medium-low heat, stirring frequently, until fragrant and golden.

OYSTERS Always buy oysters from reputable merchants who can vouch that they came from safe, clean, unpolluted waters. Fresh live oysters in the shell have a mild, sweet smell. Their shells should be closed tightly and feel heavy with water. Do not buy any oysters that remain open when touched. A strong fishy or ammonia smell indicates that the oysters are no longer fresh, so pass them by. Any oysters intended for eating raw should be bought fresh and shucked within a few hours of serving. Do not buy shucked oysters for eating raw unless you know that they were shucked especially for your order.

OYSTER SAUCE Used extensively in Chinese cooking, oyster sauce, or *haoyou*, is a thick, salty, dark brown condiment and seasoning sauce made from fermented soybeans and the liquor drawn off from fermented dried oysters. It can be refrigerated for 2–3 months.

PALM SUGAR Derived from the sap of the coconut or other palms, and sometimes called coconut sugar, palm sugar is prized for its fragrant caramel-like flavor and light to dark brown color. The sugar is often sold formed into dark, hard disks or cylinders, which may be grated or shaved for use. Light or dark brown sugar, depending upon the color desired, can be substituted.

PANCH PHORON This classic Indian spice mixture is usually made from cumin, nigella mustard, fenugreek, and fennel. It is used for flavoring seafood, vegetables, and lentils.

PARMESAN Parmesan is fashioned into large wheels and aged for 1–3 years to develop a complex, nutty flavor and dry, granular texture. "Parmigiano-Reggiano" stenciled on the rind ensures it is a true Parmesan made in Emilia-Romagna. *Grana padano*, a hard grating cheese, can be used in its place.

PINE NUTS Umbrella-shaped stone pines grow throughout the Mediterranean, and their long, slender seeds (also called *pignoli*) are high in oil and delicately flavored. As with all nuts, a gentle toasting enhances their flavor.

PRESUNTO This air-cured ham of Portugal has a sweet, smoky flavor and a deep, chestnut color. It may be served thinly sliced as a first course or used as a distinctive source of flavor in sauces, soups, stews, braises, and other dishes. Spain's finely-marbled *serrano*, Italy's prosciutto, and similar hams, including French Bayonne, German Westphalian, or American Smithfield, can be used in its place.

RICE WINE Rice wine (*liaojiu*) adds flavor to sauces and stir-fries in Chinese cooking, and works as a tenderizer and seasoning in marinades. Rice wine can be purchased at most Asian food stores. Those labeled "cooking wine" may contain 5 percent added salt, so check labels before seasoning a dish. Dry sherry is a substitute in most recipes, while Japanese mirin is the alternative choice when a mild, aromatic wine is required.

SALT Some cooks contend that the iodine added to common table salt clouds stocks and clear sauces, and that the salt's fine grains lack the texture and depth of flavor of sea salt or kosher salt. Sea salt, gathered from evaporated seawater, retains small amounts of naturally occurring minerals, and it often carries a slight tint of gray or pink from these minerals. Available in both fine and coarse crystals, sea salt is excellent used in cooking. Sprinkling it over dishes just before serving allows diners to appreciate its complex flavor. Kosher salt was originally developed for the preparation of kosher meats, but its flat, coarse grains dissolve quickly, an often-desirable quality.

SALT COD, BONELESS This strong, briny-tasting, tender fish must be soaked in cold water to reduce its saltiness before use. Be sure to use filleted salt cod. Salt cod must be refreshed in water before cooking. Refreshing will take a minimum of 3 hours and up to 24 hours, depending upon the amount of salt present.

To soak salt cod, rinse it under cold running water for 10 minutes, then put it in a large bowl and add water to cover. Let stand for 3–4 hours. Break off a small piece of the fish, poach it in simmering water for 3–4 minutes, then taste it. If it is still salty, drain the bowl, cover again with cold water, let stand for another 3–4 hours, and test again. The flavor should not be bland; you should taste a bit of the salt. When refreshed to taste, pour off the water and drain the salt cod on paper towels or according to the recipe directions.

SCALLOPS Choose scallops that are creamy white or slightly pink, rather than bright white, an indication that they have been soaked. Bay scallops should be pale pink or light orange. Although shucked scallops will have some odor, choose those with the mildest scent.

SHRIMP Choose firm, sweet-smelling fresh shrimp, also called prawns, still in the shell when possible. All but the freshest shrimp will have had their heads already removed. Most shrimp sold has been previously frozen and thawed. You may do better buying still-frozen shrimp, since its quality is the same or better than thawed, and you'll be able to decide more freely when to use it. Previously frozen shrimp should not be refrozen. Bay shrimp are usually available only shelled and cooked.

SHRIMP PASTE, DRIED Intensely flavored, this Southeast Asian seasoning paste is made by salting, fermenting, and then drying shrimp (prawns). Depending on its source, the dried paste may range in color from pinkish tan to deep purple-black. Called *blacan* in Malaysia, *trasi* in Indonesia, *kapi* in Thailand, and *ngapi* in Myanmar (Burma), it is most often sold in hard blocks from which slices can be easily cut with a sharp knife. Do not confuse the dried paste with shrimp sauce, called *bagoong* in the Philippines and sometimes

shrimp paste in English, a pungent, thick, grayish sauce sold in jars. Shrimp paste can be found in Chinese markets.

SICHUAN PEPPER The small, red-brown berries from the prickly ash tree are also known variously as *fagara,* wild peppercorn, or Chinese pepper. Spicy rather than hot, it can have a numbing effect if used to excess. When buying whole peppercorns, look for a bright red-brown color. Store in an airtight jar and use within a few weeks for the best flavor.

SORREL LEAVES These delicate, triangular leaves have a strongly tart flavor similar to that of rhubarb. The paler the leaves, the more delicate their flavor. Sorrel discolors with cooking, but it lends a bright, pleasantly sour flavor when puréed into soups or sauces.

SOY SAUCE Typically made by fermenting and aging soybeans along with wheat, salt, and water, soy sauce is an indispensable seasoning in the kitchens of China and, to a far lesser degree, in Southeast Asia. Dark soy sauce gains its dark color, thicker consistency, and edge of sweetness from the addition of caramel. Light soy sauce has a thinner consistency and a lighter flavor. Japanese soy sauces tend to be milder tasting, slightly sweeter, and less salty than Chinese varieties.

SRIRACHA Named for the seaside Thai town in which it originated, this bottled, hot or mild, sweet-tart, all-purpose sauce is made from red chiles and resembles a light-colored ketchup. Keep in mind that even the so-called mild version is still quite hot.

TAMARIND AND TAMARIND WATER The sweet-and-sour pulp from the seedpods of this tree native to India is a popular flavoring. Tamarinds are also known as Indian dates. The brown seedpods resemble fava (broad) bean pods. Tamarind paste and concentrate are also available. Tamarind pulp is sold in block form in most well-stocked Asian markets.

To make tamarind water, cut up ¾ pound (375 g) tamarind pulp into small pieces, place in a bowl, and add 2 cups (24 fl oz/750 ml) boiling water. Mash the pulp to separate the fibers and seeds, then let stand for 15 minutes, stirring 2 or 3 times. Pour the liquid through a fine-mesh sieve placed over a bowl, pushing

against the pulp with the back of a spoon and scraping the underside of the sieve to dislodge the clinging purée. Use as directed or transfer to a jar and refrigerate for up to 4 days or freeze in an ice-cube tray for up to 1 month. Tamarind concentrate dissolved in hot water can be subsitituted.

TEQUILA Young, clear *blanco* tequila has a distinct agave flavor and a less refined edge than more aged tequilas. Sharper, peppery *reposado* tequila is aged in wood for 2 to 12 months, while a smooth, subtle *añejo* tequila may have been aged for up to 5 years. For high-quality tequila, check that the label indicates the spirit is 100 percent blue agave or *agave azul* and was bottled in Mexico. Less expensive *mixto* versions may be fermented with sugar and mixed with up to 40 percent grain alcohol and other additives.

VINEGAR, BALSAMIC While vinegar is most commonly made from red or white wine, Italy's most renowned vinegar, *aceto balsamico,* or balsamic vinegar, is based on white grape juice that is reduced by boiling it down to a thick syrup, or must, then aged for many years in a succession of ever-smaller barrels made of different woods, each of which contributes its own taste to the final syrupy, sharp-and-sweet product. Rare and expensive, this true *aceto balsamico* is used sparingly as a condiment, a few drops at a time, often over Parmesan cheese or ripe strawberries. More commonly available balsamic vinegar, appropriate for cooking or salad dressings, is made from a mixture of wine vinegar, must, and caramel coloring.

INDEX

A

Aioli, 107

Amêijoas à bulhão pato, 198

Amêijoas na cataplana, 217

Anchois grillés au vinaigre de Banyuls, 126

Anchovies
  butter, 134
  and garlic dip, hot, 159
  grilled, with Banyuls vinegar, 126
  Niçoise sandwiches, 143
  and onion tart, 137
  swordfish with tomatoes and, 202

Artichokes
  fritto misto of squid, lemon, and, 42
  monkfish with olives and, 145

Atum à portuguesa, 218

Avocados balls, scallop ceviche with, 29

B

Bacalao a la vizcaína, 196

Bacalhau à Gomes de Sá, 206

Baccalà coi porri, 181

Baccalà mantecato, 176

Bacon, panfried trout with mushrooms and, 22

Bagna cauda, 159

Bai zhi xian bei pang xie, 52

Balinese fish with lemongrass and lime, 56

Beans
  ahi tuna Niçoise, grilled, 27
  salt cod with chickpeas, 212
  vegetables and salt cod with mayonnaise, 107

Beignets de morue, 116

Blanc de loup belle mouginoise, le, 142

Bouillabaisse, 146

"Broken tile" fish with sweet-and-sour sauce, 87

Butter
  anchovy, 134
  shallot, 37

C

Cabbage
  coleslaw, 30
  fish tacos, 40
  salmon pirog, 21

Cabillaud demoiselle d'Avignon, 122

Cacciucco, 182

Ca kho to, 91

Calamares con guisantes, 213

Calamares en salsa de tres chiles, 33

Calamari in zimino, 168

Calmars aux petits pois, 117

Camarão com piri-piri, 201

Camarones con naranja y tequila, 39

Cashews
  fenni, 55
  shrimp with, 66

Catfish
  lemon, with slaw in parchment, 30
  simmered in a clay pot, 91

Ceviche de callo de hacha con aguacate, 29

Ceviche rojo de camarón y sierra, 18

Cha ca Hanoi, 64

Chao pangxie heidou, 72

Cheese, red snapper with chile sauce and, 24

Chickpeas, salt cod with, 212

Choo chee hoy phat, 57

Cider, 215
  hake with, 214

Clams, 16
  -bake dinner, 16
  monkfish with greens, 191
  with sausage and tomatoes, 217
  seafood stew, 182
  stuffed, 162
  in white wine, 198
  with white wine, garlic, and tomatoes, 175

Clay pot cooking, 62–63, 91

Cod, steamed, with vegetables, 122

D

Coda di rospo piccata, 157

Coleslaw, 30

Cozze ripiene, 158

Crab
  boil, Dungeness, with shallot butter, 37
  cakes with herbed tartar sauce, 23
  in a cart, 218
  chile, 88
  fried soft-shell, 180
  with its butter and seaweed, 124
  -meat sauce, 52
  Mediterranean fish soup, 146
  seafood clay pot, 63
  seafood stew, 182
  spicy, 82
  stir-fried, with black beans, 72

Crabe à sa beurre aux algues, 124

Cream, 114

Crêperie, 119

Crevettes au fenouil, 129

Criée, la, 132

Crostini di pesce spada, 165

Cuipi wakuai yu, 87

Cuttlefish. *See also* Squid
  "pinecones," fried, with pepper-salt, 95
  stuffed with tapenade, 130

D

Demoiselles de Cherbourg à la crème, 113

Denji fry, 82

Dim sum, 99

Dumplings, steamed pork and shrimp, 98

E

Eels, 201

Eggplant
  cod, steamed, with vegetables, 122
  fish, braised, with potato and, 76

Encornets farcis à la tapenade, 130

Escabeche, 211

F

Espadarte à lisboeta, 202

Espadon des mémés toulonnaises, 139

Fennel
  ahi tuna Niçoise, grilled, 27
  salad, shaved, grilled salmon with, 45
  wild, grilled sea bream with, 154

Fenni, 55

Fish. *See also individual species*
  Balinese, with lemongrass and lime, 56
  braised, with eggplant and potato, 76
  "broken tile," with sweet-and-sour sauce, 87
  cakes, spicy, 68
  in China, 86
  and chips, 34
  deep-fried baby, 140
  Hanoi-style fried, 64
  Malabar braised, in sour gravy, 85
  in Mexico, 25
  roasted, with pine nuts and raisins, 167
  seafood clay pot, 63
  seafood cocktail in spicy red sauce, 18
  seafood stew, 182
  Sichuan chile and garlic, 79
  soup, Mediterranean, 146
  spicy, 82
  steamed, with ginger and green onions, 65
  steamed whole, with pickled plums, 96
  tacos, 40
  tandoori grilled, 71
  in a tart vinaigrette, 211
  in Tuscany, 154
  West Lake, 61

Fritters, spicy salt cod, 116

Fritto misto of squid, artichokes, and lemon, 42

G

Gambas al pil pil, 193
Gambas com caril, 197
Gastronomie, 167
Ginger juice, 52
Grand aïoli, le, 107
Gratin de coquilles Saint-
Jacques, 133
Greens, monkfish with, 191

H

Hai xian geng, 63
Hake with cider, 214
Halibut teriyaki, grilled, 28
Hanoi-style fried fish, 64
Herb sauce, 35
Hoi ma laeng poo, 77
Huitlacoche, 33
Huîtres tièdes à la vinaigrette aux
tomates, 108

I–K

Ikan goreng sambal bawang, 56
Impepata di cozze, 164
Insalata di gamberi alla sarda, 157
Jheenga masala, 90
Jiu suan la jiao xiaren, 75
Kepiting pedas, 88

L

Leeks, salt cod with, 181
Lemon catfish with slaw in
parchment, 30
Lingcod with a black olive
crust, 111
Lobster, 16
clambake dinner, 16
in the style of Cherbourg, 113
Lotte de mer aux olives et
artichauts, 145
Loup farci sur son lit de
légumes, 138
Lulas recheadas, 206

M

Machor jhal, 76
Malabar braised fish in sour
gravy, 85
Markets, Thai floating, 58
Marmitako, 202

Masala shrimp stir-fry, 80
Mediterranean fish soup, 146
Meen pollichathu, 85
Meia desfeita de bacalhau, 212
Merluza a la sidra, 214
Moleche fritte, 180
Monkfish
with greens, 191
with lemon and capers, 157
with olives and artichokes, 145
with pine nut sauce, 195
Mostelle croutée aux olives
noires, 111
Moules à la marinière, 119
Mushrooms
porcini, 160
salmon pirog, 21
sea bass with vegetables, 142
sole, fillet of, with, 161
trout, panfried, with bacon
and, 22
Mussels
with black pepper, 164
with garlic and basil, 77
Mediterranean fish soup, 146
seafood stew, 182
steamed Thai red curry, 43
stuffed, 158
swordfish, Toulon style, 139
in white wine, 119

N

Niçoise sandwiches, 143
Nonats, 140
Nuoc cham dipping sauce, 64

O

Okra and shrimp, stir-fried, with
sambal, 92
Olives
ahi tuna Niçoise, grilled, 27
crust, black, lingcod with, 111
monkfish with artichokes
and, 145
Niçoise sandwiches, 143
oil, 145, 192
sea bass with potatoes and, 172
Onion and anchovy tart, 137

Oranges
shrimp with butter and, 39
-wine sauce, red mullet
with, 208
Orata grigliata con finocchio
selvatico, 154
Oysters, warm, with tomato
vinaigrette, 108

P–Q

Pan bagnat, 143
Peas
snow, and scallops with
crabmeat sauce, 52
squid braised with, 117
squid with, 213
Peppers
stuffed with salt cod, 205
tuna with potatoes and, 202
Pescado marco, 24
Pesce al forno con pinoli e uva
passa, 167
Petite friture, le, 140
Petrale sole
cooked in butter, 127
doré with lemon-caper
butter, 38
Pimientos rellenos de bacalao, 205
Piri-piri sauce, 201
Pirog, salmon, 21
Pissaladière, 137
Pla nurng, 96
Plateau de fruits de mer, 129
Pomelo, flaked, and shrimp
salad, 59
Pork
cuttlefish stuffed with
tapenade, 130
and shrimp dumplings,
steamed, 98
Potatoes
ahi tuna Niçoise, grilled, 27
clambake dinner, 16
fish, braised, with eggplant
and, 76
fish and chips, 34
salt cod, whipped, 176
and salt cod gratin, 206
sea bass with olives and, 172
trout, oven-roasted, with, 174

tuna with peppers and, 202
vegetables and salt cod with
mayonnaise, 107
Qing chao xiaren, 66

R

Rape con grelos, 191
Rape en salsa de piñones, 195
Red mullet
with orange-wine sauce, 208
in parchment, 120
in tomato sauce, 170
in white wine, garlic, and
parsley, 168
Repas de midi, 123
Richeiado, 55
Rougets barbets en papillotes à
l'estragon, 120
Rougets grondins Monte
Carlo, 134
Rouille, 146

S

Salads
ahi tuna Niçoise, grilled, 27
coleslaw, 30
fennel, shaved, grilled salmon
with, 45
pomelo, flaked, and shrimp, 59
shrimp, with tomatoes and
capers, 157
Salmon
in cream and Muscadet
sauce, 114
grilled, with shaved fennel
salad, 45
king, 45
pirog, 21
tandoori grilled, 71
Salmonete setubalense, 208
Salt cod, 177
Bay of Biscay style, 196
with chickpeas, 212
fritters, spicy, 116
with leeks, 181
peppers stuffed with, 205
and potato gratin, 206
and vegetables with
mayonnaise, 107
whipped, 176

Sambal, 56

Sambal bhindi udang, 92

Sandwiches, Niçoise, 143

Santola no carro, 218

Sardines

    baked stuffed, 121

    with olive oil and tomatoes, 110

    in a tart vinaigrette, 211

Sardines farcies au four, 121

Sardines marinées aux tomates et huile d'olive, 110

Sauces

    crabmeat, 52

    herb, 35

    herbed tartar, 23

    nuoc cham dipping, 64

    piri-piri, 201

    sweet-and-sour, 87

Saumon à la crème au Muscadet, 114

Sausage, clams with tomatoes and, 217

Scallops

    baked in white wine, 191

    ceviche with avocado balls, 29

    gratin, 133

    and snow peas with crabmeat sauce, 52

    in thick red curry sauce, 57

    with white wine and herbs, 19

Sea bass

    on a bed of vegetables, 138

    in parchment with caper sauce, 179

    with potatoes and olives, 172

    roasted, with pine nuts and raisins, 167

    steamed, with ginger and green onions, 65

    with vegetables, 142

Sea bream, grilled, with wild fennel, 154

Seafood. *See also individual types*

    clay pot, 63

    cocktail in spicy red sauce, 18

    stew, 182

Sea robin Monte Carlo, 134

Shallot butter, 37

Shao mai, 98

Shrimp

    with cashew nuts, 66

    with chile and garlic in wine sauce, 75

    with curry, 197

    with fennel, 129

    fried, in the shell with tamarind, 83

    with hot sauce, 201

    and okra, stir-fried, with *sambal,* 92

    with orange and butter, 39

    and pork dumplings, steamed, 98

    salad, flaked pomelo and, 59

    salad with tomatoes and capers, 157

    seafood clay pot, 63

    seafood cocktail in spicy red sauce, 18

    seafood stew, 182

    sizzling, with garlic, 193

    in spiced cream sauce, 90

    spice-rubbed grilled, 55

    stir-fry, masala, 80

Sichuan chile and garlic fish, 79

Snapper

    fish tacos, 40

    red, with chile sauce and cheese, 24

    roasted, with pine nuts and raisins, 167

    steamed, with ginger and green onions, 65

Sogliola alla boscaiola, 161

Sole

    cooked in butter, 127

    fillet of, with mushrooms, 161

Sole meunière, 127

Songshu yuanzhuiti youyu, 95

Soups

    clams with white wine, garlic, and tomatoes, 175

    Mediterranean fish, 146

Spigola al cartoccio con salsa di capperi, 179

Spigola al forno, 172

Spinach, squid with, 168

Squid. *See also* Cuttlefish

    braised with peas, 117

fritto misto of artichokes, lemon, and, 42

    with peas, 213

    in sauce of three chiles, 33

    seafood clay pot, 63

    seafood stew, 182

    with spinach, 168

    stuffed, 206

Stockfish, 177

Sweet-and-sour sauce, 87

Swordfish

    toasts, smoked, 165

    with tomatoes and anchovies, 202

    Toulon style, 139

T–U

Tacos, fish, 40

Tacos de salpicón de pescado, 40

Tamarind, 92

Tandoori grilled fish, 71

Tandoori machi, 71

Tart, onion and anchovy, 137

Tartar sauce, herbed, 23

Thon à la méridionale, 135

Tiffin, 80

Tod mun pla, 68

Tomatoes

    ahi tuna Niçoise, grilled, 27

    clams with sausage and, 217

    clams with white wine, garlic, and, 175

    cod, steamed, with vegetables, 122

    cuttlefish stuffed with tapenade, 130

    sardines with olive oil and, 110

    sauce, red mullet in, 170

    sea bass on a bed of vegetables, 138

    sea bass with vegetables, 142

    seafood stew, 182

    shrimp salad with capers and, 157

    squid braised with peas, 117

    swordfish, Toulon style, 139

    swordfish with anchovies and, 202

    tuna with garlic, basil, and, 171

    vinaigrette, warm oysters with, 108

Tonno alla livornese, 171

Triglie dell'argentario, 168

Triglie in salsa rossa, 170

Trota al forno con patate, 174

Trout

    in herb sauce, 35

    oven-roasted, with potatoes, 174

    panfried, with mushrooms and bacon, 22

    in the style of Bragança, 195

    West Lake, 61

Trucha en salsa de hierbas, 35

Truta à moda de Bragança, 195

Tuna

    with garlic and chile, 218

    with garlic, basil, and tomato, 171

    grilled, with herbs, 135

    Niçoise, grilled ahi, 27

    Niçoise sandwiches, 143

    with peppers and potatoes, 202

    in a tart vinaigrette, 211

Udang goreng asam, 83

V

Vegetables. *See also individual vegetables*

    cod, steamed, with, 122

    and salt cod with mayonnaise, 107

    sea bass on a bed of, 138

    sea bass with, 142

Vieiras a la gallega, 191

Vongole ripiene, 162

W–Z

West Lake fish, 61

Xihu yu, 61

Yam som, 59

Yera varuval, 80

Zheng cong jiang yu, 65

Zucchini

    cod, steamed, with vegetables, 122

    sea bass on a bed of vegetables, 138

Zuppa di arselle, 175

ACKNOWLEDGMENTS

Weldon Owen wishes to thank the following people for their generous support in producing this book: Heather Belt, Ken DellaPenta, Julia Humes, Kate Washington, and Sharron Wood.

CREDITS

Recipe photography by Noel Barnhurst, except for the following by Andre Martin: Pages 53, 54, 60, 62, 65, 67, 70, 73, 75, 76, 81, 82, 84, 87, 90, 94, 98.

Travel photography by Michael Freeman: Pages 4 (left), ©46–47, 50, 51(left); Raymond K. Gehman/National Geographic Society: Pages ©10–11; R. Ian Lloyd: Page ©7; Jason Lowe: Pages 5 (left), 6 (bottom), 9 (left), 48 (top and bottom), 49, 51 (right), 102 (bottom), 103, 104, 105 (left), 150 (top and bottom), 153 (right), 220; Michael Melford: Page ©15 (left and right); Steven Rothfeld: Pages 6 (top), 8, 9 (right), 100-101, 102 (top), 105 (right), 148–149, 151, 152, 153 (left), 184–185, 186 (top and bottom), 187, 188, 189 (left and right), 226, 230; Ignacio Urquiza: Pages 12 (top), 13; Rachel Weill: Page ©12 (bottom); George White Jr.: Page ©14.

Recipes and sidebars by Georgeanne Brennan: Pages 107, 108, 110, 113, 114, 116, 119, 124, 126, 127, 145, 146; Lori de Mori: Pages 154, 158, 160, 161, 165, 168, 171, 174, 175, 179, 181, 182; Abigail Johnson Dodge: Pages 16, 19, 23, 34; Janet Fletcher: Pages 27, 38, 42, 45; Joyce Goldstein: Pages 191, 192, 193, 195, 196, 197, 198, 201, 202, 205, 206, 208, 209, 211, 212, 213, 214, 215, 217, 218; Diane Holuigue: Pages 111, 117, 120, 121, 122, 123, 129, 130, 132, 133, 134, 135, 137, 138, 139, 140, 142, 143, ; Joyce Jue: Pages 56, 57, 58, 59, 64, 68, 69, 77, 79, 83, 88, 91, 92, 96; Michael McLaughlin: Page 22; Cynthia Nims: Pages 21, 28, 37, 43; Ray Overton: Page 30; Jacki Passmore: Pages 52, 61, 62, 63, 65, 66, 72, 74, 75, 86, 87, 95, 98, 99; Julie Sahni: Pages 55, 71, 76, 80, 82, 85, 90; Michele Scicolone: Pages 157, 159, 162, 164, 167, 170, 172, 176, 177, 180; Marilyn Tausend: Pages 18, 24, 25, 29, 33, 35, 39, 40.

Page 4 (left): The Konkan women of Goa, India are renowned as astute businesspeople. They run, among other enterprises, the region's markets, such as this fish market in the capital, Panjim. Page 5 (left): Qingdao, China, on the edge of the Yellow Sea, is surrounded by bays that are perfect for local fishermen. Page 220: New paint refurbishes an old boat in Marseilles. Page 226: A Spanish resident relaxes on a bench overlooking the blue waters of the Bay of Biscay. Page 230: Beach chairs and umbrellas await the tide of vacationers at Monterosso, one of Italy's many popular coastal resort towns.

Cover: Dungeness Crab with Shallot Butter, page 37.

OXMOOR HOUSE INC.

Oxmoor House books are distributed by Sunset Books
80 Willow Road, Menlo Park, CA 94025
Telephone: 650-321-3600 Fax: 650-324-1532
Vice President/General Manager Rich Smeby
National Accounts Manager/Special Sales Brad Moses
Oxmoor House and Sunset Books are divisions of
Southern Progress Corporation

WILLIAMS-SONOMA

Founder and Vice-Chairman Chuck Williams

THE SAVORING SERIES

Conceived and produced by Weldon Owen Inc.
814 Montgomery Street, San Francisco, CA 94133
Telephone: 415 291 0100 Fax: 415 291 8841

In collaboration with Williams-Sonoma, Inc.
3250 Van Ness Avenue, San Francisco, CA 94109

A WELDON OWEN PRODUCTION

Set in Minion and Myriad.
Color separations by Bright Arts in Singapore.
Printed and bound by Tien Wah Press in Singapore.

First printed in 2006.
10 9 8 7 6 5 4 3 2 1

Library of Congress Cataloging-in-Publication data is available.
ISBN-10: 0-8487-3175-1
ISBN-13: 978-0-8487-3175-5

First published in the USA by Time-Life Custom Publishing
Originally published as Williams-Sonoma Savoring:
Savoring France (© 1999 Weldon Owen Inc.)
Savoring Italy (© 1999 Weldon Owen Inc.)
Savoring Southeast Asia (© 2000 Weldon Owen Inc.)
Savoring Spain & Portugal (© 2000 Weldon Owen Inc.)
Savoring India (© 2001 Weldon Owen Inc.)
Savoring Mexico (© 2001 Weldon Owen Inc.)
Savoring Tuscany (© 2001 Weldon Owen Inc.)
Savoring America (© 2002 Weldon Owen Inc.)
Savoring Provence (© 2002 Weldon Owen Inc.)
Savoring China (© 2003 Weldon Owen Inc.)

WELDON OWEN INC.

Chief Executive Officer John Owen
President and Chief Operating Officer Terry Newell
Chief Financial Officer Christine E. Munson
Vice President, International Sales Stuart Laurence
Vice President and Creative Director Gaye Allen
Vice President and Publisher Hannah Rahill

Senior Editor Kim Goodfriend
Assistant Editor Juli Vendzules

Designer Rachel Lopez

Production Director Chris Hemesath
Color Manager Teri Bell
Production and Reprint Coordinator Todd Rechner

Food Stylists George Dolese, Sally Parker
Illustrations Marlene McLoughlin
Text Stephanie Rosenbaum

A NOTE ON WEIGHTS AND MEASURES

All recipes include customary U.S. and metric measurements. Metric
conversions are based on a standard developed for these books and
have been rounded off. Actual weights may vary.